THE MISSION OF THE NEW SPIRIT REVELATION

THE PIVOTAL NATURE OF THE CHRIST EVENT IN EARTH EVOLUTION

THE MISSION OF THE
NEW SPIRIT REVELATION

THE PIVOTAL NATURE OF
THE CHRIST EVENT IN
EARTH EVOLUTION

Sixteen lectures given at various locations between
5 January and 26 December 1911

TRANSLATED BY MATTHEW BARTON

INTRODUCTION BY MATTHEW BARTON

RUDOLF STEINER

RUDOLF STEINER PRESS

CW 127

Rudolf Steiner Press
Hillside House, The Square
Forest Row, RH18 5ES

www.rudolfsteinerpress.com

Published by Rudolf Steiner Press 2021

Originally published in German under the title *Die Mission der neuen Geistesoffenbarung, Das Christus-Ereignis als Mittelpunktsgeschehen der Erdenevolution* (volume 127 in the Rudolf Steiner Gesamtausgabe or Collected Works) by Rudolf Steiner Verlag, Dornach. Based on shorthand notes that were not reviewed or revised by the speaker. This authorized translation is based on the second German edition (1989) that was edited by Wolfram Groddeck, Edwin Froböse, Anna-Maria Baiaster and Ulla Trapp

Published by permission of the Rudolf Steiner Nachlassverwaltung, Dornach

© Rudolf Steiner Nachlassverwaltung, Dornach, Rudolf Steiner Verlag 1989

This translation © Rudolf Steiner Press 2021

All rights reserved. No part of this publication may be reproduced, stored in a retrieval system, or transmitted, in any form or by any means, electronic, mechanical, photocopying or otherwise, without the prior permission of the publishers

A catalogue record for this book is available from the British Library

ISBN 978 1 85584 586 2

Cover by Andrew Morgan
Typeset by Symbiosys Technologies, Vishakapatnam, India
Printed and bound by 4Edge Ltd., Essex

CONTENTS

Publisher's Note xiii
Introduction, by Matthew Barton xv

Lecture 1
Mannheim, 5 January 1911
The Diverse Eras of Humanity's Evolution, and their Effect upon the Human Bodily Sheaths

Internalization of the soul faculties in the period between Augustine and Calvin. In the scientific age, a turning of soul powers outwards; this will be followed by a spiritual culture. Paracelsus as an example of the need to understand the world anew in every era. Religion, science and society must change as the configuration of our supersensible sheaths alters from epoch to epoch. The transition necessary in our time from the personal to the impersonal is apparent, in its declining and degenerating aspect, in the separation of money circulation from the personality; and in its upward trajectory, in the turning of the personality toward inspiring powers. Modern faith in authority and fear of ghosts. Dogma enters religion. Aristotle misunderstood. Spiritual science can lead us to religious experience, to spiritual integration of science and to a new practicality. Anthroposophy and Antisophy. A proverb by Fichte.

Pages 1-16

Lecture 2
Wiesbaden, 7 January 1911
The Effect of Moral Qualities on Karma

How teachings of karma can prove themselves in daily life. Envy can be traced to luciferic influence, lies to ahrimanic influence. Suppressed envy becomes fault-finding within a single incarnation; suppressed mendacity becomes shyness. In the next life on earth this will lead to bodily defects. Wonder—a function of the astral body. The proper mood of soul for an educator. The causes of long-lasting youthfulness and premature ageing. The fairy tale of the stork is the image of a reality.

Pages 17-25

LECTURE 3
FRANKFURT, 8 JANUARY 1911
The Inwardness of the Human Soul and its Relationship to the World

The sentient soul mediates reception of outward sense impressions. In the rational or mind soul the I awakens. Detachment from the world through the consciousness soul. Split between opinion and affect. The angel intervenes at the border between consciousness soul and rational or mind soul, the archangel between the rational soul and the sentient soul. When we relate to our surroundings, we are invigorated by the spirits of personality. Luciferic beings oppose the angels, and ahrimanic beings oppose the archangels. Without the adversarial powers, the human being could not develop freedom. Following the consciousness soul, the mind soul and the sentient soul are also to become ripe for freedom. The moral responsibility of the members of a spiritual movement.

Pages 26-36

LECTURE 4
MUNICH, 11 FEBRUARY 1911
The Connection of the Bodies of the Human Being with Humanity's Evolution and Human Biography. The Son of God and Son of Man

The loose connection of the etheric and astral body to the physical body in the Egyptian cultural period made it possible for the powers of higher beings to stream in. The human being's exterior was a reflection of his soul. Harmony of the beauty of the soul and of the body in Greek times. In future, the human being will have to draw powers consciously from the spiritual realm. The child's changing form. The art of the Greeks and the art of the future. The need to absorb spiritual ideas. The work of the I upon the bodies in the early years of life. The wisdom of the childlike soul in the ancient Indian epoch. The soul and spirit of the child in the first three years is the Son of God, the bearer of the I consciousness is the Son of Man. The decay of the earth corresponds to the drying up of the physical human body. *The Face of the Earth* by Eduard Suess.

Pages 37-51

LECTURE 5
BASEL, 23 FEBRUARY 1911
Wisdom, Prayerfulness and Certainty in Life

It is not enough to acquire theoretical truths of spiritual science. The meaning of our passage through successive cultural epochs. Numerical relationships and spiritual laws. The periodicity of life according to Wilhelm Fliess. Death and new birth. Patience and equanimity—the preconditions for spiritual development. Ancient wisdom must be replaced by Christ-imbued spirit knowledge. The mood invoked in the description of the planetary stages in *Occult Science, an Outline*. Fichte on the connection of the human being with the eternal. The pervading of the astral body with wisdom, the etheric body with prayerfulness, and the physical body with assurance in life; the meaning of these for earth's evolution.

Pages 52-63

Lecture 6
Zurich, 25 February 1911
The I at Work Upon the Child and How this Relates to the Christ Being

In the first three years of life the I, under the governance of higher beings, sculpts the brain. As the I becomes conscious, its connection with the world of spirit is extinguished. The twofold Son of God and Son of Man. The shape of the skull, a result of former incarnations. Enlivening the powers of the Son of God at a later age. Healing through laying on of hands. The connection between the Son of God in the human being and the Christ event. The deeper meaning of biblical proverbs. Three distinctions between the human being and the animal. An angelic being lived in John the Baptist as precursor of Christ Jesus. The earth as the body of humanity.

Pages 64-77

Lecture 7
St. Gallen, 26 February 1911
The Influx of Spiritual Insights into Life

The harmful effects of actions that are morally wrong. Ideals have a healing effect upon the astral body. The inadequacy of popular books on soul health. Overcoming materialism in life with a soul imbued by spiritual truths. The connection to our surroundings through the etheric streams of our hands. The etheric function of the thyroid. The relationship of the I to our environment in sorrow and laughter. Christ-permeated spiritual science engenders assurance in life.

Pages 78-92

LECTURE 8
BERLIN, 3 MARCH 1911
Ossian and Fingal's Cave

Fingal's Cave—a cathedral fashioned by nature. The revival of Ossian's songs by MacPherson and their effect upon the spirit of European culture. The core of Celtic folk culture in ancient Erin. In the song of the bards elemental passions were combined with the power of ancient clairvoyance. Fingal's battle song. The courageous deeds of battle were a preparation for deeds of spiritual life.
Address following a performance of Mendelssohn's Hebrides Overture.

Pages 93-99

LECTURE 9
BIELEFELD, 6 MARCH 1911
The Importance of Spiritual Enquiry for Moral Action

Immoral actions not only harm ourselves but humanity as a whole. Insight into our unity as human beings with the earth organism provides an enormous ethical impulse. As materialistic consciousness gains ever greater sway, antipathy to moral sermons increases. Christ as the archetype of the human being. The physical consequences on Jupiter of immorality and resistance to Christ. True wisdom emanates morality.

Pages 100-109

LECTURE 10
PRAGUE, 28 MARCH 1911
Aphorisms on the Relationship between Spiritual Science and Philosophy

The need for precise philosophical formulations. Whereas modern philosophy is an abstract pursuit, anthroposophy builds a bridge from spirit to physical reality. Concepts formed in relation to sense perception must harmonize with concepts gained from spiritual, supersensible perception. The relation of the content of consciousness to reality. The I is more comprehensive than the sphere of subjectivity. The principle that nothing transpersonal can enter the subjective sphere is true only to a limited extent. Masked materialism in conventional epistemology. Knowledge as a duty.
Reflections to complement the lectures on 'Occult Physiology'.

Pages 110-123

LECTURE 11
MUNICH, 3 MAY 1911
Original Sin and Grace

Almost all traditional religions have lost their true depths. The human being succumbed to luciferic temptation before the I entered us. We sank ever deeper in subsequent I development because the astral body became culpable. The ongoing influence of the luciferic influx on heredity. The 'original sin' allowed by the world order led to our descent from spiritual heights into physical, material existence, in order that we may evolve as free beings. The personality, within which astral drives live on the one hand, and abstract ideas on the other, must strive upward again to the spirit, where it will be filled by a higher personal principle, the Christ impulse. In this way, grace becomes the compensation for original sin.

Pages 124-137

LECTURE 12
COPENHAGEN, 5 JUNE 1911
The Mission of the New Spirit Revelation

The longing for true self-knowledge. The symbol of the Rose Cross. True and false tolerance. Knowledge of reincarnation and karma in relation to life's occurrences. The meaning of recurring lives on earth. Merely intellectual knowledge must be replaced by spiritual insight. The Christ event as the unique pivot of evolution. The danger of error and the victorious power of truth. *Introductory Words for the cycle 'Spiritual Guidance of the Human Being and Humanity'*

Pages 138-147

LECTURE 13
VIENNA, 14 JUNE 1911
Faith, Love, Hope

Socrates said that virtue could be taught. The earth's past and the past of humanity in its threefold nature. The I is our human present. The human future. The triad of faith, love and hope corresponds to the three fundamental powers of the soul. As human beings we remain united with our deeds. The idea of recurring lives on earth in Lessing's *The Education of the Human Race*. The truths of spiritual science—a living nourishment for the human soul.

Pages 148-156

LECTURE 14
BERLIN, 19 DECEMBER 1911
Symbolism and Imagination in relation to the play The Soul's Probation
The transition in Capesius's life to a spiritual outlook. The fairy tale of the miraculous spring. The world of the fairy tale as a mediating realm between clairvoyance and the rational world. The story of the Clever Cat as an example of fairy tale's world-historical nature. Imaginative clairvoyance in ancient times. End-rhyme is the poetic form of mind- or rational-soul culture, whereas alliteration embodies a will-emphasizing, sentient-soul culture. Jordan's *Nibelungen*, an attempt to renew old conditions. Language has to be returned to its origin in imaginative perception.

Pages 157-176

LECTURE 15
BERLIN, 21 DECEMBER 1911
Christmas—A Festival of Inspiration
The thought of Easter points us to conquering powers of the future while the thought of Christmas directs us back to our human origins. Originally, 6 January celebrated the birth of Christ in Jesus. In the fourth century, as ancient knowledge faded, the festival of Jesus' birth came to replace that of the birth of Christ in Jesus. In the Jesus boy of the Luke Gospel lived a soul who had not participated in humanity's downward trajectory. The connection between 'Adam and Eve Day' and the festival of the birth of Jesus. The spiritual, cosmic significance of the Holy Nights.

Pages 177-185

LECTURE 16
HANOVER, 26 DECEMBER 1911
The Birth of the Sun Spirit as Earth Spirit
The Christmas tree as a symbol of the inner, spiritual light. 'Jericho' and the 'Crossing of the Jordan' symbolize stages of initiation. The Gnostics still understood the Christ mystery. Unconscious wisdom prevailed in the shifting of the festival of Christ's birth from 6 January to 25 December: instead of the appearance of the god in a human body, henceforth people celebrated the incarnation of the innocent human soul who descends from divine, spiritual heights. The experience of the thirteen nights in the Dream Song of Olaf Åsteson.

Pages 186-197

APPENDIX

HEIDENHEIM, 30 NOVEMBER 1911

The Threefold Call from the World of Spirit

Destructive and life-creating powers. The first call from the world of spirit resounded from Mount Sinai, the second from John the Baptist, the third from spiritual science. How these three calls are reflected in child development. Penetration of the human sheaths with the power of faith, love and hope.

Notes from a lecture for the inauguration of the Heidenheim branch group

Pages 198-202

Notes...... 203

Rudolf Steiner's Collected Works 213

Significant Events in the Life of Rudolf Steiner 227

Index 243

Publisher's Note

THE current volume comprises single lectures by Rudolf Steiner given in various locations to members of the Theosophical Society, as it then was, in 1911. Marie Steiner gave the following Introduction to the Bielefeld lecture of 6 March 1911 when it was first published in the *Newsletter* ('What is happening in the Anthroposophical Society. News for members. Supplement to the weekly journal *Das Goetheanum*'), and this can also serve as a Preface for the other lectures in the volume:

> In 1911, Bielefeld was one of the smaller branch meetings. Unlike other groups that had been established for longer, it rarely had the good fortune to welcome Dr Steiner for more intimate lecture events. And yet it was often the case that his rare visits and addresses at such group meetings contained, as if in essence, what he expounded at much greater length in many lectures at the larger centres. What he said on such an evening could have a special intensity. Something like a strong, spiritual aura could emerge, and reverberate long afterwards, even in the very midst of an overwhelming throng of subsequent events and new spiritual tasks. This is particularly true of his lectures on the Christ event. Unfortunately most transcripts from that time have the character of notes, often providing only half and sometimes even only a quarter of the text. But reading between the lines you can get a sense of the substance contained there and feel it pervading you. Those familiar with Dr Steiner's mode of speech will not find it too difficult to reconstruct much of what is missing; and we can repeatedly feel astonishment at the wealth of newly emerging perspectives.
>
> The huge errors to which the Theosophical Society succumbed in its efforts to diminish the significance of the Christ event and to equate it with, or subordinate it to, other avatar appearances, necessitated a clean break between the two spiritual streams. This could only be done by making official the original name that Dr Steiner had already given to the esoteric Christianity of his spiritual science. When separation

from the Theosophical Society became unavoidable, instead of the much-loved word 'theosophy'—to which he had dedicated the whole strength of his commitment in order to increase popular regard for it, and which also, in previous centuries, had been a common designation in the West for the science of the spirit—he now chose the key term 'anthroposophy'. The aim of this was to prevent identification of the spiritual stream that he represented with the theosophical movement. The necessity for this was one dictated by outer circumstances at that time. Yet there is no contradiction between the two terms, at most only a clearer delineation, since true theosophy leads to true anthroposophy, and vice versa. The human being as harmony of the creative cosmic word, as solution of the riddle of the world, is also the content of anthroposophy. As we raise our consciousness to the divine, we also submerge ourselves in the divine. Human and divine consciousness, theosophy and anthroposophy become one.

Introduction

While the lectures in this volume were all given in the year 1911, they span the whole course of that year and were held in many different places, so that they cannot essentially be regarded as a single series, nor as anything like the linear elaboration of a theme. Much richer than that, they approach and illumine the figure of Christ in many different ways and from many different perspectives. Since 1909, Steiner's lectures had testified to a growing preoccupation with the centrality of Christ, which put him and his followers in the German section at odds with the Theosophical Society. 1911 was the year before Steiner finally split from the theosophists and founded the Anthroposophical Society over that very issue, and his intensifying emphasis on the central deed of Christ in Earth evolution can be seen at the same time as an assertion of the integrity of his vision in the face of strong opposition.

At roughly the same time as Steiner, in these lectures, was opening up profound vistas of human evolution and paths of development in which Christ is our steadfast companion and exemplar, much of the rest of the world was held spellbound by continuing human advances and endeavours in outward realms. In 1911, the hull of the ill-fated Titanic was launched, and Scott of the Antarctic, in his similarly ill-fated expedition, was struggling toward the South Pole. Despite the undoubted heroism of Scott and his companions, these two historical images can stand, perhaps, as a kind of admonition to the human race that physical exploit and technological advances can only take us so far, and cannot be the ultimate meaning and goal of our evolution. A different direction, a great deepening of our nature is needed if we are to unfold our full potential.

In Lecture 4 in this volume, Rudolf Steiner speaks of a future time, one perhaps already beginning to be ours, when the human etheric and astral bodies—which we can think of, in a kind of shorthand, as our very life and soul—will become so fully bound, chained to the physical body and the world's physical reality that we lose our human capacity for self-mastery and self-determination, which are after all spiritual capacities.

In these present 'interesting times', marked by ubiquitous alarm at a pandemic that has led, whether with good cause or not, to draconian, externally imposed societal controls and the most intent focus on *physical* survival, we may already gain more than an inkling of how thoughts and fears of bodily disease are gaining ascendancy over life and soul, relegating all other values and virtues to the vanishing margins of our existence, rendering extremely difficult our creative self-expression, our free, life-enhancing association with each other, and our very human rights themselves. As physicality alone increasingly encompasses us, says Steiner in the same lecture, we will find it ever harder to develop mobile thoughts and concepts or absorb new, creative ideas. Looking around in the world at present, it does indeed seem as if we are becoming stuck in certain fixed ways of regarding our reality, in grooves of orthodoxy that are ever harder to question, in rigid and linear forms of thought—about, say, viruses as 'enemy' and the need to combat them in more or less military fashion rather than seeing the whole ecological context of our now sorely unbalanced relationship with the planet, of which this pandemic may be a salutary symptom, an awakening call.

To many it might seem perverse and airy-fairy in the extreme to suggest, as Steiner does here, that such conditions as we have brought upon ourselves must be addressed first and foremost by turning consciously to the spirit, connecting with far broader dimensions in which life and soul are not a luxury afforded to the few but the nurturing ground of our being. What we develop inwardly as connection with realities greater than the immediate physical realm, says Steiner in Lecture 5, has value and importance for the whole planet, and can lead to an entirely different, sustaining view of the world and our place in it, countering the aridity and desiccation he speaks of as a corollary of outlooks that are solely materialistic.

Unlike previous 'war' situations, when communities pulled together and people often developed a heightened sense of caring for one another, one of the striking characteristics of our current plight is the way in which we are being divided from each other—'social distancing', the enforcement of face masks, avoidance of contagion. Such measures are presented as 'social' duty: we are told they are to protect others from ourselves. But this inversion of the whole concept of social interplay, this isolation of the individual and the fear to which it testifies, is really at odds with the idea so vividly presented here by Steiner that we are nothing as separate individuals, that we actually cannot gain anything from self-protection and self-isolation, even if supposedly to benefit others. As has become apparent, we are *not* 'all in this together': the wealthy have known how to use their advantage, with some huge corporations of course even benefitting greatly from the crisis, while poorer folk have suffered the brunt of the pandemic, often losing their livelihoods altogether in lockdown situations. There is a crass immorality at work here but, as we can read in this volume, immoral action anywhere on earth is like an abscess that makes the whole body sick, and, since this will ultimately come home to roost, it is an illusion to think we can gain advantage for ourselves alone. Extending this thought, Steiner develops the overarching, all-embracing idea—or rather living picture—of the reality of Christ who, he says, is for the body of the whole Earth what the heart is within our individual organism. Here all the threads come together in Steiner's invocation, from many different angles, of the exemplar and epitome of humanity, of a figure toward whom we can slowly work our way; of a reality that can descend upon us as, and only if, we raise ourselves through inner endeavour that nurtures in us qualities such as hope, love and trusting but also clearsighted vision of the future.

To me it seems that the polar contrast to authority externally imposed, and authority blindly followed—as urged upon us all at present—is the cultivation of love. 'What would we be without love?' asks Steiner. 'We would inevitably become isolated and gradually lose all connection with our fellow human beings and our fellow creatures in the natural world.' In a world increasingly manifesting traits of lovelessness—of isolationist self-protection and compliance not only with authoritarian rulers but with the 'authority' of a rigid worldview, as well as destruction of the planet of which we should be benevolent, loving custodians—these lectures are extraordinarily timely. They can help us broaden our vistas again and affirm our creative spirits in community with the whole world, physical and spiritual, of which we are a continually evolving part.

Matthew Barton
March 2021

Lecture 1

THE DIVERSE ERAS OF HUMANITY'S EVOLUTION, AND THEIR EFFECT UPON THE HUMAN BODILY SHEATHS

MANNHEIM, 5 JANUARY 1911

It has been some time since we were able to hold a branch meeting here in Mannheim, but today we may take up this task once again. Over the past few months, my dear friends, you have been attentively and eagerly absorbing the more important ideas and insights of our spiritual-scientific worldview. It is therefore perhaps not inappropriate to speak today about something that, on the one hand, can direct our gaze to the whole scope of our spiritual-scientific movement, but on the other also gives us the opportunity to evaluate a little the spiritual knowledge we have acquired, in particular as it relates to the human being and his evolution; to appraise it, if you like, in the service of something to which all human beings should be dedicated and which, for anthroposophists in particular, should assume a distinctive form by virtue of their insights, by virtue of the feelings that they can gain through the spiritual-scientific worldview. As you know, my dear friends, humanity's evolution advances, progressing through eras and epochs, and each such era and epoch has its own particular mission. In the history of humanity we can distinguish longer and shorter eras, and in each period, in turn, there are particular points at which the true task and mission of this age must not be neglected or overlooked—when it must be fully embraced. In successive eras, as we can discern, tasks are required by the worlds of spirit, tasks particular to this or that epoch; and then, for us human beings, it is a matter of acting rightly so as to know something about these tasks, so as to take up into our souls an awareness and knowledge of these tasks.

We live in an age when it really is an urgent matter for a number of people to gain knowledge once again of what, today or in our present era, needs to be done first and foremost in the spiritual domain. I would like firstly to draw your attention to just two epochs that closely concern us, one of which belongs to the past and much of whose spiritual riches and effects still extend into our present age. The second epoch, on the other hand, has scarcely begun. We stand at the beginning of a new era, a shorter cycle or epoch of humanity; we stand as it were, at a critical juncture, and this is why it is especially important to understand the nature of these two eras a little. The first comprises roughly the epoch that began with Augustine,[1] and ended as the sixteenth century was dawning. In esoteric science we regard this period as extending from Augustine to Calvin. Then comes a subsequent era comprising the period from Calvin[2] through to the last third of the nineteenth century. Now we stand again at the beginning of an era with new challenges and tasks, and meeting them will be extraordinarily important for humanity's immediate future. Let us therefore form a picture of what commonly and especially occurs at the start of new periods in evolution. As one era passes over into the next, something grows old, outmoded, and something new and fresh dawns. Something goes into decline while the other is germinal, starts to root and grow, begins to shine like the dawn of a new day—the sunshine of a new era that is arriving. And the distinctive thing about such a transitional period—as you know, people speak in various ways of 'transitional eras', but today it really can be said that a transitional age is arriving—is that human culture must start to be informed with new forces.

To characterize this I want to consider a great mission for all humanity: the rise of Christianity. If we picture how Christianity arose, we must say that those at the pinnacle of culture rejected it. Yet these same cultural leaders had reached a point of decline. Try to form a picture of Roman culture and its incipient decline, and try also to picture the kinds of communities to whom Paul preached: they were people who, with naivety if you like, but also with fresh powers, stood outside the prevailing culture, and harboured a living sense of what must come. They did not really figure amongst that culture's full flowering. New forces were coming to birth but appeared sometimes even amongst the lowest orders of society. Having developed for a period, the complex social existence of higher, influential echelons of society must decline again, and in particular the prevailing knowledge and disciplines with their concepts, ideas and so forth arrive at a point when they can no longer develop. Then something new emerges inevitably, rises from the people, and we can observe a radical change at work. In certain respects today we again stand at such a moment of upheaval. The scientific ideas achieved with such dedication have actually come to a point where anyone with insight must say they are faltering. The scientific concepts and ideas promoted and perpetuated by the mainstream are now on the brink of decline. And in fact the whole way in which people pursue cultural life, the mainstream of this cultural life, is in great decline. I'd like to outline very roughly and bluntly the symptoms of this decline which is really proceeding apace now, symptoms that can be observed by those who have any awareness of it.

If one has participated in cultural life in the past, as it came to expression in literature, books and so forth, and in science, then one will have grown up with a certain sense of seriousness in regard to these pursuits, a seriousness that is nowadays already seen as outmoded—a seriousness that is no longer understood. The whole tone of weekly journals, for instance, was very different in the 1870s from what it has become. If we can say this, it was far, far more dignified. In those days, within the cultural mainstream, people held very particular views about our relationship to drama, to lyric poetry and so on. In those days, too, you could write poetry or drama of less strict standards—plays, for instance, that were written for little festive occasions, more as light entertainment or for fun. Sometimes these showed talent. Students, especially, performed plays that showed talent. But as one grew older, and gained an overview of literary schools, one found that works were now valued that had once been regarded as having only ephemeral value. These same things gained literary and cultural acclaim. I don't wish to cause offence by naming names. Today we have reached a point where published trivialities are now the order of the day—whole bookshops are filled with them. Even 30 or 40 years ago, writers would have thought it a waste of ink to write such stuff. When you're in the midst of a transition and upheaval like this, you don't judge things severely enough, but cultural historians will one day characterize the end of the nineteenth century in such terms. We are currently facing a deterioration in traditional cultural life, and this could easily be demonstrated by the decline in scientific theories. We should not be surprised therefore if what is now to arise as a new spiritual and cultural movement, and is to give human evolution a new impetus, meets with little interest from mainstream culture; when those who move in the latter circles regard anthroposophists[*] as associations of semi-idiots, as, largely, very uneducated folk, and so on and so forth. This is inevitable in every age of transition. Fresh forces have to rise up from below, and what springs and germinates in this way will become essential in a subsequent era to really develop a new upward momentum.

Now, I spoke of two eras. The period from Augustine to Calvin was primarily one in which all human soul forces, all human powers, sought to become more inward. In all fields, a greater inwardness was apparent during these times. Outward science was pursued to a lesser degree, and the human being focused less on outward laws of nature and natural phenomena. At the beginning of this period, with Augustine himself, who in a sense prefigured our own spiritual-scientific view of the human being's configuration, we find the idea of the influx of supersensible powers that employ the human being as their instrument. In the further course of this epoch, we encounter remarkable mystics such as Meister Eckhardt, Susos, Johannes Tauler[3] and many more. While outward science receded during this period, there comes to the fore another, singular way in which people encompassed nature with a brilliantly intuitive gaze. We see this enhanced in figures

---

[*] The lectures in this volume were given before Steiner separated from the theosophical movement and founded anthroposophy. All references to 'theosophy' have therefore been changed to 'anthroposophy'. See also remarks on this split by Marie Steiner in Publisher's Note, on p. xiii.

such as Agrippa of Nettesheim. Then we encounter others, like Paracelsus and Jakob Boehme,[4] who appear as the fruits of this deepening of the human soul during those centuries. Such a current in culture can only last for a certain period. It rises, culminates, reaches its zenith and then declines again. Usually, every such current is superseded by something that in some respects appears as its counter-image.

Indeed, the subsequent centuries are like a counter-image of this current. Gradually, humankind forgets the picture of the human soul's inwardness. Times arrive when science achieves its endless triumphs. Great figures such as Copernicus, Kepler and Galileo appear, followed in the nineteenth century by those such as Julius Robert Meyer, Darwin and so on. A plethora of outward facts holds sway.

And yet people at the beginning of the new epoch are different from those who come later. Someone like Kepler, for instance, who exerted such a decisive influence on the physical sciences, was a pious man, and felt deeply and inwardly committed to Christianity. He discovered three laws—known as Kepler's three laws—which basically are nothing other than laws of time and space clothed in mathematical formulae.[5] In other words they are something entirely mechanical; and yet this same man spent far more time than he did on these discoveries in explaining the configurations of the cosmos at the time of the Mystery in Palestine: the interrelated positions of Saturn, Jupiter and Mars at the time Christ was born. It was on such matters that Kepler's thoughts were focused. He bequeathed to humanity his purely mathematical discoveries about the science of astronomy. But what he carried inwardly in his deepest heart remained his own inmost concern in an age that served only outward life.

Or consider Newton.[6] Universally known for his discovery of the laws of gravity, his Christianity is scarcely ever mentioned—Haeckel for instance ignores this when he speaks of Newton's decisive influence. Yet Newton was such a firm Christian that he wrote a commentary on the Apocalypse in his quietest and most sacred moments. But he could not bequeath this to humanity. Instead he left us with the purely mechanical law of gravity in an era that was dedicated to an outward grasp and comprehension of natural phenomena. And this era ended with the last third of the nineteenth century.

At this point an era begins that must necessarily appear as a counter-image to the preceding one. And the task of preparing this new direction, which is to work on so that everything we have often spoken of may arrive, falls to the spiritual-scientific worldview, which must once again engender a deepening of the human soul. Every age must work in a different way from previous ones. It would be mistaken simply to study what was once the right approach in the epoch extending from Augustine to Calvin. We can dwell upon such times, but we must know that today, following the era of natural science, we have to seek the world of spirit in a different way. Now is there anything, apart from abstract considerations, that can enable us to discern the need to grasp the world anew in every succeeding epoch?

Consider Paracelsus, for instance. He really is an unfathomable mind for our modern, very trivial and external forms of enquiry. He had deep insights into the secrets of healing, of medicine. It is possible to learn things of wonderful grandeur from Paracelsus if you study what he had to say about healing various illnesses. But let us imagine that a physician at the very pinnacle of our modern culture were to study Paracelsus with a view to making practical use of his directions. In relation to certain major things, this would lead to very true results and insights. But some things would be of no use any more to a modern physician. If he were to use some of the medicines that Paracelsus recommends, this would be of no use since human nature has changed already since the sixteenth century. This is because everything in the world changes and progresses. Outward things do not conform to the gradual development of our arbitrary knowledge. They advance; and it is our task to follow their progress with our knowledge and powers of enquiry. We have to learn anew continually, as Paracelsus learned. And if we proceed as faithfully as he did, we will, in some respects, find quite different results than he did. In our era, the tasks that face us are very much spiritual ones.

Now I would like to outline in broad strokes how, as it is written in the stars, human culture must progress in the near future. It is not up to human beings alone to give this culture its direction. Old views will not be able to match the radical change in actual circumstances. Things take their course, and spiritual science has the task of describing this course; it shows us how we can understand our era.

We stand at the dawn of an entirely new form of human life and thinking. Human culture has three especially important aspects, which are: religion, science and, thirdly, human society and co-existence in general, the feelings that people develop for each other, all that unfolds in social community. These three aspects are the most significant, and so it is especially important to trace, in succeeding epochs, what form these three aspects must assume—religion, science and social co-existence. And here there are certain requirements that we must simply understand as human beings, which do not lie within our power to determine.

Why must religion, science and social community keep changing from epoch to epoch? They do so simply because human nature changes. It is not insignificant to learn how our human nature consists of various levels or aspects. That we consist of physical body, life body and astral body with sentient soul, rational or mind soul and consciousness soul should not be a merely theoretical consideration, knowledge that can be acquired by just a few as a handy classification. We learn about these because they have a deep significance for human life. And you can have an inkling of this deep significance if you think back to the predominant role, say, of the sentient soul during the Egyptian and Chaldean era. Higher beings primarily worked upon this aspect of human nature. And in the Greco-Roman period, the period during which Christianity first arose, all influences upon humanity from divine, spiritual heights were working upon the mind soul. And today these influences work upon the consciousness soul. We will understand nothing at all of the human being's relationship to the great powers at work in the world if we do not know how this human nature is configured. What after all are we preparing as we concern ourselves today with spiritual-scientific insights? In our time, the consciousness soul is primarily being cultivated. All outward thinking and knowledge, all utilitarian thinking— this thinking that accords with principles of usefulness—depends in a certain respect upon developing the consciousness soul. And this is already being permeated by the intrinsic light of the spirit self.

Now the remarkable thing is that in our age we have two currents that flow side by side: one that is tumbling into decline, and one that is now rising towards a future blossom. The one that is tumbling towards decline has not yet reached its nadir. And from this still grow great human discoveries that will have a huge future. This also has its blessings. It is true that humanity will long continue to reap blessings from what is moving towards decline. But the kind of thinking that invents zeppelins is one wedded to decline, whereas the form of thinking that concerns itself with the configurations of human nature is that of humanity's future.

But these two do have a common meeting ground, as we can see in all realms. I'd like first of all to offer you a very practical example, that of monetary transactions. During the nineteenth century this changed to a very considerable degree. There was a huge turnaround. If you look at the period directly preceding the last third of the nineteenth century, all financial speculation attached to the individual person. It was Rothschild's purely financial and speculative genius that conducted money everywhere to and from financial centres. And if we study the history of the large banking companies, we find exemplary instances everywhere of how monetary transactions arose entirely in accord with the type of human nature that was founded on the consciousness soul, on the individual person. Then this changed. But nothing much is said about it since it is still in its infancy. Nowadays, by contrast, it is no longer the consciousness soul that predominates exclusively in financial transactions; today we find a kind of aggregation or centralization: share capital, the company, the association—something that goes beyond the individual person.

Try to see what is only now just beginning but will increasingly become apparent. Today it is almost irrelevant which person is in charge. The processes that people have developed for monetary transactions are already working in an impersonal way, are acting by themselves. Here, in a descending momentum, you can see how the consciousness soul reaches over toward the spirit self.

Here it manifests in a current of decline; but it manifests in the current of regenerating life where we seek what a committed individual has achieved; where we seek through Inspiration to gain the help of the powers who will once again furnish us with Inspiration from the world of spirit. Here too we pass from the personal to the transpersonal. Thus we can discern common characteristics in our era both in the currents of decline and regeneration. Especially however we must beware of attending too much in any era to what emerges as authority. As long as we lack spiritual insight, this can seriously mislead us.

This is particularly true in one area of human culture, the field of materialistic medicine. Here we can discern the decisive influence of authority, and the ever increasing claim to authority, which is in fact far, far more dreadful than any kind of medieval tyranny. We find ourselves in the very midst of this tendency, which will keep increasing. People may mock the ghosts of medieval superstition, but we can ask if anything much has changed. Has this fear of ghosts faded? Aren't people actually far more afraid of ghosts than they were back then? What happens in the human soul when people are told they carry 60,000 bacilli on their hands, is far more terrible than generally acknowledged. In America statistics have been calculated about how many such bacilli can be found on a man's moustache. At least the ghosts of medieval times were, one might say, decent ghosts; but modern bacilli-ghosts are too minuscule to grapple with. The fear invoked by them is only just beginning, and leads, in health matters, to people succumbing to a really terrible belief in authority.

Everywhere we see the character of this transitional era. It becomes apparent if we can observe phenomena in the right way.

But now let us ask what the doctrines and revelations of anthroposophy teach us about the further development of these three major areas of life. How must things develop in future, and how do we need to work so that the creative, fruitful spirit self can be rightly introduced into the consciousness soul, in a spiritual way? The prophetic stars—that is, the teachings of spiritual science—tell us the following: in the whole way in which people have tried in preceding centuries to introduce religion into human culture, it is a mingling of two things, one of which cannot be called religion at all in the strict sense, while the other is indeed religion.

What is religion in reality? We must characterize it ultimately as a mood of the human soul: a mood that opens to the spiritual, to the infinite. We can characterize it well by starting with its simplest manifestations, though these can later be raised, enhanced, to the highest level. If we walk across a meadow and our soul is open to all that grows and blossoms there, we will feel a sense of joyfulness for the glories revealed there in flowers and grasses, for each gleaming bead of dew. Finding such a mood within ourselves, so that our heart opens, is not yet religion. It can only become religion if this feeling intensifies into a sense of the infinite behind the finite, of the spirit behind sensory reality. If our soul feels communion with the spirit, this mood corresponds to that of religion. The more we can intensify this sense of the eternal within us, the more we cultivate religion within ourselves or others.

But in a necessary evolution, such impulses that lead human feeling and sensibility from the transient to the everlasting, have become mingled with certain views and ideas about the nature and properties of the supersensible realm. And in consequence religion has in a sense become linked with what is really the science of the spirit, with what must be regarded as a science. And today we see how, in this kind of ecclesiastical faith, religion can only be sustained if certain doctrines are preserved at the same time. Yet this gives rise to what we can regard as rigid dogmas, fixed adherence to certain ideas about the world of spirit. Such ideas ought naturally to develop and progress since the human spirit itself progresses. True religious feeling ought to rejoice at such progress, since it reveals the glories of the divine, spiritual world in ever more grandeur.

True religious feeling would not have delivered Giordano Bruno up to the stake. Instead it should have said: How great is God that he sends such people to earth and reveals such things through them. Then, alongside the religious aspect, it would inevitably also have acknowledged the realm of scientific enquiry, a field that extends both to the outer world and the world of spirit. Progress must necessarily adapt to the human spirit which itself progresses from epoch to epoch. As the sixteenth century arrived, a great change occurred in relation to this quest for knowledge. Before the age of Copernicus,

Galileo and Kepler, what was taught in universities and great centres of learning had assumed strange forms. Aristotle[7] is certainly a great source of wisdom, but what he accomplished embodied the greatest learning *in his own time*. The medieval period greatly misconceived his thought, and ultimately no longer understood at all what he had meant. And yet his doctrines continued to be followed and taught.

To avoid misunderstandings, and to show you how knowledge must change from epoch to epoch to accompany the evolution of the human spirit, I would like to speak in more detail about something that occurred in connection with Aristotle. Aristotle's work was embedded in an age when people still had a sense that human nature possesses not only blood and nerves etcetera but also an etheric body. If one were only to depict the etheric body, it would appear very different from the picture given by modern anatomists. In the era when Aristotle was working, no great importance was attributed to this flesh-and-blood picture, since people in those days were still aware of the etheric body. If we were to draw the latter, we would have to see a centre here, where the heart is, and then draw rays, important ones, emanating from it, directed toward the brain and connected with the whole way in which a person thinks. If we consider the etheric body we see how thinking is regulated from a centre located close to the physical heart. And Aristotle depicted this to make clear the singular nature of thinking. Later people no longer understood what Aristotle meant. They began to confuse a word in Greek that corresponds to our word 'nerve', but which is decisive for the organism of thinking, with material nerves. They thought Aristotle was speaking of physical nerve cords when in fact he was describing etheric currents. As the materialistic age dawned, people no longer understood Aristotle. And so you can see how they taught his doctrines in a completely erroneous way. They stated that the main nerves issue from the heart. And then along came scientific, materialistic research as introduced by Copernicus, Galileo and others, and it was discovered that the nerves issue from the brain, the physical nerves and spinal cord. And so they said that Aristotle was wrong. Thus Copernicus, Galileo and Giordano Bruno disputed the doctrines of Aristotle. You see, medieval Aristotelians did not adhere to what Aristotle actually taught, but to what they imagined he meant. And thus it happened that Galileo showed a friend of his, who was an Aristotelian, that the nerves in a corpse issue from the brain; yet this friend preferred to believe Aristotle rather than his own eyes. He believed in his own mistaken view of Aristotle's teaching. And so we can see how at this time the stream of spiritual science as promulgated by Aristotle, the science of the etheric body, was led over into material science. Its merits should not be denied; it has brought great blessings and benefits to humanity and does so still. But now we are in an era when we must once again ascend to the spiritual.

A time is swiftly approaching when science must once again learn to understand the intrinsic nature of spirit, when it will need to become what in esotericism is called 'pneumatology', or teaching of the spirit. What was science in the last century? The doctrine of abstract ideas and natural laws that no longer had any connection with the reality of spiritual life. Science now stands at a point when it must become pneumatology, when it must return to the spirit. This is written in the stars of anthroposophy. And since religion always invokes a mood that opens to the spirit, science and religion will inevitably work in harmony in eras when science integrates the spirit and thus becomes pneumatology. Then science can properly explain the life of spirit, and sustain and support the mood which in turn should live in religion.

What is now beginning stands in crass contrast to what has now lapsed. Let us for example consider how the waning, declining principle manifests in the various evangelical faiths: people sought to exclude scientific thinking altogether from the realm that is meant to be dedicated to faith. Think of Luther and Kant. Kant said that he had to suspend knowledge in order to give full scope to freedom, immortality and God.[8]

Here science was focused on outward, sensory physicality and excluded a supersensible, spiritual aspect to reality. Therefore, in this view of Kant, it was necessary to preserve untarnished the traditional sacred testaments. There were good reasons for this. But now a different age is coming, when anthroposophy leads us into the world of spirit; and now we will see the gradual approach of something that must be developed and accomplished through anthroposophy's support and illumination of science. Religion and science will once again go hand-in-hand in the next epoch. Science will gradually come to have validity for all. It will become comprehensible to all. For this reason, the parallel course of religion and science that is now beginning will give rise in the fullest sense to what we may call individualism in religion: each separate heart will find its way into the world of spirit in its own individual, religious way. A common and shared science of the spirit will serve to guide and accompany each person in the most individual and personal way in the realm of religion. This will be the hallmark of our age.

Once again, remarkably, we can see here how a personal moment points to something transpersonal. The symptoms of decline also show this. And how do we discern this pointer to a transpersonal level in certain ecclesiastical contexts? What did it mean when, in a certain Church, its guardians appealed to Inspiration? [... gap in the text].Things have to be seen in relation to their spiritual character. Much that is apparent today especially in religious life, in the various confessions, points to this luminous influx of the spirit self into what we call the consciousness soul, whether this be in a waning or ascending momentum.

This is apparent especially in the third of the three named spheres of human culture. Here an insight and understanding will spread of which modern pragmatism as yet has no inkling at all. A principle of this new understanding will be that the happiness of an individual can never be purchased at the cost of the lesser happiness of others. In future, therefore, the personal moment will be led on, led over, into something transpersonal; egoism will be led over into something that surpasses egoism, into a realm where human beings are united. Gradually no one will wish to be happy without knowing that others are equally so. This mood, in stark contrast to the pragmatism of today, is slowly emerging. There is only one means to engender this mood, and this is to gain knowledge of the true core of the human being and its nature and composition, as spiritual science teaches us. We have to know the human being if we wish to be human.

We see these three things at the start of their development. What is the role of spiritual science? It should teach us to understand everything that is inevitably coming. Let me state in radical terms the stance we can take. Let's assume hypothetically for a moment that today's anthroposophy, which is still a very small current in the world, were to be regarded as deluded fantasy by those who encounter it, and suppressed by them. Imagine that all who embrace 'antisophy'[9] were to make it simply impossible for anthroposophy to thrive (for science tends in that direction). Then people would be unable to gain any understanding of what has been described to you here as a necessary evolution, one inscribed in the stars, of science, religion and human co-existence. Imagine that people isolated themselves from any understanding of such things. What state would humankind be in, in that case? Human beings on the earth would then be like some herd of animals that has found itself in very alien climatic conditions where they cannot survive. In consequence these animals would waste away and atrophy; gradually they would succumb. Similarly, in such a case human beings would succumb to decline, to decadence, to premature downfall—though not through extinction. Much worse than extinction, they would turn animal-like, and so only their lower passions, drives and desires would remain. People would be interested only in their food, their fodder, and they would employ all their thinking to produce this food. They would build factories to produce the best flour, the best bread; they would build ships and zeppelins to convey produce from faraway lands and to supply products they wished to enjoy. They would employ enormous ingenuity upon 'increased cultivation'—which is the term they might use for culture. Endless intelligence and ingenuity would be used, but all ultimately directed to putting food on the table. What really does the term 'cultural advance' mean today? If we send telegraphs only to say 'I need so many sacks of flour', this focuses all our ingenuity on producing something that really only serves what we can call the 'animal in man'. Spirituality and intelligence are two totally different things. The materialistic age leads to a culmination of intelligence and 'intelligent culture'. But this has nothing to do with spirituality. If we assume that humankind were to be isolated in this way, so that truly human qualities are excluded, what would the gods have to do? They would say: 'Here is a race that has failed to understand the mission of the earth. Now we must send down a different race, a lineage of souls who can fulfil the earth's mission.'

Yet small circles *will* develop understanding for the necessary spiritual life of the future, and so humankind will bring the mission of the earth to fulfilment. The sixth epoch, which will succeed the fifth post-Atlantean era, whose culture is dedicated to the consciousness soul, will be fulfilled by a small circle of human beings who spread far and wide throughout the rest of humanity. Yet this can only be accomplished if human free will comes in to its own. You see, once the I has taken root in human nature, the human being must also develop free will to develop this I. And it depends on each separate individual whether he wishes to bring understanding to bear on spiritualization, or whether he prefers to pursue the downward path that modern humanity is taking at present.

Social practice must develop towards a fulfilment of the principle that the happiness of the individual cannot be gained at the cost of the happiness of others. If people refuse to understand this, they are cultivating a downward path of evolution, one that brings with it aridity and animalization. Today you can say that we face a decision as human beings: either to desire and seek spiritual science, or not to do so; and this means either to seek the ascent or the decline of humanity. We need to have this sense in everything we do; we should feel that our karma has placed us into humanity's evolution like a new material, to offer our powers as elementary forces that must work their way upward.

If we gain this sense, then anthroposophy will soon become practical feeling, practical sensibility, and in our heart will take root an awareness of what we are actually doing when we undertake seemingly insignificant work in anthroposophical branch meetings. We should do so not as some kind of hobby on the side, not as the eccentricity of a few, but in understanding of the deepest needs of a newly resurgent epoch.

I wanted to show you how things are interrelated, so that we can properly understand human progress. Let us recall that we are self-aware beings, that we must therefore know what we are, and that only by virtue of self-knowledge can we fulfil our destiny in the world. All those, therefore, who do not wish to know anything about human nature, lack the will to place themselves rightly into the world. Let us recall the words of someone who had an intimation of much that is today emerging as anthroposophy—Johann Gottlieb Fichte. In his lectures 'On the Vocation of the Scholar', he once spoke of his lofty ideas. When he came to write a Preface to these lectures, it occurred to him that publication of this book would meet with a general sense that the ideas contained in it are very fine but impractical. How, he wondered, can such thoughts be introduced and integrated into life? Yet Fichte was fully aware himself that life is continually governed by ideas.

Let me give an example. Who built the Simplon Tunnel? No engineer today can work without differential and integral calculations. So basically it was Leibniz, the inventor of differential and integral calculation, who has built all the tunnels and bridges of our time. The spirit everywhere governs everything in life, and we can learn from what Fichte has written—can learn to fortify ourselves, strengthen our anthroposophical awareness, when people say our ideas are eccentric and impractical. Fichte says that it is common knowledge that ideas cannot be directly implemented in life;[10] that we hold this knowledge in common with others who object to our ideas, and that maybe we even know it better than they do. But the fact that these others wish to know nothing at all about ideas only proves that the wise guidance of the world, the sway of divine powers, will not be able to count upon them. Therefore Fichte asks that a benevolent natural world, in which they do believe, may send them sunshine and rain when they need it, good digestion and, if possible, also a few good thoughts.

We can to some degree fortify ourselves by saying this: We know that as anthroposophists we must cultivate understanding for what must inevitably come. May a benevolent nature give the others what Fichte describes; but also what they need in the spirit, though they believe they have no need of it. May the spirit give them ever keener and keener thoughts, so that they no longer regard spiritual science as fantasy, but recognize it as an important impulse needed by humanity.

Lecture 2

THE EFFECT OF MORAL QUALITIES ON KARMA[11]

WIESBADEN, 7 JANUARY 1911

In the course of our spiritual-scientific reflections—which often after all lead us into very lofty heights of existence—it is surely sometimes a good idea to take a look at daily life, this life that continually surrounds us. With a little good will and perspicacity, you see, the application of spiritual science to daily life can give us very important insights into the truth and cogency of what we seek in this realm.

What we call karma, preceding factors that have a causative effect in a succeeding life, is doubtless amongst the most important teachings we meet in the field of spiritual science. Now, in most cases where karma is mentioned, the anthroposophist no doubt thinks of causes that originate in previous lives. And those, therefore, who are still highly sceptical about spiritual-scientific endeavours, can easily ask how such things can be proven. Of course we basically know that such an objection is childish. If we take the trouble to delve deeper into what spiritual science offers us, we can discover that everything that can be said about karma is in fact well-founded. And yet it is also good to point to experiences and observations accessible even to those who are far from developing clairvoyant faculties or from espousing anthroposophical methods of observation. Understood rightly, you see, karma does not only proceed from a previous life and act causatively in this one, but also is very much at work already within a single life. It is just that, ordinarily, the span of our observation in life is so short that not much can be detected of how earlier causes create subsequent effects. If we consider a period of five or six years, nothing much will emerge from this. But if we observe longer spans of time, even between birth and death in a single life as far as this is possible, we can find much evidence already of the workings of karma. We can discern this even in very outward matters.

These introductory words are not intended as something especially anthroposophical in nature. I wish only to show that, even for the most ordinary things, larger spans of time are necessary for discovering connections of cause and effect. I myself have had much opportunity to observe children. I taught children, though it was a long time ago.[12] But if you have taught four children in a family over many years, you have an opportunity not only to observe these four children themselves, but also the children of family friends and so on. You are well-placed to see what any of these children do or what is done with them. Back then a particular medical condition existed which, thank goodness, is now very much on the wane; and it was thought necessary to strengthen the little ones by giving them a small glass of red wine, not just at one meal but at several meals. This was thought an excellent idea. I was able to observe many children who were raised on red wine in this way, and other children whose parents declined to do this. The children who were aged two-and-a-half to four at the time are now over thirty, or close to forty. And you can see that the children treated with red wine, supposedly to strengthen them, have become fidgety, nervous people. There is a marked difference, for those who wish to observe it, between them and the children who did not drink red wine when they were young. Almost a quarter of a century is necessary, it turns out, to be able to observe this.

In the same way it is particularly important to consider longer spans of time when studying karmic consequences involving human moral and ethical qualities. Today I want to point to a few such qualities and their effect upon the soul, upon the sensibility: the workings of karma even within a single life. I would like to consider several good and several bad qualities: envy, jealousy, mendacity; then benevolence and—something we find so often in younger people—wonder, wonderment and similar things. So let us first take the negative qualities of jealousy and deceitfulness.

Let us assume that we discern jealousy or envy in a child. From our spiritual-scientific observations, we know that particular powers are at work in the bodies that constitute our being, of which we are normally unaware, in the astral body and etheric body: luciferic powers in the astral body, ahrimanic powers in the etheric body. These powers are adversaries to human evolution. Everything related to the astral body such as jealousy comes from the temptations of Lucifer. Everything related to the etheric body such as deceitfulness involves the temptations of Ahriman. In a jealous child, Lucifer has seized the astral body in a sense: here the luciferic powers have their point of entry. It is a singular fact that everyone, from the most primitive peoples to the most evolved leaders of humanity, regard jealousy and deceitfulness as reprehensible qualities. The moment someone recognizes they are jealous or deceitful, a sense rises within them of the very objectionable nature of these qualities, and they will seek to do all in their power to rid themselves of such feelings. Envy and deceitfulness, jealousy and lies, are instinctively felt to be wrong. Goethe says that he finds in himself many faults upon deep self-examination, but no hint of jealousy.[13] Benvenuto Cellini[14] says the same thing about mendacity. If someone notices that they are a jealous person, they will instinctively do what they can to rid themselves of this habit. Jealousy is a luciferic quality. If someone sees that they have a tendency to jealousy and therefore works to rid themselves of this habit, Lucifer will say: 'There is a danger this person will evade me.' Both Lucifer and Ahriman harbour equal enmity for the human being but themselves are bosom friends. So in this case Lucifer will call upon Ahriman for help, and he will transform the envy into another quality. Envy undergoes a metamorphosis, one that turns the person, who previously begrudged another something, into a fierce critic who seeks for everything and anything in the other that can be condemned. This urgent need to find fault is nothing other than transformed envy. And when this happens, Ahriman has you in his grasp. This transformed envy is very widespread. If it did not exist in the form of critical gossip, an urge to say bad things about others, many social gatherings would fall silent for lack of subject matter.

In terms of karma, interestingly, jealousy in its original form, or in its metamorphosis as criticism, leads to the same consequence. If you study someone who was jealous in their youth, or highly critical of others, you will see that those consumed by jealousy in youth become uncertain in their later years. They can find no solid ground, find it hard to relate to others, cannot rely on their own counsel; are glad when someone else advises them what to do. In a single life already this is the karmic consequence both of jealousy and its metamorphosis.

Lying is a quality inhering in the etheric body, and originates from Ahriman. If, at a certain age, a person becomes a habitual liar, or if they lie a lot due to bad upbringing, in later years this will always manifest as a certain shyness, an inability to be straight with others. Certain moral proverbs are spot-on in this respect: 'He can't look me in the eye' is one such saying, referring to a deceitful quality. Shyness and lack of independence emerge as soul qualities within a single life. If we try to observe life in the same way that a physicist, say, observes the outward course of the world, we can discover these things, and they illumine our understanding of life.

The consequence of such a quality resides within the mind and soul in one life. But if, through spiritual science, we trace the effects of one life into the next, we find that the karmic effect apparent within the soul in one life acquires greater power in the next. Here we can demonstrate that lack of independence, appearing as the soul consequence of jealousy in one life, and shyness as the effect of deceitfulness, come to be formative upon the structure of the body in the next life. Here they take a hold upon our corporeal nature.

People who were very envious in a former life will be reborn with an outward bodily organization that renders them helpless. Those who lied a lot will be reborn with no proper relationship to the surrounding world: they cannot be loved by the people around them, and feel rejected by them; it is hard for love to enter their lives. Spiritual science must be regarded as pragmatic. What I'm saying now has direct, practical repercussions.

Let us assume that a child we know cannot develop a relationship with us, that it withdraws from us in timidity, or that this child is weak and pale. The anthroposophist will say: this pallid frailty, the disposition to all kinds of illnesses, has to be ascribed to an envious disposition in the previous incarnation; and shyness can be ascribed to deceitfulness. But it is not by accident that this child is born in our circles, for an individual can only be placed into a situation that belongs to them. Before long, people will come to recognize the law of karma as self-evident. People are born into circumstances to which they belong. Frailty and helplessness are the consequences of envy in a former life, and we are connected with this child because it envied us. It comes to us in its new being, because we are the ones to whom this being lied so often in a former incarnation. How should we behave in such a case? There is no need for long reflections here, for we should behave in the most moral and ethical way, also in ordinary life.

When a person envies us or criticizes us about everything, it is best to meet them with benevolence and love. That is the best conduct. In our unnatural, materialistic times, of course, this cannot always be done. But it is the best way to behave towards a child who is born with these particular kinds of disposition. As well as recognizing that this child envied us or lied to us in a former incarnation, we take the firm resolve to show this child especial benevolence. Let us summon a warm feeling for such conduct. Try to observe these things and you will find that the cheeks of such a child can start to grow red, that the child begins to strengthen. We must simply keep behaving to it in this way. The same is true of deceitfulness. Someone who lies to us the whole time is best served if we do all in our power to give them a resonant sense of the love of truth. If we behave like this toward a shy or timid child, we will find that we effectively counter any increase in the conflict.

And so we find that we can do life enormous services. This is an example of how spiritual science can have practical results. We should never forget that we can keep on finding evidence of the workings of karma everywhere. And similarly we should always remember, especially when such children are entrusted to our care, that we are here given the means to show how spiritual science has gone deep into our very being.

We can consider other qualities too in the light of spiritual science—for example wonder, astonishment.[15] The ancient Greek philosophers heeded a fine instinct when they said that philosophy starts with wonder.[16] What is this quality really? We meet the phenomena around us with wonder and amazement. Then sometimes too, this wonder is replaced by something different, when we start to *understand* the realities that first astonished us. So let us now ask about the nature of this wonder. We encounter a phenomenon, and it elicits wonder from us. Here there is no relationship yet with our reason and intelligence since these latter seek understanding, and do not express themselves in wonder. The relationship we have with things through wonder is far more immediate. Understanding concerns itself with analysis of constitutive parts whereas wonder arises directly in response to the whole of a phenomenon. The reason for this is that understanding, reason, involves the I in relationship to what is observed, whereas wonder involves the astral body. The latter is not fully conscious; it is a kind of subconscious. When the astral body has a relationship to a phenomenon, and this relationship does not as yet raise itself to the level of the I, wonder appears. It is because we can feel wonder about something that we can enter into a connection with it that lies below the threshold of consciousness. This subconscious connection is in many cases very important, in the same way that the ancient Greeks regarded wonder as an important prelude to philosophy.

It is good for people to encompass something with their astral body before they apply their intelligence to it. This creates a foundation in their feelings and sensibility into which understanding can immerse itself. This is quite different from tackling something rationally from the outset, and means that we greatly broaden the basis of our understanding. In turn this leads to richer, fuller understanding. This is why it is so important for a teacher first to develop a sacred wonder toward the child, toward the child's individuality which surfaces, as it were, from darkness; to keep an open mind for things we cannot survey at all with our intelligence alone: the infinite depths of an individual. Encountering this individual we intentionally engender a sense of wonder in ourselves. This wonder will come, for there is always rich opportunity for wonder and amazement toward each person. These feelings are not spoiled by our narrower intellect but are sometimes much surer, richer, truer than what is grasped by the narrow intellect. The foundations for insights we can apply to practical life can be gained through wonder, through our life of feeling. And something very important depends upon this: the trust that one person feels toward another. It's true, isn't it, that we can often feel trust or mistrust in someone—for the negative is equally true—before we encompass them in thoughts and concepts, with our rational mind? People often regret that they didn't 'trust their instincts', their first impressions, instead overriding truer inklings. And they are often right to say this. Our social relations, our relationship to life, should grow forth from our feelings and sensibility. Some people are little disposed to feel such vague intimations. There are those who can gaze up at the starry heavens for hours on end without knowing much about astronomy, while others remain unmoved by such a sight until they read a book that can explain it all to them. The latter lack this feeling foundation, and can also often pass others by insensibly until or unless they find sufficient time to bring intellectual analysis to bear on them.

This is also apparent in people's reaction to spiritual science. Really we can only speak to someone's reason in their earliest youth. Later it becomes impossible, for reasons cited by Goethe: you can't, he says, persuade people their assertions are untrue, for their view is based on holding true what is false.[17] If someone feels that there is in spiritual science something that fulfils their whole longing, they will always be able to find logical proofs that can be found everywhere. Things are basically very clear; they need only be seen in the light of a spiritual outlook.

Let us imagine that in youth a person encounters someone older and feels a sacred reverence for them, without knowing exactly what elicits this feeling. If we consider the broad feeling disposition such a person possesses, we will find they stay youthful for a long time, that a young heart beats in their breast even when their hair has long since turned grey. They retain a certain mobility in life. In particular, they retain throughout life a capacity to adapt quickly to situations, to be skilled in the way they meet all circumstances. Someone who opens themselves so fully to life when they are young finds that life opens before them increasingly in their later life. They become ever more able to gain insights, find it ever easier to feel the spiritual element behind things. They become ever more spiritual. It is different for someone who especially developed their rational mind when young: they tend to become old prematurely. This is not the fault of the individual but the karma of the community. A rational person increasingly sunders themselves from the world, and it becomes ever harder for them to understand it. This is why many criticize everything around them. In my youth—they say—everything was beautiful, but all is spoiled now. This grumbling and complaining, this dissatisfaction with everything, and living entirely in childhood memories, is connected with the soul's rational inclinations in youth. For this reason we must do everything in our power to found education on the broad basis of feeling and sensibility, especially on the quality of pictorial imagination.

In our era, humanity in general is sailing in the opposite direction. For instance, the legend of the stork that brings a baby is not a lie told to children—it is simply an image truer than the ideas people think should be imparted to them: that a child only originates with its father and mother. The picture of the stork—or other similar tales—points to something in the child that descends from lofty heights. Hearing such tales, the child gazes into regions that are far beyond physical mundanities, and develops a sense of things from which, at a later age, truth emerges. To regard the picture of the stork as untrue merely testifies to a lack of imagination, to an inability to clothe the process of reincarnation—which cannot simply be described to them prosaically—in a fitting image. It may be objected that children today do not believe this tale anyway. Yet this is because the adults who tell it to them do not believe it themselves. The moment I myself do not believe what an image expresses, children will not believe in it either. But if we see in it an image of the reality and truth that underlies it, if we have sufficient imagination to transform this truth into an image, then children will feel it to be true. Actually it is a lovely thing to say to a child that a part of them comes from their father, a part from their mother, but other beings carry down a third part from heavenly heights, bear this upon their wings and entrust it to father and mother. To say this is very accurate, and we are speaking the truth. The astral body of children to whom we impart rich, pictorial thoughts is nurtured, and we give them the blessing of a youthfulness that will reach far into their old age. This pictorial quality cultivated in education, which will also above all underlie children's play, is infinitely important. Here too we can see how karma is already at work within a single life.

And so spiritual science, as it engages in education and culture, will reveal itself to be true in the very way in which life thrives and flourishes in consequences, whereas materialism will display its untruth by rendering life arid and prematurely old.

Lecture 3

THE INWARDNESS OF THE HUMAN SOUL AND ITS RELATIONSHIP TO THE WORLD[18]

FRANKFURT, 8 JANUARY 1911

Today and tomorrow evening, drawing on Goethe,[19] we will discuss various matters of interest to the pupil of spiritual science concerning inner aspects of the human soul, its evolution and its relationship to the world. Since questions considered in both lectures will be centred on Goethe, it seems sensible firstly to ensure that you possess a certain acquaintance with the basic elements of human soul life by speaking, separately from Goethe, of the inner nature of the human soul, drawing instead on spiritual-scientific sources as we usually do.

If we consider the evolution of the human soul we must clearly distinguish between the sentient soul, the mind soul and the consciousness soul. In speaking firstly of the sentient soul, we are not referring only to that aspect of soul capable of connecting to the outer world through perception and sense impressions, but also to the centre within us of what we can call drives, desires and passions, and also all impulses of will. Actually, consideration of everything of the nature of will, everything that arises as an inner impetus in our quest for a relationship with the outer world, is most useful when it comes to forming an idea of the nature of the sentient soul within us. This is the very essence of the sentient soul; and at the same time it is the most important mediator, too, in our reception of outer impressions facilitated by processes of perception. For this reason it is called the sentient soul. The sentient soul holds sway whenever we receive an impression of colour or tone. It holds sway largely too when passions arise in us, such as anger, or strong feelings such as fear.

What we call the mind or rational soul only slowly emerges from the sentient soul, and in certain respects is already more lucid than the sentient soul. In the mind soul we find capacities to clothe in thoughts what has been felt in the sentient soul, the instincts and emotions we experience, and to elucidate them into a more human form of soul life. If, for instance, affects that are otherwise only focused on self-preservation clarify into benevolence, and even into loving conduct toward one's surroundings, then the mind soul is already at work. In the mind soul dawns the I, the true centre of our soul life.

In the further evolution of the I, during which we come to feel our interiority, and our capacity to work and act out of our centre, we can form our thoughts and mental pictures into great ideas with which to encompass nature, or into moral thoughts, or ideas of duty. In all that we relate to in this way, we speak of the consciousness soul. There are no hard and fast divisions between these different aspects of the soul but it is necessary to distinguish between them since each relates to the outer world in a different way.

If we first consider the consciousness soul, we find it initially to be our highest aspect of soul, but at the same time the part which has most clearly separated itself in a sense from the rest of the world. It is the most autonomous aspect of the soul.

When we steep ourselves in the consciousness soul, we can be most alone in our soul life, most isolated from the outer world. This is the part of the soul which, by its very nature, erects the most barriers and boundaries against the surrounding world. In consequence it is more predisposed to succumb to mistakes and errors. It is the aspect of soul most detached from the universe. And yet the errors it succumbs to are limited in scope. This is the most important aspect of what we call the consciousness soul. Above all, it expresses itself as logical thinking, as conceptual analysis, also as calculation and mathematical thinking, as all activity intrinsic in certain respects to human beings alone and not found in animals.

The powers of the sentient and mind soul rise up into the consciousness soul. The drives, passions and desires, the will impulses of the sentient soul, and the feelings and intellectual judgements of the mind soul, penetrate it. Yet in the consciousness soul all this is processed by logical thinking, and therefore our opinions are formed primarily within the latter. And since the consciousness soul is the most isolated part of the soul, people's opinions are all very divergent. If we think of things we hold in common, which have developed within our nation, our family circle, because they are customary in our surroundings, these are elements that reside in the rational or mind soul. Yet things that first have their seat in the consciousness soul can migrate into the mind soul—for example, an opinion we once formed can become habitual. Or a capacity we develop can transform into an habitual skill, and has then descended into the mind soul.

The consciousness soul is also the most isolated aspect of the soul because it is from there that we directly extend our feelers into the world around us. When we consider what we wish to do, we are living in the mind soul. When we observe what is around us we extend through our senses our feelers directly out of the consciousness soul, and return again to what makes us the most isolated of beings. You see, what our senses offer us makes us into isolated beings. We isolate ourselves precisely because we must establish a relationship with the outer world in an entirely local and temporary way through the consciousness soul. But opinions reside most strongly in the consciousness soul. First an opinion asserts itself, and takes root in the consciousness soul. This is why we are isolated beings in respect of our opinions. In respect of habits, people understand each other better already. We are most independent, but also most isolated, within the consciousness soul, and thus it is difficult for us to gain access to the content of the consciousness soul of another person. We do not even know whether the other sees the colours red and blue in the same way that we do.

But apart from this, let us now consider the content of the consciousness soul that consists of views and opinions. Let us consider something that may appear extremely logical, opinions which we may imagine to have the soundest possible logical basis. Nevertheless, we cannot get very far with our fellow human beings with these logical reasonings. Logical reasons do not initially have any traction in outer life, and this is actually the normal state of affairs. It is therefore easy to win young people, children, round to our view of things. Later it will be increasingly difficult. Children meet us not only with their consciousness soul but with their mind and sentient soul too. They meet us with their whole personality. And our powers to persuade and convince are dependent on far more than the consciousness soul. The will, the feeling is predominant. The most logical justification can be found for the most varied points of view depending on differences of will and feeling. Yet in the present cycle of humanity, people are properly independent only as far as the consciousness soul is concerned, and less so in respect of the other aspects of the soul. Try to sense how opinions form: a person is entirely free to form an opinion, a context of concepts and ideas. They are less free in respect of the content of the mind soul. Here a person does not feel free at all, for otherwise their feelings could not play such havoc with them as they often do. In our views and opinions we can be fully convinced in ourselves that something or other must displease us—but our feelings speak differently, and allow us to find a pleasure at odds with our opinion. The fact that our feeling sensibility can contradict our opinions can show us that we are not as free in regard to feeling as to opinions. We feel ourselves least free of all in everything that concerns the will, in the whole nature of the sentient soul. The discrepancy can sometimes be very great indeed between the finest principles—between the view that something or other is not good—and the drive, the emotional urge. Here's a drastic example: the mind soul of a teacher in charge of an angry child recognizes that this anger must be expunged. But since he does not succeed in achieving this by beneficial means, he throws an inkpot at his head. Here we see the greatest discrepancy.

What is going on in the soul to give rise to this discrepancy? It is because, at our current stage of evolution, we are isolated in the consciousness soul but that nevertheless, at the boundary between this and the mind or feeling soul, an influence upon the soul is at work from beings higher than the human level. And again, at the boundary between the mind soul and the sentient soul, a similar influence exists from powers outside and above the human being. The same is true at the boundary between sentient soul and sentient body.

I am describing the situation in our present era, in our century. Circumstances are different in other eras. We can easily discover how other powers are at work upon us when we consider the will. When we think, we reside with ourselves. We can sit down in a corner and dwell in our thoughts. But to carry out a will impulse, we must move hands and feet; we must initiate a physical action. In passing from one thought to another, your consciousness remains present. But initially we have no idea what happens at the transition between the thought, 'I will pick up the clock,' and then actually performing this action. This is quite different from passing from one thought to another, during which we can observe the whole sequence consciously. And this is an instance of other powers intervening to aid us. At the boundary between the mind soul and the consciousness soul, beings intervene whom we can call angels or angeloi. They are beings who condense what otherwise occurs consciously in opinions, condense these into what we can call feelings. The expression 'feeling' is a little vague. What we inwardly feel is already a condensing of thought. And underlying this are powers that aid us.

Let us now look at the boundary between the mind soul and the sentient soul. Here there are still higher beings that intervene. They stir the will in us, empower thought to become will. These are the archangels or archangeloi. But when we enter into relationship with the surrounding world, the Spirits of Personality are at work. Here we already feel the world's opposition or resistance when we engage and intervene in its fabric. Thus in the intermediate realms between different soul forces dwell spirit beings that lead us and strengthen us, and have the mission of transforming into deeds, into powers, what we can only otherwise experience as thought if left to ourselves.

Now when we descend into these subconscious regions of soul life, immediately it is possible that the battles that occur and must occur within the world of spirit intrude also into the arena of our consciousness. Where angelic beings intervene, luciferic beings, adversaries of the angels, are also immediately present. If only the angels intervened, our feeling sensibility, our mind, would reach out only to what is beautiful, to what corresponds to our human dignity. The luciferic beings lead us toward things we would not be in agreement with if we reflected calmly, but which we are drawn to nevertheless. Where the archangels intervene, ahrimanic beings can do so likewise, and can succeed in turning our judgement into misjudgement, our search for truth into lies. Logical opinion is freely given us human beings. But the moment we arrive at feelings, at impulses of will, other beings play in, including ones who oppose the benevolent beings. Anyone who acquaints themselves in any way with esoteric investigation must be aware of this.

In ordinary life, things are established to ensure that the luciferic and ahrimanic powers opposing the angels and archangels can nevertheless be beneficially directed in all their workings. There is no point in seeking to be wiser than the wisdom governing the world and to ask, Why do we need these luciferic and ahrimanic beings? Human beings could not be as free as they are if they were not given a counterweight to the angelic beings in the nature of these two powers. We must be able to lie so that we can come to truth by our own powers. We must achieve truth autonomously, and therefore we need Ahriman. We have to resist Ahriman and pursue the path toward truth. By this means we have become an autonomous being in whom the sense of truth inheres. The most sublime powers governing the world have established things so that their adversaries, Lucifer and Ahriman, do not take all before them. They exist, surely, to serve our freedom and the evolution of consciousness by compelling us strongly with impure urges, desires and also false judgements which, in the course of karma, can be rebalanced and redressed, and ultimately cannot disrupt the mission of the earth. Among the loveliest and profoundest insights we can gradually develop through esoteric studies is this: that all untruth and all that is bad can ultimately be transformed into the good.

But there is a pressing question that everyone should really ask themselves: Apart from this fact, is there another reason why we must pass through all our incarnations and only perfect ourselves by first committing all kinds of error? Yes, there is a reason for this. It is beyond the scope of this lecture to elucidate why human beings, through their previous earthly lives, have come to a point when they can only gradually mature. Presently we are only independent in respect of the consciousness soul. But a time will come when, despite all inclination for error, we will have a sure command of our actions and their effects. If we had no sign of this as yet, we would be plunged in continual conflict and quarrel. As humanity is at present, it is ripe to acquire freedom in the consciousness soul; but people are not yet ripe for freedom in the mind soul and sentient soul. Progress never occurs in a completely linear evolution. In all cultures we can see how some souls hurry on ahead, take leadership and prefigure what other souls can only develop in later eras. Today, human souls are only ripe for freedom in the consciousness soul. But spiritual wisdom gradually leads us to gain freedom in the mind soul and sentient soul too, to gain more isolated autonomy so that, to find what is good, we no longer have to look to traditional and habitual tenets or customs. Instead, the impulse for good will stream from our own soul. This is also a necessary interpretation of the Pauline saying: Not I but Christ in me.[20] When Christ lives in human beings, they will be able to be free also in respect of the mind soul and the sentient soul. Humankind has already developed a somewhat dispassionate outlook as far as the most trivial, logical matters are concerned: in mathematics. Here passions have withdrawn far enough from human hearts for people to be able to discover the truth for themselves. But as far as the mind soul and sentient soul are concerned, people continue to adjust the truth as required and even consider such adjustments to be the key thing since luciferic and ahrimanic powers are everywhere at work.

You will understand that in a movement founded upon spiritual wisdom, where the aim is to awaken deeper powers of the human soul to isolated awareness, mere curiosity about the worlds of spirit is not enough. This simply cannot be the motivation for spiritual enquiry at all. Instead what is needed is a sense of responsibility. Through this movement, future human capacities are drawn in advance into our time: a seed of the future is awoken that in general is not yet ripe. We must be aware of this; we must be careful and attentive in ensuring that, even if the soul remains fine and congenial within this spiritual movement, we must nevertheless remain alert to the dangers that threaten it, and awaken a sense of responsibility. When the soul approaches spiritual things without the required maturity, there is indeed a danger, and not everyone will notice it. Those who stand more deeply rooted in this movement will know, must know—if they are not to collapse under the unendurable—that they must always be careful to utter only things that have first passed a hundred times through their soul, and not just once or ten times. It is difficult when speaking of spiritual matters to formulate words in a way that is fitting. Within the whole circle of anthroposophists, a particular view must become current: the view that we require of those who represent the movement that they pay due heed to the truth in this sense. It should not be thought that someone can simply stand up and deliver a lecture every evening without repeatedly and continually allowing these truths to pass through their soul, so that the right words and formulations are found. One aspect of this is the difficulty we face in even opening our mouths to express spiritual matters. The other is that those who belong to such a movement must actually ensure that this feeling exists in those who represent the movement. Yet even those who do not yet stand deeply within it must take care that certain things do not happen to their soul. They should keep asking themselves this: Am I mature enough yet to represent a spiritual movement? Do I need to place myself more fully within this movement so that the world of spirit can act more strongly upon me? No one should be discouraged by this; but they should awaken in themselves the sense that previously they may have done what is good and right under the compulsions of tradition and upbringing, and that there is a boundary where, in representing the truth, not only the angels, archangels and Spirits of Personality stand, but also Lucifer and Ahriman. We can repeatedly discover that people who previously loved the truth begin to lie when spiritual-scientific truths work upon them; and this is because they have not sufficiently recognized that they must, above all, grow mature, must allow spiritual truths to work upon them, and must not let *themselves* speak. We have to be aware of this need for responsibility. But it would be cowardly to refrain therefore from joining this spiritual movement. Right conduct is not to evade a duty to be careful but to take proper heed of this duty. These things I have spoken of now are deeply connected with what has, in every era, distinguished the character of progressive spiritual movements.

There are the great lights who seek to advance humanity. But wherever great lights are found, deep shadows are often present. And this can explain the not always unjustified accusations we hear against those who seek to bring down truths from the world of spirit to the physical plane. In every such movement, those who wished to do nothing other than help spiritual truths flow down into the physical world have been joined by others who did not care to practise self-criticism, nor to tame their pride and vanity. We can observe plentiful instances of this within spiritual movements, and we have to recognize that, unfortunately, the outer world is unable to distinguish between such advocates and those who truly embody the movement. The reverse is sometimes also true. Especially in our spiritual-scientific movement, people should appeal to independent judgement and sweep away all sense prevailing in society that *what* is said is less important than *who* says it. We should attend only to what a person says if, when we bring our sense of truth and open minds to it, we find it illuminating. Our movement is in the highest degree fit to help independent judgement germinate and take root. Yet in our time there is a strong dose of what we might call comfortable belief. Great obstacles to the spiritual-scientific movement are created through this comfort-seeking dependency. To believe something simply because a particular person says it hampers free judgement, free human soul life, hampers the developing autonomy also of the mind soul. It is so comfortable not to have to think for oneself, and to accept something as truth because this or that person said it. It is much easier to believe a person than to check and test what they have said.

I have often asserted that we can initially offer stimulus only within the spiritual movement. But if you take all the historical accounts of, say, Zarathustra, nothing in them will refute what has been said about him here if you really survey them fully. These things can be examined and checked, and the more rigorously this is done, the more agreeable it is to someone who wishes to represent the spiritual movement in an objective way. Such a person has the will to examine and test statements. But it is so much more comfortable and easy to believe, simply to say that this or that clairvoyant said something was so. This is a danger for both real and supposed clairvoyants until they are fully sure of their perceptions. It is certainly tempting to tell people things they will believe. It is all too easy to lurch into something that lurks in wait as a person seeks to ascend to the supersensible world. Such a person is rising into a world where things really cannot so easily be checked as they can in the physical world. It takes quite a bit of checking to ascertain rationally that angels and archangels intervene at certain boundaries. Belief often depends only on the impression that we have gained of someone else. We can see from mass suggestion how easy it is to exert an influence on people and get them to believe things.

The most wonderful discoveries will be made in future about mass suggestion. In earlier times it was quite different because the consciousness soul was not yet so independent. Today we are at a point where the consciousness soul is becoming emancipated, and yet at the same time we are still completely caught up in the unfreedom of the mind soul. How does suggestion work? It isn't only through the sympathetic or unsympathetic qualities in a person. It is also at work, for instance, when someone has taken up a certain post and, having to support his five children, say, believes he is compelled to stay in this job. People often prefer to attend to what charlatans say about their spiritual insights than to things based on sound enquiry. You see, the former will have two qualities: first of all it will be very trivial in nature. For instance, the things mediums write down in automatic writing are often such that another could easily work it out for themselves; people believe it because of the way it is conveyed. They think something is being communicated to them from the world of spirit. The very triviality of such pronouncements recommends it to people. Or alternatively, these 'insights' are so incomprehensible that no one can understand what they mean. The more incomprehensible they are, the more 'mystical' they are often thought to be. At the boundaries between supersensible and sensory reality, charlatanism can easily combine with things that do derive from serious enquiry. It must be emphasized that we only fulfil our duty here if we are alert to the workings of our own soul, keenly attending to everything that can be muddied by instincts. We may think we are advancing the concerns of humanity whereas in fact we may only be advancing our own; or, unnoticed, untruth, the temptation of Ahriman, can mingle with our words.

We can only truly make progress by being continually awake to all these things—only by repeatedly reminding ourselves that if we join a spiritual movement there is a great danger of becoming vain and arrogant. This is self-evident. There is nothing intrinsically wrong with it unless a person does nothing to recognize and deal with these attributes. There is a huge temptation to depart from the truth a little when associating with people who believe you. You can pull the wool over people's eyes if they take what you say as authoritative. People should not be reproached for the fact that, as they come nearer to the world of spirit, mendacity appears in them; but they must not excuse this in themselves. They must make every effort to root out this tendency. This is the meaning of the phrase, 'Man know thyself'. We must seek moments of secluded reflection when we can come to see that, yet again, a danger threatens and we must be on our guard. If we do not have these secluded moments, if it is too unpleasant for us to acknowledge things in us that are not good, and if such recognition does not become the point of departure for combating our flaws with all our might, then we are on a slippery slope: we will slip downwards instead of ascending.

These are things we must consider if we are to affirm our stance toward esoteric enquiry—the mode of enquiry that is the highest gift of grace flowing into the physical world from worlds of spirit, toward which we should feel the greatest responsibility.

The duty should awaken in us to enter the world of spirit with others who make up part of humanity, because this is the only possible way to make progress. At the same time this should be accompanied by a sense of responsibility; the sense that, having once become acquainted with these things, it becomes our duty to engage with them. Those who represent spiritual science are often accused of paying too little heed to moral questions. Yet we do often engage with such questions, as we have done again today, so that, as our spiritual movement progresses, and leads us toward the sources of the spirit, the impulses that flow from those sources can increasingly be heard.

Lecture 4

THE CONNECTION OF THE BODIES OF THE HUMAN BEING WITH HUMANITY'S EVOLUTION AND HUMAN BIOGRAPHY. THE SON OF GOD AND SON OF MAN

MUNICH, 11 FEBRUARY 1911

As we study spiritual science, we first acquaint ourselves with what we call the human being's different levels or aspects, distinguishing the physical body, etheric body, astral body, I and so forth. To many it might seem that by doing so, by ascertaining that we are constituted of these different bodies, we have already to some degree encompassed the whole of human nature. Many do indeed think that they possess the most intrinsic and essential knowledge about the human being once they know this, once they can list these various aspects or levels, as well as knowing how each of these behaves as it passes through diverse incarnations. On the one hand, while it is necessary for us to take these bodies as our point of departure, we must recognize that this is really still only a first and very preliminary step. You see, it is not a matter only of us being constituted of these seven or nine aspects, but the key thing is how the different levels interrelate, how each stands in relation to the other.

In fact, this interrelationship does not remain constant for all human beings and in all eras, but varies. Above all, this interrelationship of the human bodies changes over the long course of human evolution. If we look back to humanity of four or five thousand years ago, these bodies were connected to each other in a way quite different from today; and in future they will become very differently related once again. The nature of this union, the interplay and interrelationship of the different levels of our being, alters as time goes by. Our continual sequence of reincarnations gains significance by virtue of the fact that, as we pass through our own individual evolution from incarnation to incarnation, in the course of the whole of the earth's evolution this complex of physical body, etheric body and astral body evolves in its interrelationships, and therefore with every new incarnation we encounter, if you like, a new configuration. Because of this, by virtue of this encounter with a repeatedly new configuration of our bodies, we keep having new experiences. What I mean can be illustrated by considering an ancient point in time with our own era.

If we looked back to the fifth and fourth millennium BC, to Egyptian culture, and studied the people of those times, we would find a far looser relationship between physical body, etheric body and astral body than is the case today. In those ancient times, astral and etheric bodies were more tenuously bound to the physical body than today. That is precisely the tendency of our current evolution: astral and etheric bodies seek to unite ever more closely and firmly with the human physical body. This is very significant: as evolution advances toward the future: astral and etheric bodies are tending to become ever more firmly chained to the physical body, and in consequence the human soul no longer has the same kind of influence over our physical body as it did in ancient times. In those eras, the astral and etheric bodies were freer, and the laws of the physical body did not inform them so vigorously as they do nowadays. In olden times, when a person entertained a feeling or an idea, the power of this feeling or idea swiftly transplanted itself into the astral and etheric body, and, since people at that time had mastery over their etheric and astral body, their soul could in turn hold sway over the physical body. This capacity of the soul to rule the physical body is continually waning nowadays as the astral and etheric body become ever more integrated with and into the physical body. But this also has another consequence: it means that over the course of the ages, our natural constitution becomes ever less available to the powers and potencies that work down upon us from the world of spirit. In ancient times, therefore, we had what can be called 'natural Inspiration and Imagination', an ancient clairvoyance, since the etheric and astral bodies were freer then. Into this free astral and etheric body streamed the powers of the hierarchies, working into these bodies. Now, by contrast, in the process of humanity's development, the physical body sunders etheric and astral body from our intrinsic interiority, lays claim to them; and in consequence the direct influence of worlds of spirit grows ever weaker, can gain ever less purchase upon the human being's etheric and astral bodies.

We can trace this in the human being's outward form. If we were to go a very long way back, to the humanity, say, of ancient Egypt, we would find that a passion or drive at work in the soul in those days worked on into the astral and etheric body, which in turn impressed these drives and passions into the physical body. For this reason we would also find that in very ancient times of Egyptian culture, but altogether in eras of ancient culture, the external human form was a kind of imprint of the soul. In those days you could read from a person's countenance, their physiognomy, what lived in their soul. There was a full accord, one might say, between outer physical appearance and the soul. Then came the Greco-Roman era—these remarkable people, the Greeks, in the middle of post-Atlantean times. In them was a kind of balance in which, in general, the powers of the world of spirit flowed into the soul and came to expression in corporeality. This gave the Greeks their remarkable harmony between outward physicality, the beauty of their outward corporeality, and the beauty of their soul. This loveliness of soul, since it was free of the physical body, was in consequence capable of opening upward toward the hierarchies. There was an influx of the powers of the hierarchies, coming to expression in the physical body, and therefore the whole physical body of an ancient Greek became an expression of the beauty of his soul. Thus we find that, to a great degree, a transpersonal quality came to expression in the human body in the Greek era, a universal human quality.

In the future—and this is the important thing which we now inscribe in our souls—this will change radically. In future, the human physical body will assert itself more forcefully, will chain astral and etheric bodies to itself. Only if we consciously approach the world of spirit, absorbing ideas, concepts and feelings from it—as we are now beginning to do in the spiritual movement—can we then ourselves develop the powerful forces that formerly flowed into the physical and etheric body from the hierarchies. As the future approaches, we can only retain mastery of our physical body by consciously drawing strong powers from the spiritual world that can overcome the resistant energies of the etheric body, bound up as this is so closely with the physical body.

We can put it like this: in ancient pre-Christian times, human beings were endowed with a natural capacity to act upon their physical body. In future people will only have this capacity if they themselves do something to ensure it. But in consequence, a difference and distinction will increasingly become apparent within humanity—between those who reject spiritual teachings and insights, and those who gladly, willingly and instinctively approach such knowledge. As we know, the latter group as yet remains small. But this division will occur between those who reject the spiritual and despise it, and those who willingly embrace spiritual movements, initially through a certain kind of instinct. This will become apparent in the features of those who resist spirituality; they will have no power over their gestures, their physical exterior—it will become clear that their physical aspect is stronger than they are themselves. By contrast, it will be evident that those who embrace spiritual teachings will acquire strength to overcome the resistance of their physical body.

In their outward form and development, human beings will in future display very different characteristics from those of ancient times. Returning once more to the ancient world, we can say that in the Egypt of the fifth or fourth millennium BC, children at birth did not yet appear properly human. They looked as if an angel had landed, as if the child had received its soft bodily forms from the world of spirit as the direct expressions of the spiritual within the physical. As these children grew, they became ever more human in appearance. They developed downward into humanity. In the Greeks we find a great similarity between people at a younger and older age. Already in early infancy one could observe the imprint of a universally human quality which continued as the child grew. For this reason it is right to see the Greeks as a kind of childlike people.

In future it will become ever more apparent that at birth, children—and especially the most significant individuals—will be ugly, truly ugly compared to the ideal of Greek beauty. But the more a person acquaints themselves with spiritual ideas, the more their form and figure will acquire a characteristic appearance: what was at first vague and undefined, or even ugly in the child, will transform as they become acquainted with spiritual ideas. It will be noticeable how a person's features express ideas and concepts drawn from the world of spirit. This will increasingly grow to be the case.

What manifests in the outward features of humanity sometimes appears in a compressed form in art. It is true to say that the material for the humanity that is to advance toward the future is, as it were, drawn from the European peoples, whereas the material for a humanity that once had the old kind of sway over the physical body arose in southern lands. In art too, in Greek art, we find an expression of universal human beauty. Greek sculptors endowed even the figures of their gods with the expression of human beauty, and this continued right up to the Renaissance of southern Europe. If you compare a Madonna by Raphael to one painted in northern lands, you can see that art prefigures what is actually to come. Here you have the more characteristic form, a predominance of characteristic qualities. In the echoes of Greek art beauty appears as a self-sustaining quality. A strong inwardness of soul is what humanity will require in the near future. We are advancing toward such an era, and this very fact must be connected with another: that these different bodies of the human being possess a different interrelationship at different eras of evolution. In the past they were more loosely connected, but now the lower aspects are becoming ever more closely bound up with one another.

Now various things are connected with this fact, and in our time they can become a very tangible reality for an attentive observer of life: for instance the inability of some people to form concepts that correspond with the world's realities. Today there are numerous people whose ideas have been so firmly drilled into them that they become completely unable to take up new ideas later on. What causes this? The elasticity of an etheric body that is less firmly connected with the physical body enables it always to absorb new ideas. An etheric body strongly bound up with the physical, on the other hand, first acquires a sum of concepts, and then the physical body reciprocally imposes upon the etheric body the definite form it has thereby acquired. Thus it is that many people in cultured and educated circles, in later life, can no longer alter what they have inscribed in their brains. Their concepts become rigid and inelastic. Their etheric body can no longer free itself—the physical body will not let go of it. This tendency can then only be overcome by the strength and penetration of spiritual concepts and ideas. You see, here people have to overcome a cosmic tendency through their own powers. This is in fact the human mission: to overcome a cosmic tendency by our own efforts.

A comparison can help clarify what I mean. Imagine a plant pervaded by sap, which renders it fresh and green. Let the plant's sap and moisture stand for the etheric body, and the rest of the plant for the human being's physical body. This human physical body becomes powerful, as I said, by virtue of drawing the etheric body and also the astral body toward it. It gains ascendancy over them. In consequence, the etheric and astral body become weak and powerless, as if moisture were withdrawn from the plant so that it dries up, gradually becomes woody; and this is due to impoverishment of the powers of the etheric and astral body. Similarly a brain that becomes 'woody' can absorb only a few concepts since it wishes to stick with the ones it already has. We must enliven our astral body and our etheric body by taking up spiritual ideas and concepts.

And so we see that the spiritual movement of today contains a necessity intrinsic to the future of our mission as human beings—something as necessary as anything that has affected the human race without our human involvement. However, people will long vociferously dismiss such truths, though to do so will not do any good. People will come to see from developments in culture that come increasingly to the fore in the near future that things are as I describe them. Realities will demonstrate this to them.

Now this altering interrelationship of the bodies or aspects of the human being is not only a factor that concerns all human evolution but it also affects each single human life. The relationship between etheric body, astral body and I is certainly not the same in infancy as it is in old age. This relationship changes in each individual as it does through evolution. The first three years of a child's life must be regarded as very important. Basically a person is quite different then from how they will be later on. We know that these first three years are sharply separated from the rest of a person's life by two facts: one is that we only learn to say I to ourselves at the end of this period, to know ourselves as an I. The other is that, when we look back on our life later, we cannot remember further back than this point, which separates early infancy from the rest of our life. Normally, at any rate, people do not remember what precedes this point in time. In certain respects we are quite different beings before it. And even if modern psychologists say the most inane things nowadays, we must hold fast to this fact: that really we only come to conscious awareness of our I-nature after this period of three years has elapsed. Today we even have books on psychology that state children learn to think before they learn to speak. Such nonsense, as found in popular psychology manuals, is possible only in an age when psychologists working in some official capacity are regarded as serious scientists. One of the most important facts they overlook is this distinction between early infancy and the rest of a person's life. We can even say that a person is quite different in nature in the first three years than after this period. Only later does the human I appear, that principle to which everything else is related. No one should claim, though, that this I was inactive beforehand. Naturally it was not. It does not come to birth only in the child's third year. It was there already, but it had a task different from engaging in the activity of consciousness.

What task did it have then? It is the most important spiritual factor in developing the child's three sheaths, the astral body, the etheric body and the physical body. The brain's physical sheath is continually transformed and here we see the I continually at work. This cannot become conscious because its task at this time is a different one: it has to shape the instrument of consciousness. The principle that later comes to our awareness works upon our physical brain in the first three years of life. In a sense this only represents a change in the task of the I. First it works *upon* us, and then *within* us. It is really a sculptor initially, this I, and what it accomplishes in shaping this physical brain of ours is inexpressible. The I is a mighty artist. But who gives it the powers it possesses? It possesses this power because, basically, the forces of the next higher hierarchy, that of the angels, stream into it during the first three years of life. This is not a metaphor but a reality: our angel, that is, a being of the next higher hierarchy, does actually work in us through the I. This angelic being works in the I, and through the I upon the human being, forming and shaping us. It is as if we possessed the whole stream of spiritual life, as if we flowed upward to the higher hierarchies where the powers of these hierarchies poured into us. But the moment we learn to say I, it is as if something in us is separated from these powers; as if we are now called upon to do something that the angels previously did for us.

Thus in infancy we have something that actually appears as a last echo of what to some degree persisted throughout a person's life in the first post-Atlantean period. For almost the whole of their life, or at least for the first half of it, people directly after the great Atlantean catastrophe were as infants are today. We can see this clearly in early Indian culture. The great teachers of the Indian people, the holy Rishis, were the most childlike of people in early Indian culture. I have often spoken of them. Conceiving of them in terms of a modern scholar would be very mistaken. If you met them today you would not think very much of them—you would think they were simple and childlike, naïve peasants. Nowadays, perhaps, the childlike nature of the Rishis is nowhere to be found any longer. But in their era an influx of Inspiration streamed through them and they uttered things that were mysteries of the higher worlds, and this was because they really never spoke the word 'I' throughout their lives, at least in the way people do today. They never said 'I'. They were not children as such, therefore, because a child's thinking is as yet primitive. But into this same form of soul life flowed the greatest treasures of wisdom. It was as if a child in their first three years of life were to utter the greatest wisdom. Children do not utter wisdom in this way—or at least not in the sense understood by a portion of humanity. But it is also true to say, as I have often remarked, that the wisest person can perhaps learn something from the child. And in fact, someone who can see into worlds of spirit, observing a child before them with the current that ascends from this child into the spiritual world, has—and forgive me the mundane comparison—something like a telephone line to the worlds of spirit. Worlds of spirit speak through the child, it is just that people are unaware of this. The wisest can learn most from children. The child does not utter wisdom as such but the angel does so through the child.

And now the question is this: If the infant's I is not merely their fourth aspect or level but at the same time the lowest aspect of an angel, how does their whole constitution at this point relate to their subsequent life? At this period of childhood, you see, we could categorize the child's I as the lowest aspect of the angel. The bodily sheaths or aspects at this period interrelate in a quite different way from how they do later on. And so we must ask how this changes in the course of life. What occurs later? The living stream is, as it were, cut off and we lose our living connection with the spiritual world. Thus in these earliest years we can observe most keenly the powers a person brings with them from their previous incarnations. At this period the spiritual core of a person is working most intensely to configure and shape the body so as to fit it for this incarnation. How does our later, ordinary consciousness relate to this? A person today no longer has the etheric body and its relationship to the physical body as this existed in the holy Rishis. Throughout the life of such a person, the etheric and astral body retained an inherited configuration enabling the I to sculpt and model the human being's outer body. Nowadays, at birth already, we inherit a physical body that is so dense and exacting that the I can only perform a small part of the work that it once performed. Our physical body is no longer fit material for what we are in our first three years. We inherit the physical body we need for our later life, but it is not suited for raising our gaze to worlds of spirit. The child does not know what is streaming down, and those around him certainly do not, for the physical body has changed, has become more dense and dry. We are born with a soul which in the first three years of life still reaches aloft into worlds of spirit, yet we are born with a body destined to develop the consciousness in which the I lives throughout the rest of our life. If we did not have this dense physical body, we would remain childlike in this current cycle of human evolution. But because we do have it, we cannot become fully aware of how we live in communion with the spiritual world during our first three years.

What is needed now in human evolution? What is the only sound and healthy thing? We can most easily express this healthy principle if we use two terms from olden times for the two beings within us. The one is our being of soul and spirit in the first three years of childhood: this is no longer properly adapted to our outward nature and cannot develop I consciousness. In olden times people used the phrase 'Son of God' for this being. By contrast, the being that nowadays has its physical body such that I consciousness can dwell within it, was called the 'Son of Man'. And thus the Son of God lives within the Son of Man. In today's conditions the Son of God can no longer become conscious in the Son of Man but must first be choked off, cut off, if modern I consciousness is to develop. But our human task is to reshape, to overcome the Son of Man, the outward sheaths, through conscious assimilation of the spiritual world, to gain mastery of them in such a way that gradually the Son of Man will become entirely pervaded once more by the Son of God. By the time the earth reaches the end of its evolution, we must have rendered conscious what we cannot any more render conscious from childhood onward. We must have completely pervaded our Son of Man with our divine aspect. What is it that we must fully imbue and infuse? What must pour itself into all parts of the physical, etheric and astral body so that we completely pervade our whole Son of Man with the whole Son of God? What lives in the first three years of childhood must—now fully conscious and pervaded by the I— infuse and inform our whole human being.

Let us assume that a being were to appear before us as an ideal exemplar of what we need to become, to evolve into. What must be fulfilled in such a being? The soul dwelling in this being is of no use for it cannot pervade the outer sheaths. An ordinary person at the present stage of evolution would not be able to realize the human earthly ideal, would not be able to embody it. We would have to tear out the soul, and, as it were, have it standing there before us, tear out the soul as it is in the Son of Man, and implant into our being the nature of the soul in the first three years, but now fully imbued with I consciousness. There is no other way to conjure before us an ideal of earthly evolution than to picture someone whose soul we tear out and then into whom we implant a soul such as that of the first three years, a childlike soul yet one that possesses full I consciousness. That is what we would need to implant. But how long would such a soul endure existing in a physical human life on earth? The physical body can only bear such a soul living within it for three years, and then it must subdue it. In other words, in such a person the physical body would shatter after three years. The whole karma of the earth would have to be such that the physical body shatters after three years. For in a person of today what lives for the first three years is subdued. Were it to persist, it would instead have to subdue and burst the physical body asunder. And so an ideal of the human earthly mission would only be fulfilled if the human being's physical body, etheric body and astral body remained as they were, ordinary soul nature were torn from it, and the soul nature of our first three years, possessed of full I consciousness, were implanted in its place. Then the soul would burst the human body asunder, but during these three years it would offer an exemplary picture of what the human being can attain.

This is the Christ ideal, and what occurred at the Jordan Baptism is the reality of what has been described. What we must understand to be the human ideal was actually presented to earthly humanity. It cannot be otherwise. The ideal we envisage happened. At the Jordan Baptism, the soul under whose sway we are during the first three years of childhood, but now fully pervaded by the human I, in full upward connection with the world of spirit, was implanted into a human body whose previous soul had departed; and after three years this soul from worlds of spirit burst the bodies asunder. In our first three years of childhood, therefore, we have a weak image before us, as it were an entirely revealed picture, of the Christ being who lived on earth in the body of Jesus for three years. And if we try to develop within us a human being that is like the young child's soul, but fully imbued with all the content of the spiritual world, then we can form a picture of that I-hood, that Christ being of whom Paul speaks when he urged upon us the thought of 'Not I but Christ in me': the child soul filled with I-hood. Then we become able to pervade our Son of Man with our Son of God, and will be able to fulfil our earthly ideal, to overcome all outer nature and rediscover our connection with the spiritual world.

And how should we grow to be? In religious testaments, every saying has multiple meanings. We must become like little children[21] if we wish to look out into the heavenly realms yet possess also the full maturity of the I. This is the prospect awaiting us by the time the earth has fulfilled its mission. We can feel very curiously moved if we realize how, on the one hand, our physical body is facing a process of increasing desiccation, while on the other the process of spiritualization is being initiated and will in future overcome the part of us that grows arid. Out of worlds of spirit, inner life must become so strong that resistant outwardness conforms to its character; then as human beings we will be in harmony with our earthly evolution. Spiritual science teaches us that the earth has long since passed the point when the mineral realm, which forms our soil from granite through gneiss, from slate through to fertile soil, retains its vigorous, ascendant powers. Everything is, rather, involved in a continual process of degeneration. We do not walk about on a ground that is being newly formed but, since the earth has passed the midpoint of its evolution, upon a ground that is already decaying, is already breaking down. Our own development is in full accord with the development of our planet. We possess a physical body that is slowly growing arid, and which we are overcoming, but in the ground beneath us, too, we have something involved in decline, and the forming of valleys and mountains is now a matter of erosion of the earth's crust.

Spiritual science teaches us that we dwell upon a declining earth. If you climb a mountain, you must recognize that it is composed of broken and fragmented boulders, and that these processes of erosion are not ones of regeneration. Since mid-Atlantean times we have passed the midpoint of earth's evolution. Since then we have been living on an earth destroyed, which will eventually fall away from us as a corpse. This is one of the finest examples of the full accord between spiritual science and the mainstream science of today. You see, anthroposophists should learn to distinguish between real science and everything that poses as science in countless popular media but which in fact is nothing but a sum of preconceptions and suchlike. If you go to the real source of each scientific discipline, you will discover that spiritual insights are in full accord with science. This is one of the finest examples. There is no more rigorous geologist than Eduard Suess, and it is no doubt correct, as another geologist has said, that his work *The Face of the Earth* recounts the earth's geological epic.[22] But Suess proceeded very carefully and rigorously. This monumental work of his gives us everything we can assert about geology today without succumbing to preconceived theories. Unlike, say, Buch or Humboldt,[23] who investigated phenomena with predetermined ideas in mind, Suess keeps to the facts. And there is a very interesting thing he says about the forming of the earth, based on his careful collation of facts. In the development of the earth and the soil he ascertains precisely what spiritual science ascertains, though he draws his conclusions from purely physical realities and knows nothing about spiritual science. He says that valleys formed when certain forces caused rock and stone to collapse, giving rise to depressions, leaving higher ground standing and so forth. Everything came about through collapse, overthrow and folding over, in which destructive forces were at play. I'd like to read you a passage from his great work, and you will see that it accords with spiritual insights. He writes this:[24]

> We are witnessing the collapse of the planet. It did of course begin a long time ago, and, since the human race has not yet been here long, we remain confident and cheerful. The traces of this collapse are apparent not only in the high mountains. Massifs have in some cases sunk by many thousands of feet; and the existence of fractures is shown not by the slightest difference in elevation on the surface but by the difference in rock types, or is brought to light by deep mining. Time has smoothed and levelled everything. In Bohemia, in Pfalz, in Belgium, in Pennsylvania: in numerous places on the earth, the plough draws its furrows over the mightiest geological breaks.

I say this only to show you how our planet earth displays the same process of desiccation and decline as the physical body. Those today who establish 'worldviews' do not look to real science. It takes much effort even to study the whole of this mighty work by Eduard Suess. And doing so would be of no use without acquainting oneself with all modern geological knowledge insofar as it supports and leads to such a book. If we go to the real sources of knowledge and science, we invariably find absolutely reliable facts.

And then on the other hand we have a spiritual science which tells us—for instance about the course of earth's evolution—that once upon a time, before organisms existed, the earth was not in some imaginary state where granite was fluid fire, but where the earth was pervaded by the same kind of activity as, for example, a person is when he thinks. This process of disintegration was initiated, and gave rise to what we can describe as follows: from the earth organism, like rain, fell chemical substances that this organism now no longer contains, for instance the substance of which granite consists. These substances filtered down and basically these were processes of destruction which, combined with the chemism of the earth, made it possible for granite to emerge as the earth's solid foundation. A process of disintegration began at this time, and what exists today must be its consequence. Our mineral processes are the consequences of that disintegrative process which continues apace. What must real science teach us? That really the processes exist that must inevitably exist. This is apparent everywhere in true science. Nowhere does true science contradict the tenets of spiritual science. It continually confirms them.

This confirmation extends likewise to reincarnation and karma. But we must eventually get beyond all the theories, preconceptions and suchlike that exist here. We must always resort to facts, not confused hypotheses, such as assumptions made by theoretical geologists about the state of the earth when granite formed, let alone philosophical theories today about the world around us, which are more or less devoid of all spirituality. We should not let ourselves be over-impressed by those who tell us, for instance that human individuation, which we see as founded on reincarnation and karma, originates in the 'endlessness of spiritual evolution'. A person may be world famous and teach that human individuation and development 'originate in the endlessness of spiritual evolution'—but this, however much it is promulgated as official philosophy and associated with the grand name of Wundt,[25] is no more than artificial thunder. Here, in fact, we stand at the boundary between two cultural worlds, and we must be aware of this. One is real science, which, insofar as it is founded on actual facts, continually confirms spiritual science, while the other consists only of diverse philosophical theories, hypotheses and all sorts of 'ingenious' inventions about what may underlie outer processes. True spiritual science must distinguish itself clearly from the latter. And then we will also increasingly recognize how what we learn through spiritual insights—this configuration of the human being and the interrelationships between these bodily sheaths and the diverse eras of humanity's evolution, and also of each individual's evolution—point us to profound secrets of the world. A true understanding of the first three years of childhood, for example, offers us the first level of approach to recognizing the truth of the Mystery of Golgotha, and to understanding the biblical phrase, 'Unless ye become as little children, you will in no wise enter the kingdom of heaven'!

Lecture 5

WISDOM, PRAYERFULNESS AND CERTAINTY IN LIFE

BASEL, 23 FEBRUARY 1911

Properly perceived, spiritual science gives certainty and strength. How can it engage positively in life? Many people think that it impedes rather than supports us in leading a really good human life if we study this realm and gather spiritual insights. Why do we actually need so much spiritual knowledge, why do we need to learn so much about the evolution of the earth and of a whole planetary system? Simply seeking the higher self within us, they think, and becoming a better person in consequence, makes us the best anthroposophists. Other minds of a more theoretical bent, on the other hand, like to hear about what constitutes the human being, to exert their intellect in studying how humanity has evolved through the different cultural epochs, to enumerate all these eras. They wish to learn such things as soon as possible, and preferably note down the most important teachings in summarized form, and be able to disseminate them as a kind of catechism.

Neither of these two outlooks in any way encompass what the science of the spirit can be for a person, and what it can become for someone who, by means of it, is able to find their right footing in life. Certainly it is true to say that we are constituted of a physical, etheric and astral body, and I. But it is mistaken to think that simply listing these facts is enough. This gives us nothing but a schema. Only when we apply such knowledge to life itself do we really learn anything about the human being. But we cannot do so until we recognize that merely knowing these names is not the important thing so much as perceiving how these four aspects are connected and interrelated in the human being. The important thing is whether, say, the etheric body is more or less strongly connected to the physical body, whether the etheric body and the astral body have an affinity and seek a close connection with each other or whether they are more loosely connected. If we consider these matters it becomes apparent that this interrelationship of the diverse bodies changes during the course of humanity's evolution on earth. Compared to today, it was different in the past and will be different again in future. If we look back to the ancient Egyptians in very early millennia of Egyptian culture, and thus to ourselves in former incarnations, we find a loose connection in those days between physical, etheric and astral bodies. Today we have a far denser connection between them. And in future this connection will become ever more compact. In this light we can discover a meaning in our passage through the different cultural epochs. Why do people continually reincarnate, we may ask? Since the nature of the interconnection of our being's sheaths keeps changing, we repeatedly encounter a different kind of outward human existence. As Chaldeans, you see, we had a very different configuration of these bodies than we do today, and in future this configuration will again be different. Our experiences of life are different in consequence.

And now it is important to ask—so that we can form the right thoughts about it—how the inward core of our being, which passes from one incarnation to the next, relates to the garment in which it is clothed each time, to the astral body, etheric body and physical body. External science basically only investigates the outer sheath and knows nothing of the deeper laws that hold sway from one incarnation to the next. But actually mainstream science also overlooks the real, deeper meaning of this outward body. We can discover this if we consider the frames of reference of outward science, and others which it dismisses. Here it is very interesting to note that for a long time science tended to ascribe free will to human beings. But, as I have pointed out previously, in more recent times science often disputes or rejects this idea, citing empirical research. This directs us to study the course of outward life. For instance, you can use statistics to ascertain how many suicides occur in a particular region, and this will show a certain regularity in the suicide rate. Statistics show this to be a regular occurrence. A certain number of people are simply condemned to commit suicide, so how can one speak of free will? Then we could go a lot further in this direction and point to insurance procedures, which calculate and formulate the number of people who survive beyond the age of 30. In other words, there are numerical formulae that can establish how many of those born today will still be here in 30 years. Thus life and death are subject to strict outward laws.

Mainstream science has acknowledged these things. But it will be compelled to acknowledge others too. Realities are coming to light that will compel people to think in spiritual-scientific terms. Science is generally little inclined to assimilate new ideas swiftly but adheres to a curious habit. You often hear rather grand assertions that in the 'Dark Ages' there were people who resisted the teachings of Copernicus. His ideas had a hard time making headway against the dark minds of those times. Yet those most vociferous about this are precisely the ones who not only behave in the same way toward spiritual science but toward scientific facts that now compel us to seek spiritual laws. For instance, a physician in Berlin has discovered certain numerical ratios in human life. This physician, Wilhelm Fliess,[26] has started to record how, in particular families, births equate to the number of deaths. For instance, let us say that a woman dies on a particular day. 1,428 days before this, this person's first grandchild was born. 1,428 days after she died, the second grandchild was born. Thus we have here the death of the grandmother, and, in symmetrical relationship to it, both before and afterwards, the birth of a grandchild. As if this were not enough, in a period of 7 times 1,428 days after the grandmother's death, a great-grandchild is born. If we study this we keep finding very specific numerical relationships which ultimately, and very wonderfully, reveal a connection between births and deaths. Fliess has discovered such things in numerous instances.

Yet science seems reluctant to acknowledge such a thing, since it stands in too great a contradiction to it. Even improvements in health are subject to numerical factors. Certain numerical factors can be seen to govern the number of deaths from tuberculosis in a particular period compared with the number of such cases from previous decades. Physicians say they have reduced the number of cases through hygienic measures. But Fliess proved that this can be calculated according to arithmetical factors. Modern science dislikes this, but is being compelled to acknowledge that objective arithmetical factors hold sway. It will eventually return to the old saying of Pythagoras: number governs everything that exists. While we do calculations inwardly, the higher spirits have long since performed calculations that they embody accordingly in living reality. The saying of Pythagoras that God is a mathematician seems to be gaining credence. But on the other hand, this will also reinforce the view of external science that our human interiority plays no part in our destiny. If it is arithmetically determined when we must die, if births and deaths are connected, say, by periods of 1,428 or multiples of these, it seems that our inward life is harnessed to mighty outward laws and conditions.

It seems we might have to give up speaking of particular laws that hold sway within us. Yet we can cite outer reasons that will demonstrate that this is not entirely true. However carefully it is calculated that a certain number of suicides occur in a particular place, or a certain number of robberies, does this prove that people are compelled to be robbers? Laws of probability can enable us to calculate the probable length of a person's life. But I do not think that anyone will admit they must die on the day determined arithmetically. Our inner being is not compelled to follow this lawfulness of mathematical formulae.

What is happening when Fliess proves that 1,428 days pass between a death and the birth of two children, respectively before and after it? Does this prove something about the inner lawfulness of our I being? The relationship between our inner core and the outward course of life is not easily discernible. How does this accord with the fact that we are subject to karma and that we must follow the dictates of our inner I-being? It is not easy to understand, but I will try to clarify it with a metaphor. It is perfectly possible for two occurrences, two currents, two realities, that do certainly relate to one another, nevertheless to unfold independently of each other. Picture this: If you want to go from here to Zurich, you take a train. You can see when the train departs from the timetable, which contains all sorts of numbers. So in a sense you have an inward connection with these numbers. In your thoughts, aims, inward experience, you feel yourself to be dependent on the numbers in the timetable. But beside this fact of being able to study the timetable, surely there is another that relates to you inwardly, your will and motivations, the fact of wishing to board the train. By studying the timetable you will never decipher whether you are a good or bad person, a wise person or a fool. And in the same way that it is immaterial for our inner soul which timetable we study, it is immaterial for our karma in life which numbers are ascertained by calculations such as those conducted by Fliess. We embark upon the stream of life that is governed by laws that are connected with our own inner lawfulness only by virtue of what we ourselves cause to happen. We must decide to board the train. And it is equally true that we must determine, through the inner laws of karma, to embark upon a stream of life which is then in turn governed by arithmetic.

Why am I saying all this? It is because the spiritual seeker should increasingly acquire a feeling for the complexity of life; should recognize that life is something we should not imagine we can encompass with the easiest and most comfortable thoughts. It is wrong to think, as many do, that life can be understood by citing a few phrases drawn from spiritual science. We need to have the will to delve ever deeper into these matters. We must gain the sense that the thoughts that structure the world also apply to human beings. If there were no connection at all between outward laws and human karma, the whole of life would fall apart.

This can be shown by two facts. In spiritual science we try to present comparisons that are as valid as possible. The numbers on a train timetable are of course connected with practical realities. Although it has nothing to do with the timetable whether or not we go to Zurich, the timetable is nevertheless connected with human circumstances. People have compiled it so as to accord more or less with actual circumstances.

It is generally adapted to human life and needs. Something similar is true of our karma and the flux of our life, which karma governs. Here too the beings of the higher hierarchies have 'determined' the timetable according to numerical relationships that statistics can ascertain by arithmetical calculations, so that they correspond to general human circumstances. On being reincarnated, one person will encounter a comfortable set of circumstances, while another person will meet uncomfortable ones. It is not true to say that in every family this law applies, of a grandchild being born always 1,428 days before the death of the grandmother. But if we consider that the number 1428 is divisible by 28—it is 51 times 28—we can understand this numerical relationship better. In these calculations we will not always come to the number 1428 but usually, between death of a family member and the birth of another, a multiple of 28 will be in play. The multiple may be 13 or 17 or something else, but it will contain the number 28. There is a patterning regularity at work here. The timetable allows us to board various trains. And similarly our karma allows us to arrange our lives, whether comfortably or uncomfortably.

I am saying this not only to suggest how complex these outward conditions are, but I would like to show at the same time that we can draw a moral consequence from such insights. And this is the infinite importance of what spiritual science gives us. We can say that we stand in the world and find within it the numerical relationships that show how our outward life is governed. It took long ages of human cultural evolution to discover this. But how much do we actually know about such lawful regularity? Infinitely little, if the truth be told. Slowly and gradually we discovered something about divine wisdom. But the loveliest and most important wisdoms are the very ones that urge us to be humble: they show us how little the thoughts we have can encompass life. This recognition can spur us on to strive further toward the light.

This moral sensibility, this reverence towards the wisdom of the cosmos, is something we can acquire that makes us better people. And we acquire this feeling towards wisdom, it comes over us, when we recognize that this wisdom stood close to us in our existence between death and a new birth. When the need arises for us to descend again to earthly existence, we choose which train we must embark in to fulfil our karma. We are faced by a decision, and we decide whether this or that family union, these or those parents are the ones we choose. But if we were asked today which the best conditions for our incarnation would be, which family it would be best for us to come to, we would not find the answer. In other words, before incarnating we are more perspicacious than we are in our physical existence, for then, before we were re-embodied, we made the right choice. The sense that we have not become cleverer since incarnating than we were before cannot lead to pride about the things we may have achieved.

Why are we so much cleverer before birth, and able to make the right choice? We would not be so, alone, but in our life between death and rebirth we are pervaded by other forces before we enter physical existence. When we enter upon physical existence, we are pervaded by the substances of the earthly realm that surround us, by oxygen, nitrogen and so on. We absorb them and they are then contained in our bodily sheaths. When we lay aside the body again, and pass through the gate of death, living between death and rebirth, we are absorbed by the beings of the higher hierarchies. In the same way that we live here on earth with the diverse realms of animals, plants and minerals, we live together there with the archai, the archangels and angels. We are integrated into their being in the same way that we are here integrated into physical substances. In the same way that these substances assert their laws here on earth—the iron in the blood, for example, pulsing according to its laws—so between death and rebirth the beings of the higher hierarchies are active within us, and their wisdom pushes us into the right stream of existence. The beings of the higher hierarchies bear wisdom within them in the same way that we bear physical substances within us. And it is only right and proper if the moral consequence of this for us is a sense of humility, when we rightly discern what a small portion of the sublime wisdom of these beings we have assimilated so far in physical life. Between death and rebirth we are embedded in the womb of these beings of the higher hierarchies and must surrender ourselves to them. Not to want this would be like trying to live without absorbing the physical substances of hydrogen, oxygen and so on. It would be absurd to try to live without surrendering ourselves fully to the beings of the higher hierarchies.

If you consider that you must surrender yourself to the beings of the higher hierarchies between death and rebirth, you may ask how best to prepare yourself for that existence. The very best preparation is, now already, between birth and death, to unfold this feeling of devotion toward the divine, spiritual world. All that we assimilate in life becomes reverence and devotion if we imbue ourselves with the right feelings. Humility and devotion to the world of spirit will pervade all our feelings.

If we start to think and to live in this way, we will also find balance in our relationship to the surrounding world. These thoughts regulate and harmonize the rest of our feelings. Many sullying influences from the outer world find their way into anthroposophy. They do not originate in anthroposophy itself but people convey them into it from outward life. Let us imagine someone who is industrious and hard-working in the world and yet to others it appears that this is driven by ambition; he overdoes things, saps his own strength, fails to observe the healthy limits to work. And now he engages with anthroposophy where he encounters ideas very different from those he had previously. And yet he can carry this general quality he possessed before into anthroposophy. He may hear, for instance, that study is necessary to help the soul progress. And so he studies, but does so like a student who wants to be top of the class. He should learn to achieve more balance in the expenditure of his energies—should learn to see what he is capable of achieving according to the powers that karma has assigned him. He ought not to go overboard in his studies of anthroposophy. Or maybe he has heard that it is good for spiritual development to refrain from eating meat, but he forgets to ask whether this is good for his body. He refrains from meat to hasten his development. But anthroposophy should teach us that we must first examine our karma to see if we can immediately adhere to the loftiest rules or not. Calm, humble observation of our own karma, of our own capacities and powers, is something we acquire if we rightly engage with what spiritual science can give us. Those who have made the most progress in esoteric matters are most careful about observing this rule of balance. Sometimes, however, the opposite occurs: when outward circumstances obstruct proper schooling, people may do violence to themselves, push through toward the goals they have set themselves, do themselves spiritual mischief so as to be able to gain an answer immediately to whatever question arises. More advanced pupils will never do this. They will consider the question that faces them but then ask themselves whether they are at present capable of finding a full answer to it. Let us first wait, they will say, to see if the beings of the world of spirit grant us the answer to it. And rather than go at the question full tilt they will hold back initially. They know that they must wait. And they can wait because they are so full of the knowledge that life lasts eternally, and that karma, which they never ignore, gives each person what is right for them. And then, at some point or other, they will receive an inner sign: the powers of the spiritual world will reveal the answer to them at last. This may take years, or perhaps several incarnations. And this characterizes the right outlook: being able to wait, patience, finding balance, never being in too great a hurry.

Those who allow the teachings of spiritual science to work upon them will learn to master their feelings in such a way that this balance, this harmony, becomes observable. With this outlook we penetrate the astral body with the I such that this astral body absorbs truths from the spiritual world, like—to use a trivial expression—a sponge absorbing water. Spirit knowledge gradually informs the astral body and imbues it. Today we live in an era in which it is necessary, and will become ever more necessary, to pervade the astral body with spiritual knowledge. The changing times are leading toward a situation when the human astral body, on passing through the gate of death, and subsequently embarking on future incarnations, will be plunged in darkness and will fail to find its way in the world of spirit unless it has already filled itself with spiritual knowledge. But if it is pervaded by the knowledge of the spirit that we are now absorbing, it will become a source of light and illumine its surroundings. The wisdom we absorb here becomes light in the spiritual world.

If we ask ourselves why anthroposophy has only arrived on the scene now and did not previously exist, the answer is because there was once a primordial wisdom that shaped and informed people without them needing to do anything about it. This was a kind of inheritance that people received from Old Moon, and with it they could penetrate the world of spirit. It lasted until the Christian era, and then people ceased being able to directly assimilate spiritual wisdom. Now we must first imbue the soul with spiritual-scientific knowledge, and this will become the power enabling us in future to enter the world of spirit and illumine it with our inner light. Conditions alter from era to era as humanity evolves.

All esotericists know that there is a wisdom that originated on Old Moon whose vestiges still worked on into the fifteenth or sixteenth centuries. This meant that when people entered the world of spirit they perceived the light there that shone without their involvement. But today we could assimilate as much as we liked of this ancient wisdom passed down as legacy to humanity, and it would no longer shine once we had passed through the gate of death. Only the wisdom we absorb through Christ by saying 'Not I but Christ in me'[27] will be a beacon for our future passage through the gate of death. And so we absorb a science of the spirit pervaded by Christ and thereby possess a source of light in the astral body when we cross the threshold.

But when we absorb this Christ-imbued spirit knowledge, when we fill our astral body with it, it does not remain mere wisdom. It penetrates our feelings too. We learn what occurred on Old Saturn, on Old Sun and on Old Moon, and what the mission of the earth is. If you read your way into the accounts I gave in my *Occult Science, an Outline*, you will feel that the description of Saturn strikes a quite different tone from that of the other planetary conditions. In the description of Saturn conditions you can feel a certain austerity or acerbity. You can feel this inwardly, and this is necessary. Sun existence can be felt as blossoming, burgeoning life. The description of Old Moon can convey a certain dark and melancholy feeling informing all the thoughts about this planetary embodiment. A sensitive person can perceive this, even as far as tasting it on their tongue.

Dullards will say that the descriptions are uneven, the style erratic. But we should know that this is necessary, and we should also know why this is so. We must know why a melody composed of three particular tones is necessary to embody and resonate with accompanying words; and when we know this we can also transform it into feelings, and send these feelings out into the world. The feelings we kindle within us in this way transform themselves. The wisdom that is absorbed by the astral body transforms into a voluntary surrender to world conditions, and this then takes a hold of our etheric body. If we are wise, we prepare our future path. The powers with which we descend into our next incarnations form and penetrate the etheric body. If we have imbued our etheric body with true and genuine prayerfulness and piety, and it is then dissolved into the cosmic ether, we have given to the cosmos an etheric body pervaded by prayerfulness, and it will benefit the whole world. But if we are unpious, materialistic, then we lay aside an etheric body that has a destructive, eruptive effect when it is dissolved into the world ether. The wiser we are, the more we serve ourselves directly, but indirectly also the world. The more prayerful we are, the more we directly serve the world, for piety is communicated to the whole world. And spiritual science can give not only wisdom and prayerfulness, but also certainty and awareness of the life forces of the body. Conscious connection with the spiritual world already gives such life forces.

I have often mentioned that Fichte, who stood at the threshold of anthroposophy, knew something of these matters. There lived in him such a certainty that, in speaking of the nature of the human being, he could say this:[28]

> I raise my head keenly aloft to the plunging mountain slopes and to the thundering waterfall, and to the crashing clouds afloat in a sea of fire, and I say this: 'I am eternal and I defy your power! Break upon my head all of you; and you, the earth and the skies, whip yourselves together into a wild tumult. You elements, rage and foam and pulverize in your wild conflict the very last solar particle of the body I call mine—nevertheless my *will* alone, with its firm intent, will hover keen and cold above the ruins of the universe. For I have grasped my destiny and it is more enduring than you; it is eternal, and I am equally eternal.'

Certainty in life springs from the awareness that the human being walks within the eternity of the spirit. Can a person thus rooted in the eternal spirit grow weak? And it is spirit knowledge that pours ever more such strength into us.

What do we gain from this strength? Wisdom gives the astral body [Mars] what raises us increasingly over inhibiting forces. Prayerfulness governs the powers and the right structuring of the etheric body. [Bors] But what streams into our body when we know ourselves to be connected with the eternal, is assurance in life, and this imparts itself to us right into the forces of the physical body. If we possess this certainty, then maya, illusion and deception fall away. It is illusory to say that our physical body decomposes only into dust at death. No. It is not a matter of indifference to know how the physical body was first configured, how we formed it. If such assurance in the eternal imbues this physical body, then we give back to the earth what we acquired as assurance in life. We fortify our planet earth through what we acquired during our lifetime. Through our physical body we give our certainty in life to the world. In the degenerating physical body, the degenerative part is only maya. If you continue to observe the physical body beyond death you see that the degree of assurance a person acquired in life flows back into our earth.

And so, through wisdom, prayerfulness and assurance in life we fortify in the astral body, in the etheric body and in the physical body what we can develop as our greatest virtues for the whole evolution of our earth. Thus we work upon our whole planet earth, but at the same time we acquire a sense of the fact that we do not stand here in isolation but that what we develop inwardly has value and importance for the whole. And just as there is no solar particle in us that does not bear within it the laws of the universe, so no single human being fails either to enhance or degrade the universe through what they do or omit to do. We can give to the ongoing world process as much as we take from it—and we can degrade it by omitting to concern ourselves with its enhancement, by failing to fill ourselves with prayerfulness and failing to develop assurance in life. By such omission we contribute as much to the destruction of the planet as we enhance it by acquiring wisdom, prayerfulness and assurance in life. And so we gradually come to intimate what spiritual science can become for us in our feeling life if it takes hold of the whole of our being.

Lecture 6

THE I AT WORK UPON THE CHILD AND HOW THIS RELATES TO THE CHRIST BEING

ZURICH, 25 FEBRUARY 1911

In giving a public lecture such as yesterday's[29] about 'Spiritual Science and Our Human Future', or something similar, one has to take account of the receptivity of our modern world, its rather limited receptivity. One has to recognize that, while insights necessary to humanity are flowing down from worlds of spirit in our era, very few people are able to absorb them with an open mind. Most people, without due preparation to absorb such things, would experience the deeper quality of our spiritual science as a shock, as something that appears to them fantastical or dreamlike.

This makes it all the more necessary for us to deepen our consideration of the most important questions and embed them more fully in our feelings. And here I want to point to the need to examine more closely the great truth of the implanting of the I in human nature, a truth that is in fact rather more complex than we usually realize.

We know that during the period of Old Saturn the human being first acquired the foundation for the physical body, then during Old Sun the foundation for the etheric body, during Old Moon the foundation for the astral body, and that the task really of our earthly evolution is to incorporate the I into these other members of our being. Only when we arrive at the end of earth evolution will we be fully pervaded, as far as this is possible, by I nature. If we consider the earthly human being altogether we can say that I nature is the true centre of our being. And yet it must be evident that this I is connected with us differently at different periods of our present life, not always in the same way. And in general we must recognize that we do not as yet grasp the different sheaths of our being if we know only that we are constituted of physical, etheric and astral bodies and the I. Let us now consider how these aspects of our being can be interrelated, both in the different eras of human evolution and in a single human life.

Let us first look at the child. As we know, children learn to say 'I' relatively late. This is deeply significant, even if modern psychologists—who think they practise a science—fail to understand what it means that a child comes relatively late to the thought, the inner experience of the I. In early infancy, indeed until about three or three-and-a-half, though children may sometimes babble the word 'I' in imitation, they do not as yet have a real experience of the I. There is a book, *The Soul of the Child* by Heinrich Lhotzky,[30] in which you will find the curious statement that a child learns to think before learning to speak. This is nonsense. The child learns to think through speaking. Those seeking spiritual-scientific knowledge must be wary of accepting the statements of supposed science today. Children only learn to live fully in the I, and to have knowledge of it, around three or so.

And something else is connected with this: namely that in ordinary awareness— thus not in higher clairvoyant consciousness—we can only remember back to a specific point in our life, and never before that. If you think back over your own life you will see that memory halts at some point and does not reach back to birth. Sometimes people confuse things they have been told with their own experiences, but the thread of memory starts roughly from the point when the experience of the I first appears, and our dimmest memories reach back to this time.

Now let us ask this: If the I experience was not present in our first three years, does this mean the I itself did not live in us in infancy? In fact we have to distinguish whether we always know about what exists within us or whether it can be there without our knowledge. The I is present in the child, but unknowingly, just as we are connected to the I when we're asleep, but know nothing of it. The fact that we know about something is not decisive for its being there. We have to say that the I is present but is not conscious in the child.

How is the I at work? Well, that is quite distinctive. If you were to study the physical human brain you would find that after birth it looks relatively imperfect compared to its later form. Some of its fine convolutions are elaborated later, are sculpted and configured in subsequent years. It is the I that does this in us, and because it has this task it cannot come to conscious awareness in us. It must elaborate the brain and reconfigure it in finer form so that it can later think. The I is hard at work in these early years.

Once the I has become conscious we would ask in vain how it has done this, how it shaped and configured the brain. You will admit that in our whole life from birth to death, the I does not come to conscious awareness of how it has shaped the brain. And yet we can still ask this question. And the answer we receive is that in this activity the I is guided by the beings of the higher hierarchies. If we have a child before us and look at this child with clairvoyant perception, the I is certainly present as I aura, but from this I aura currents pass to the higher hierarchies, to the angels, archangels and so forth, and the powers of the hierarchies stream in. The popular idea that children are protected by their angel is in fact a very real truth. Later this closer union ceases: the I experiences itself then more in the nerves and can become conscious of itself. A sort of narrowing and closing off occurs. Thus in the child we find a sort of 'telephone connection' in that the I extends into the divine, spiritual hierarchies. We have to pay serious heed to spiritual-scientific assertions. I once said that the wisest person can learn a great deal from children. This is because they do not need to confine their gaze to the child but can extend their vision on into the world of spirit, for the child has this 'phone connection' to the spiritual world which is later ruptured. Thus in the first three years we have a quite different being before us than we do later on. We have the I of infancy that works sculpturally under the guidance of beings of the higher hierarchies to elaborate the human instruments of thinking. But then the I enters these instruments and can no longer work upon them from without. By that point, these instruments must have been configured. Though they can continue to develop as the child grows, the I can no longer work upon them.

We can therefore make a clear distinction between a child in the first three-and-a-half years, and the rest of life. In esoteric parlance, we call the first the 'human divine' because it stands in relationship to the higher hierarchies, or the Son of God. The other we call the Son of Man. In the latter dwells the I and moves our limbs, and works, insofar as this is still possible, from within outward. Thus we have to distinguish between the Son of God and the Son of Man.

In other words, we have to conceive of a gulf separating the Son of God and the Son of Man. The Son of God, who is primarily active up to the age of three-and-a-half, contains all enlivening powers, spurring us on to pour ever more and more life forces into our organism. These forces also contain something upbuilding, healing, enlivening by contrast to the being we later are. If at a later stage of life, we wish not only to have a human nature dependent on the senses and the instruments of the physical body, through which we relate and connect to our surroundings, but also seek to extend ourselves upward into the world of spirit, then we have to try to awaken something of these powers in us voluntarily. We have to appeal to the forces that live in us in earliest infancy, except that we now waken them consciously whereas the child unconsciously invokes them. We can see therefore that in this respect we possess a dual nature.

What appears in these powers of the first three-and-a-half years? Working under the guidance of the higher hierarchies something comes to expression that works over from former incarnations. You can easily confirm this by studying the human skull, which contains different ridges and depressions depending on the individual. No skull is identical with another, and so you can't have a generally applicable phrenology either. The powers at work in the human skull come from former incarnations, and cease to have any momentum after these three-and-a-half years have elapsed. During this period everything is still mobile and the spirit can still work upon it. Later everything becomes fixed, and it can no longer do so.

What does it mean that we cannot work with these powers any more later on? What is this due to? It is due to our specific evolution on earth. Once the I has become conscious of itself in the body, this presupposes that the body is stable and fixed, and can no longer be receptive to the work of the powers I have spoken of. We are concerned here with powers intrinsic to us as a species, which build up our human architectural form. If we were to work with these forces of infancy in the physical body for longer than these three-and-a-half years, which is the right and proper period for this, the physical body could not endure it. It would come asunder, break apart, for now the forces that give us stable fixity through physical heredity come into play. If the other powers did not cease, the body would break apart, could not endure it. Instead we sink down into our Son of Man; the Son of God can no longer make headway against our Son of Man after three years. But we still bear this Son of God within us nevertheless. These powers keep working within the physical body throughout our life, but can no longer directly participate in upbuilding processes. If we inwardly examine ourselves, we can find, though, that the I with its 'telephone connection' survives. But the physical body is now too coarse, too dense, too 'woody' for the Son of God to continue shaping it sculpturally.

The best powers are present in these first three to three-and-a-half years, and we continue to be nourished by them for the rest of our lives. They are dimmed, and yet they still remain present in later years in the most varied ways. It is as if we were imbued by these powers yet cannot give direct expression to them. If we seek to absorb ideas of higher worlds through spiritual science, we can do so all the better the more we still contain within us of what lived in us in our first three years, when the I acted selflessly within us. The fresher and more mobile these forces are, the less aged they have become as we advance into old age, the more it is possible for us to transform ourselves through these powers of the spirit. What we have around us in these three years is the best portion of our humanity. Only the dense physical body hinders us, sadly, from making full use of these forces. Developing them to a special degree in our later years—although we can no longer alter our physical body by this means for we are no longer soft as wax—we can nevertheless, by making full use of them through esoteric wisdom, enable this power to flow out of us through our fingertips. We gain the special gift of healing, of curing someone by laying our hands upon them if these spiritual forces are still active. They no longer reshape our own body but they bring blessing and benediction to others as they flow out of us.

The goal of earth evolution is gradually to unfold these powers within us. When earthly evolution comes to an end, and we have passed through our many incarnations, we will have had to entirely pervade ourselves consciously with what we possess unconsciously in our early childhood years. It makes a difference whether we possess these powers unconsciously or consciously. By then people will have to have become fully imbued with this form of childlike consciousness. And then it will no longer burst the confines of the body because it will only slowly have expanded it.

In world evolution an archetypal prefiguring was needed for this influx of the power of infancy into humanity. It is self-evident that this paradigm could not be given in the form of a young child. A human being who had attained a certain age had to be pervaded consciously with the same forces that in childhood unconsciously pervade us. If we had a human being before us whose I we extracted, removing it so as to make him empty of this I, and if we were instead to pour into him what the child possesses in early infancy, he would bring it to consciousness with his developed brain. Then he would be conscious of what lived in him during the first years of childhood. How long can a human being on earth endure these elements? Three years, no longer, and then he must fall apart. If this principle cannot transform itself—in ordinary human development it does transform—then the human body can endure it for no longer than three years. If it were to be possible at all for a being to bear the forces of infancy consciously within him, then this person's karma must be such that the physical body in whom this being is implanted falls apart after three years.

It is therefore conceivable that what the human being will attain by the end of earthly evolution is prefigured in the world by someone whose corporeality is such that his I can be removed and, his incarnations making this possible, another being can be implanted into him. Then the human body would tolerate this implanted being for no longer than three years. By its rightful karma this human body would then break asunder. And that is what happened. At the Jordan baptism was present a human body of such a kind that its I, the I of Zarathustra, could depart; and then a being could descend into this body. The Christ being filled it, but could only remain there for three years. After these three years, this body broke asunder in the Mystery of Golgotha.

What was able to live for three years in that human body is something we must, as human beings, cultivate and nurture and gradually through incarnations bring to living reality within us so that, at the end of our incarnations, it can be fully and entirely present in the human being. We see here a remarkable connection between the Son of God in the human being and the Christ event. For all the things we find in esotericism can be illumined from various angles. Evidence such as ordinary science requires cannot suffice for esotericism. Evidence is compelling here only when truths are brought together from all sides, reciprocally supporting each other. We can come to know the Christ event from yet another angle by deriving it as we have done today from human nature itself. We have seen how we can best understand the Christ by developing an outlook that arises from such a truth. We must recognize that at the Jordan baptism there came to dwell in the fully developed body of Jesus of Nazareth a being that lives in every human body, but only unconsciously, in the first three years of life. And here we must look upon the three years of Christ as a time in which this child being is transposed into consciousness. That is the best way to acquaint ourselves with the Christ being.

Old sayings can be variously interpreted. One such is that 'Unless ye become as little children, ye will in no way enter the kingdom of heaven.'[31] Here we see deep into the profounder meaning that sometimes lies in the verses of religious testaments.

Let us consider life in childhood especially at this period, as it properly unfolds. Modern scientists do not yet know a great deal about what can help us study the true nature of the human being. We have to recognize firstly that the human being is radically different from the outset from all other creatures. If you study a creature close to us, an ape, you find that from the beginning its stance is intrinsic in it through a singular balance of weight and posture, the singular balance and distribution of its limbs. To begin with a person cannot walk at all but must first develop and achieve this distribution of balance and posture. Through the work of our I we have to bring our limbs into a position in which we can remain upright and walk. In these early years of childhood, therefore, this I not only has to work at modelling and configuring the brain, but also at achieving balance and stability that is not naturally given us as it is to animals. We have to first bring our bones into angles, relative to our centre of balance, that are necessary for walking. The animal, right up to the highest animals, has this as a natural endowment from the beginning. In the human being, by contrast, the work of the I is needed to achieve this gradually. Prior to this we crawl or fall over. Thus we would be bound to one place, to the ground, if our I did not do its work in the first years of infancy.

As we saw, the I works upon its brain, chisels at it and shapes it like a sculptor so that we can later become discerning beings. And so we can say that we acquire discernment of the truth in life by virtue of the I shaping its instrument. We have to realize that no further life is possible for us without us achieving it in this way.

Another thing that radically differentiates human beings from animals is our speech. Speech too must first be achieved by the I. We do not have a predisposition for speech—it is not one of the capacities we are naturally endowed with. A cow says moo, but this is not yet speech. Acquisition of language depends upon the I dwelling amongst other human I beings. If a person were to be transported to a distant island and lived alone there, he would not learn to speak. Second dentition is an inherited characteristic, and we would still get our second teeth on this lonely island. But speech is something we acquire through the I in engagement with the human life round us. These differences are important. Thus in what we call human life, speech is the third thing that our I acquires.

By activating these powers the growing person finds their path on earth, discerns truth, and lives a human life in engagement with their surroundings. To express what is acquired in this way, the child might say, if it could: 'The I within me transforms me such that I am the way, the truth and the life.'[32] If we conceive of this transformed into a higher, spiritual realm, how must a being that lives for three years in a human body with fully conscious powers of childhood speak to humankind? It would say, 'I am the way, the truth and the life.' And indeed, as these powers of childhood ascend to a higher, fully conscious level, we find again the great exemplar of what becomes apparent in the child at a lower level. This is conveyed through Christ Jesus as a primary truth. The saying, 'Unless ye become as little children ye will in no wise enter the kingdom of heaven' cannot be comprehended unless we know what spiritual science can teach us about our connection with enlivening forces of childhood. And it is equally true that what rings out as a radical statement, 'I am the way, the life and the truth', is best understood if we see it as a paradigm for what the I achieves in the body of the child.

From such things we gain the possibility of accessing, for the soul at least if not for the body, a portion of the enlivening powers which we need on earth. People today, insofar as they do not acknowledge a world of spirit, have no proper feeling of such realities. If you go to numerous people who live in the mainstream of life today, and say to them what I have now said to you—about the need to become as little children in order to enter the kingdom of heaven—you will see what kind of response you get. They will acknowledge that such comments are ingenious comparisons but that they can't get anywhere with them. They will find it more useful to go and watch some sensational play, or even worse. If people have no real feeling for the meaning of these truths, they will find little justification for them. You see, in the feeling for such things lies the very capacity to introduce a childlike gift of apprehension into our life. If we are unable to have sympathy and enthusiasm for something like the comparison between Christ and the activity of the human I in early childhood, if we regard this as merely childish, then we lack the ability or gift to awaken the originating powers of childhood. All the arid academics have very little ability to waken these primary powers of childhood, and thus to reach the world of spirit. If we have enthusiasm for pondering on such things, it works in our soul so that we can penetrate ourselves with these powers of infancy.

But this gives us a portion of what enables us to retain a broad-hearted and open Christianity. I have often said, haven't I, that we are only at the beginning of our understanding and apprehension of Christ? For centuries, through to the twelfth and thirteenth centuries, a Christianity existed whose faithful had no means of reading the Bible, who depended instead on sermons and on the teachings of inspired people. Then came a Christianity that stuck to the Bible, that drew its knowledge from the biblical texts. And we are unaware of the power of Christ if we do not recognize that his statement, 'I am with you always unto the end of the ages'[33] is something he made real. We are Christians if we recognize that Christ, after his first manifestation, will manifest again in every age for every person who wishes to see him. The Christ is not so poor that he says only the things recorded in the Gospels. We should not repeatedly cite the words, 'Ye cannot yet bear to hear it',[34] but let humanity, rather, make itself mature enough to perceive the Christ.

This will include becoming able to find the right stance toward what pours in through the Jordan baptism, toward the sound, fruitful powers of infancy. This would be a deep and fruitful, germinal idea. Even if people did not know the name of Christ or anything of the Gospels—names are certainly not the primary thing to consider—what counts is the being and the reality. We can leave it to others to say that faithful adherence to a religion means invoking particular names. We adhere not to names but to realities. And we do so, for instance, by discerning the powers at work in early childhood that once descended upon the body of Jesus of Nazareth.

Imagine you lived on a lonely island where no news of the Mystery of Golgotha had ever arrived. Nevertheless, if there were people living there who, in their spiritual life and work, absorbed the power of early infancy in full consciousness and cultivated it through into old age, they would still be Christians in the true sense of the word. Then there is no need to search in the Gospels, for Christianity becomes something living and will go on and on developing. This is a distinction we must keep clearly in mind; and then we will increasingly recognize how intimately, really, the Christ mission is connected with the whole nature of the earth. We will be able to see that this

Christ mission is something that we can discern in the nature of modern humanity itself. The need for permeation by Christ, of living the Pauline saying 'Christ in me',[35] becomes apparent when we can acknowledge that we need to transform what lives in us in early childhood, and pervade the whole of our life with it. Then the Christ is in us.

This enables us to encompass Christianity in the broadest and most heartfelt sense, and gives us a perspective in which Christianity can assume quite different forms. Times will come when Christ will be called by a quite different name, when quite different sacred texts will exist, and when people will no longer refer at all to an outward history that recounts that Jesus of Nazareth once lived in such and such a place. Instead through their consciousness of humanity, people will discern this reality.

We present such things because they enable us to show, time and time again, how the science of the spirit can engage in the deepest conceivable way in the whole shaping of human feeling and how it must become a living practice. Only then will we be able to understand what we find in historical documents. For many the sacred texts are a book with seven seals. Consider people today: by the end of earth evolution they will have reached the point of inwardly permeating their souls with Christ, but today they are only at the beginning of this work. Yet Christ still lives in us, and through all our subsequent incarnations he will increasingly live in us in an ever broader and deeper sense.

How were things back in the time before Christ revealed himself on earth? As yet the I was only in preparation. The Christ is what gives meaning to the I, and before this the I was only being prepared. Whenever an entity is still in preparation, the beings who preceded it must help it. The human being was preparing to give the I its meaning, up to the point of the events at Golgotha. Until then other beings had to help us, ones who had previously attained the level of humanity, that is, on Old Moon. We know that these are the beings of the higher hierarchies of the next level, the angels. They stand one level higher than the human being. The primary mission of these beings was to guide and direct humanity as long as human beings themselves were not yet able to look to Christ and to say 'Christ gives my I its meaning.' For this reason human beings were not able to guide themselves toward Christ but had to be guided by beings who are their elder brothers.

The Bible conveys this with wonderful precision. Consider the precursor of Christ, John. If he is really to be the precursor, he cannot be the figure of which outward history tells, for he does not yet possess the I in the sense I have described. Therefore we cannot say that Christ's precursor, John the Baptist, preceded him. Remarkably, the Gospel of St. Mark begins with these words of the prophet: 'I will send my angel before you, who will prepare the way.'[36] In other words, we must take note of something acknowledged in the abstract in theological circles, but ignored in its actual reality. The outer world is initially *maya*, illusion. We have to first learn to perceive it in the right way, and then it is no longer maya. When outward events on the physical plane are related by John, this is maya. We do not understand them. The Bible regards the person of John as maya. Within John, taking possession of his soul, lives an angelic being who leads human beings to Christ. John is a carapace for the revelation of the angelic being. The angel was able to enter him because the reborn Elijah was ready to assimilate him. The angel then spoke through him, was sent, and only makes use of John as a mouthpiece. The Bible is very precise in this respect.

And so we can say that humankind could only be led toward the I by virtue of the fact that those beings who had completed their 'humanity' stage on Old Moon became the guides of earthly human beings in the pre-Christian period. All ancient leaders of humanity were so because angels worked through them. How is this now for modern human beings? In pre-Christian times, angel beings worked into their nature since they did not yet have the I within them as their own exemplar. But now that we possess the sun light of Christ, we are able to turn our countenance toward Christ, and through this a power enters us again which the angels once emanated. In the same way that we once received the angels, we must now receive the Christ through devotion to the Christ being. In his day John said: Not I but the angel in me has been sent as a messenger and uses me as an instrument to prepare the path; and in the same way, today, we must say like Paul: Not I but Christ in me. We must learn to understand the Christ in terms that spiritual science teaches.

We need not hold back in stating what, for instance, I said today about the first three years of childhood. We Christianize ourselves by emphasizing how infancy sheds its sunlike glow over the whole of our life, whereas modern science causes people to grow old prematurely: they fail to imbue themselves with the sun powers of infancy, instead rendering the brain and other aspects of their being desiccated.

Among other truths, therefore, let us take up the idea of being able to discern the true nature of Christianity without relying on written documents, reflecting only upon the nature of the human being instead. Rather than seeing spiritual science in terms of theoretical categories, and citing the fact, say, that we consist of four members—the physical, etheric, astral bodies and the I—we can try to see how these different aspects are connected within us, and will then discern how the I of infancy bears an affinity to another being. We will discern that this I is, as it were, like a sheath, and after three years entirely shifts its role in relation to the other members, the rest of our human nature.

This insight acquires its proper value when it becomes an actual power in us, and when we say this: We must pass through many incarnations on earth in future; we know that we can develop what is within us to an ever greater and broader degree, and bring it to ever greater awareness. We know that we can entirely pour out the higher human being, the Son of God in us, upon the Son of Man, and thereby continue to ascend and advance from incarnation to incarnation until the earth arrives at its goal. At that point the earth will become a corpse just as each single person becomes a corpse. Just as each person's corpse returns to the earth while the soul rises to the world of spirit, so it will be with the whole earth.

If we regard the whole earth as the body of all humanity, we can say that the earth will die and become a corpse, will dissolve into the matter of the universe, will be pulverized so that its substance can be used anew. But the human being will rise into worlds of spirit so as to pass on into the next planetary stage. And we must keep in mind that these words are not abstract ones.

It is strange, isn't it, that there are people who think that our earth with the sun and the other planets originated in a great fog-soup and nothing more, and that from it emerged the sun, the earth and, through confluence and amalgamation of matter, the human being arose; and that our human evolution will simply continue and eventually come to an end in the grave of earth, the whole thing a meaningless episode! The future history of culture will find it very hard to understand this morbid fantasy—to understand how human imagination could ever have become so morbid as to seriously accept this idea. To formulate the Kant-Laplace theory is tantamount to explaining humankind in terms only of the dust into which we return at cremation. Such a science is deadly, it does not enliven the living power in our soul. Spiritual science seeks to enliven this power, to develop it within us to ever higher forms, and enable us to see ourselves as more than a configuration of dust. It enables us to develop towards a new planetary existence.

Lecture 7

THE INFLUX OF SPIRITUAL INSIGHTS INTO LIFE

ST. GALLEN, 26 FEBRUARY 1911

In our branch meetings we acquire ideas about the nature of the human being, about human evolution, learning for instance that we are constituted of physical body, etheric body, astral body and I. While this is certainly a gain relative to the general knowledge prevailing in the world today, we cannot say that this more or less theoretical understanding of ours as yet amounts to what anthroposophy can in truth be for human beings. Anthroposophy will only become what it should be for each individual and also for our human community if it passes into life, if it becomes living practice. And on occasions such as this when I myself can see you again, dear friends, I am glad to be able to turn your attention to the fact that the ideas, the laws at work in the universe and in humankind, which we otherwise learn about in the annual programme of these branch meetings, play an important role in human life itself. Today I would like to reflect upon how anthroposophy actually flows into life.

Those who may as yet know little about anthroposophy may often wonder this: Yes, we speak here of the realities and truths of supersensible nature, but how can someone who is not yet clairvoyant say anything much about these worlds of spirit, how can anything be known of these worlds except the things that others relate? This is a very common preconception, but it has very little justification. It is true that without clairvoyance we cannot, for instance, perceive the human being's astral body; but what happens to and with this astral body can be experienced first hand, and here anthroposophy is extraordinarily helpful.

Let me cite an instance of how someone can experience the fact that they do possess an astral body. As you know, in daily life people are used to doing many things without thinking, many things too that they do not even intend to do. Consider how many people do things from morning to night without fully reflecting on what they are doing, without being fully present. And later they may realize that they themselves were not entirely happy with what they did. Isn't it true to say that we then do things that we only partially consider or reflect upon, only partly accompany them with our thoughts? Such unthinking habits are often due to our tendency to absorb things from without that we would not do if we reflected consciously on them or if we educated ourselves differently.

From a materialistic point of view, it might seem as if it were a matter of indifference whether we act in ways that accord with our intentions or not, whether we do things that we can justify to ourselves or not. To clairvoyant perception this is not so. To clairvoyant vision it is apparent that every act, every action that is not morally justifiable to us, makes an impression or imprint upon our astral body. It is like a blow to our astral body. And of those who act in such ways you can say that they have many ruptures, many pits and hollows in their astral body because they do many things that they would not be able to justify morally if they thought about it.

I am not now thinking of professional matters but of habitual actions. Here, every such impact affects the astral body, and because it does not fade but resides there, it acts further upon the etheric body too, is imprinted there like a signet impress, and remains there so that the person walks around with all these signet imprints in their etheric body. Those who are not clairvoyant can say that— up to this point—that they have no way of knowing this; yet what occurs here is actually experienced. Things remain present in a certain way, really for the whole of the rest of a person's life, and work back upon them so that they may sometimes feel they have had enough of life. Or they may display sullen ill-humour to those around them, and this sullenness works back upon their own health.

It is extremely important to be aware of such things. Often, you see, for instance around the age of 37, something will emerge that makes us inwardly morose, without any apparent cause, that puts us in ill-humour, makes us melancholy—and will then have a harmful effect on our health. It can play havoc with our digestive system, and cause other such conditions. This may have been set in motion when we were, say, 20 years old, when the imprint of the astral upon the etheric was first instigated.

Thus we can say that only the clairvoyant can perceive what lives in the astral body, but that everyone can experience its effect. Some people would never become morose, displaying a certain instability and sense of inner helplessness, nor would their bodily organism become so debilitated, if they considered that actions whose consequences do not immediately become apparent in the world nevertheless enter our invisible being and only later come to view. If someone were to decide to observe whether what the clairvoyant says is true or not, they would soon see, and feel, the truth of such things. The actions and deeds we do everyday but cannot justify to ourselves, lead to consequences for us.

Let us consider the opposite case, someone who can think and reflect in broader dimensions than they can actually bring into effect. This is the case for every idealist. They know they cannot realize all their ideals but only some of them. If we harbour great ideas, we must be happy if we can realize just a portion of them. If we are able to reflect on matters that go far beyond what life allows us, this also works back upon the astral body, but differently, so that a person then imbues it with healthy forces that render them strong, inwardly stable and tranquil. If, say, a person was an idealist around the age of 20, and, not crediting materialistic views, retained belief and trust in their ideals, this will become apparent later on in life in that they will not be too shaken by every little mishap, nor by ailments: they will remain more steadfast and be content to let be what will, as opposed to others who did not develop ideals in earlier life.

Thus ideals we have that go beyond what life allows us to realize can give us stability and tranquillity. Mainstream physicians are already becoming aware of this, but they do not know how to make real use of it, how to encourage people to have a full range of positive thoughts that surpass mundane realities.

Certainly, there are popular books that are thought to be beneficial for mental health. Such books recommend developing calmer and more consistent thoughts to achieve stability, tranquillity, equanimity and so on. This is a very good place to begin for some people, though it does not take us very far down the road toward finding real soul nourishment. Books by authors such as Duboc and Ralph Waldo Trine[37] are very good as a starting point. As far as the real requirements of soul health are concerned, however, they offer no more than would be gained by asking what we need to be physically healthy, and getting the answer that we need to eat healthy food, food whose substances can easily be absorbed by the organism. It's true of course! But this leaves unanswered the question as to what food this is exactly. It leaves unanswered what the actual steps are for achieving soul health.

These books, which have as much to say about mental health as such rules would have to say about physical health, are fine as a first step, but will not offer any real assistance in the course of our further quest. By contrast, spiritual science offers us thoughts of the most precise kind, very specific thoughts about how people have engaged in self-development in all eras and how they can do so today. This becomes ever more apparent through the treasures of anthroposophic wisdom, so that we can say this: spiritual science gives us great opportunities to reach in our thoughts far beyond what we can actually realize in life. Anthroposophy therefore makes us inwardly stable, enabling us to draw forth from within a balance and equanimity whenever something occurs in our close proximity and threatens to unsettle and upset us.

Whether something unsettling reaches our ears is not what matters, but the attention we give to it, and how we engage with it. Things that occur outside us play in to our inner state, which can fluctuate between being over the moon at one moment, and deeply downcast the next, and these volatile excesses of feeling undermine our moral and physical health. There are plenty of painful states of soul, and these can be compared to the clattering of the mill wheel.

The miller who works in the mill no longer even registers the sounds. Thus we can surrender to every least painful incident, and magnify the sound, if you like, of our own clattering mill wheel, or we can divert our attention from it. This will not work if our soul is empty, but it will if we possess an inner content of soul from which we can draw strength.

Let's take an example. Imagine two people, one of whom goes to the office every day and works. At lunch time he has a drink or two, and talks to people. In the evening he has another little drink and then he goes to bed. When something disrupts the normal rhythm of his life, such a person will immediately be overwhelmed by it: he attends to the clattering of his own mill wheel, his own hurt or pain, for he possesses nothing within him he can draw upon to drown out the noise of it.

A second person likewise fulfils his daily tasks, but unlike the other he harbours within him many thoughts of great scope, such as spiritual science affords us. These resound from within him so that he no longer hears the outer clatter and rattle. It is not that we need make arduous efforts to draw such content forth; it simply appears by itself by virtue of the fact that we have attached strong feelings to it. Therefore we will suffer less from the slings and arrows of life, finding ever more comfort from what we have acquired within us through years of spiritual effort. This becomes a possession, a special and precious one that no one can take from us. Everything else we acquire in the world, or that is given us, can be taken from us. But what we acquire for the spirit becomes a possession that henceforth we can never be deprived of.

People like saying that death is the great leveller. Certainly, but it is equally true that there is no conceivable situation where what I have said would not hold good. Being rich, belonging to an aristocratic family, will not help us here. To gain this spiritual possession, we must all pursue one and the same path. It is not only death that makes all one, but the life of the spirit too, before which all are equal. And this endows this life of the spirit with a far-reaching significance, for from it flows something that raises us above the illusions of the sensory world.

Someone might object that a slate might fall on my head, and cripple me. Or I could suffer a brain injury and lose my mind. But if we really make the treasures of anthroposophy our own, so that we possess them inwardly, we will know that such a condition is only a passing one. Even if our brain were gravely damaged, this would only be like wishing to make something and finding the tool broken that we wanted to do it with—for instance wanting to hammer in a nail and finding the hammer broke as we did so. All we can do then is find another hammer. The same is true of the brain. Consciousness can lose its tools but in a new life we can remake them. We need not let our sense of eternity fail in relation to the inviolability of our spiritual possessions. It is not a matter of knowledge alone, but of this knowledge penetrating our heart, and doing so in such a way that we retain fruits which lead us even beyond the loss of the tool and instrument of our cognition.

All this testifies to the fact that such things act upon our astral body. How exactly they do so is something only the clairvoyant can know, but the consequences can be experienced by each and every person in their daily life. Someone who often acts in ways they cannot morally justify, and who becomes morose in consequence, will easily suffer pain whenever something unsettling happens. But if, in response to the same occurrences, a person can rate them as little compared to their inner experiences and ideals, this certainty will emanate a healing effect. They will be able always to hold to the eternal that lives in them. And if, in this fulsome way, the spirit of eternity approaches us, as is the case in anthroposophy, then we are safe in all of life's circumstances.

Now, my dear friends, there are other things that can convince us that the spiritual treasures we assimilate, which we imbue ourselves with, have a very close connection with our whole happiness in life, our full engagement with it. Just as someone can have good moods, so they can also suffer bad moods that may continually return and plague them, that dominate their whole inner soul configuration. Here the spiritual researcher will say that such moods come to expression in a person's supersensible nature; they lodge in the etheric body, imprint themselves in the physical body and act upon the blood. When a mood affects the etheric body, an action is exerted upon the blood, and the result of this is a tenor of mood that continually returns to plague someone throughout their life. This impairs their blood circulation, makes their blood heavy. And here we have an instance where we can say that the effect of what occurs in the soul passes into the physical body. Even someone who is not clairvoyant can notice this and say that their body hampers them, that they suffer from it and that this results from their whole mood. If they could change this, they say, then they know that they could exert a healing effect upon their whole constitution.

Now it might be thought that we then need only free ourselves from the physical body. But it is not a question of requiring someone to recognize the body's dependence on the mind and spirit, but of the reality that the strength of the spirit allows us to become independent of the body. We become independent precisely by making the body an instrument of the spirit.

The materialist who believes the teachings of materialism, is better off than someone who is actually dependent on energy and substance—so that, for instance, they can be in only one place in winter, and spend the summer only in some other place. To avoid ailments such as neurasthenia they become entirely dependent on physical conditions. Thus it is not a matter only of believing in these teachings of energy and matter, but actually becoming dependent on material conditions. What kind of life is it after all if we are always obliged to spend winter only in the city and summer only in the country? Prayer and belief do not help such a person, for they are a materialist in the full sense, they have actually become dependent on 'energy and substance'.

If we allow thoughts derived from spiritual enquiry to work upon us, our connection with the world of spirit becomes apparent to us. But we see something else as well. If we are very unhappy, to an extent that someone else could not deal with, we find that an anthroposophist can deal with it. Imagine someone who is 18 years old, who has been used to having things paid for by his father, but now his father goes bankrupt. Suddenly he has to work. He may experience this as misfortune. Time goes by and he reaches the age of 50. Then he can look back and say, 'Thank God this misfortune occurred, for otherwise I would have become a good-for-nothing.' Once we are no longer embroiled in misfortune we can regard it as an instrument of our development. We must be able to say that our own karma presented us with this misfortune, and that we needed its educative effect in our lives. Someone who can form such thoughts, at least, will not grumble at the world at times of misfortune but recognize the validity and wisdom in it. But gradually this will create in us moods that have a quite different effect from our feelings of dependency on 'energy and substance'. Now we know, rather, that we are dependent on the guidance of the spiritual cosmos. This imparts itself to our mood, and through the resulting effects upon our etheric body we remove ourselves from dependency on 'energy and substance'. And then we do not need to go to the Riviera in order to improve our mood, but instead our spiritual possessions enable us to shape our inner instruments so as to become independent of external factors.

Ways to sustain such a mood are not found in the writings of Ralph Waldo Trine and others. But pouring the wisdom of anthroposophy into our mood does render us independent of matter and energy, opening us to a source that raises us beyond time and space. Then we remove ourselves from the power of matter, and work back upon the instrument of our body. Gradually, by this means, we acquire practical benefits for the way we live. Not everyone believes this straight away, my dear friends; since all are so dependent on matter and energy, very few are disposed to recognize such things. Experience could teach them that these things are true, for experience can offer us living proofs. Spiritual science has practical fruits, you see, that become apparent in very mundane ways, in our actual lives.

I'd like to offer examples of what spiritual science teaches, and to do so will cite some very mundane circumstances. Because we engage with outward matter on the physical plane, in certain situations we must be able to discern the spirit at work in this matter surrounding us—for matter is only an illusion, maya, and everything is really concentrated spirit. In ordinary life we must gain a sense of the spirit within material objects. Thus our outward relationship with things must be such that we can still find what you might call intimate connections with them.

There are people who often wash their hands, and others who rarely do so. In some ways there is a big difference between the first and the second. In respect of our various bodily parts, we are in fact pervaded by the supersensible in very different ways. For instance, the etheric body does not pervade our chest and upper thigh to the same extent as it does our hands. From the fingers, especially, powerful etheric rays stream out. And because this is so, we can develop a wonderfully intimate relationship with the outer world through our hands. Those who often wash their hands have a finer relationship to their surroundings, are more subtly sensitive to them, because, through the spirit materialized in the blood, an effect issues to make a person more sensitive in their hands. Those with thicker skins for the surrounding world do not often wash their hands. You can observe how insensitive such robust people are to the singularities of their fellow human beings, whereas those who wash their hands often enter into a more intimate relationship with their surroundings. If someone were to try to bring about something similar elsewhere, say with the shoulders, if they were to wash them as much as the hands, they would likely develop neurasthenia. What is healthy for the hands is not good for the shoulders. Our organism is such that we can develop this intimate relationship to our surroundings through our hands.

It would also be detrimental to wash the face so often. To treat the face like this would not be beneficial for health. Things are quite different for other parts of the human body. People who have not been properly schooled in spiritual science, physicians with a materialistic outlook for instance, do not notice the difference, and recommend cold ablutions for children. Such things are done to a fanatical degree. People ought to realize that such a measure is worse than anything else! It creates the tendency for neurasthenia, is an absurd undermining of health. The hands cope with it, whereas it makes the rest of the body receptive to materiality. Here you see the effect of materialism. I'm speaking here in general terms. Things are different in cases where such a measure is used temporarily for a curative purpose.

The youngest children are washed down in cold water systematically every morning, a torment for them. But that is not all. They are made to run about naked in the sun, go sunbathing, so that the material aspect of the outer world can act upon them. We should be glad that we can work outward from our inner centre, and should not render ourselves ever more dependent on matter. This complete exposure of the body to outward influences is the same as if the miller did everything possible to hear the clatter and rattle of the mill wheel, and was displeased if he could not hear it. There are exceptions of course, cases where a temporary remedy of this kind is needed. But if this is done throughout childhood a person's organism will become susceptible to every least influence. The organism hardens itself, inures itself so that in the end it is entirely hardened and no longer feels outer influences.*

Such insights do not arise simply from ordinary pragmatism. That isn't possible. We can only assess such things once we understand the whole human being. But you can deduce from very simple things that the human being is complex, and that the most diverse interrelationships exist between our physical, etheric and astral body and so forth. You may perhaps have found it difficult to take seriously what was said today about the particular ways in which the astral and etheric bodies are connected with the physical body. On the one hand I have said that the removal, or the illness, of a particular organ can bring a person close to a condition of idiocy. But if you give the thyroid extract of a sheep,[38] say, to such a person, they will regain their faculties again. This is a well-known fact. But it is one we can only properly evaluate through spiritual science. Why does this happen? Well, not only in the thyroid but also in the far larger number of glands, we find instruments built up from the etheric body. We need our tools in the physical world to do all sorts of things. In the same way that we need a hammer to hammer in a nail, so we need the tools or instruments for the purposes for which they are given us. If they are removed, we no longer possess them. But this does not mean it is impossible to substitute something else that acts

---

* The transcript of this whole passage records only single key words and phrases, and we have not been able to accurately reconstruct it (editors).

in the same way. We have to know, though, that such an action is only possible if the etheric body is functioning.

In the case of organs that are related to the astral body, we cannot bring about an organic change by substituting their secretion. I have witnessed how people with a brain defect ate sheep brains or suchlike without any improvement in brain function, since the brain is an organ that relates to the astral body. We can see here how spiritual science sheds light on these things too. We do not understand the human being if we cannot study these higher, supersensible members of the human being, for basically we then have no idea at all of what is at work.

Accounts in modern medical books seem to suggest that a person loses their reason when the thyroid is morbid or has been removed. This is not so. They lose only their participation, their interest, they grow dull and do not apply their reason. Not being able to think does not mean we are stupid. If you have no interest in something, your reason is still intact. What is lost is the living engagement we have with things, our interest, attention to things. Someone devoid of interest does not direct his attention to anything since he lacks the tools for this. We do not give him reason with the thyroid but we give him a tool for engaged participation with the world. We judge a person quite wrongly if we know nothing at all about the supersensible world, and a great portion of what is taught in our scientific and popular books is at this level. When you read that loss of the thyroid renders people idiotic, and that they become brighter again by consuming thyreodine, this is not true. What is true, rather, is that their attention is re-engaged. Wherever you look you can ascertain that what clairvoyant enquiry discovers is not fantastical. Though not everyone can see it, what the clairvoyant perceives can be proven to exist. I would urge you to reflect on this: though you may not be able to accept communications based on clairvoyant enquiry, you can experience their validity first-hand in the world, gaining indirect evidence of the truth of such communications.

I have said various things about the way in which the astral body's influence becomes apparent in life. I have described the living effect of the etheric body. Now I would like to make a few remarks about the I, which will enable you to connect anthroposophic theory to lived reality.

As you know, weeping and sorrow are universal phenomena. What does it signify in life to feel an externally caused sadness that manifests in physical tears, or to have an inward soul experience that likewise expresses itself in tears? We have in us something that enables us not only to experience what lives within our body but—in ordinary, normal awareness—that allows us to experience and empathize with what is occurring around us. We participate in our surroundings when we are saddened by some loss, and weep. What does this tell us? That we can take into ourselves what lives in our surroundings, and can bear it fully within us, in our heart. It signifies that we have an I within us, which has a mysterious, magical connection with our whole surroundings. Through this magical connection with things that do not live within us, we experience our connection with the world outside us.

The I can live in us in two ways: firstly in an egoistic way; then we are concerned with our tears primarily as a way of gaining relief from our pain because we do not wish to [truly] engage with it. Or secondly, sadness can also be fully justified because we absorb into us something that lives in our environment. For this reason tears are most precious in someone who is saddened by things that have as little as possible to do with them personally. There are people who weep in mere egoism, because they cannot cope with what is happening in their life, or cannot bear their own loss. And then there are indeed those who weep about things that do not directly concern them—cry like a baby as the phrase has it, about something in a novel or a play. And this capacity, a certain shimmer, can pass from their own sadness also to encompass all other tears and sorrow; for the more we are moved about everything else in the world, the greater does our sadness become. And in our sorrow we are in a sense led toward our I by means that are not egoistic. A creature devoid of the I cannot weep or be sad. The claim that animals also cry is therefore nonsense. Certainly animals cannot cry or sorrow as human beings do. The dog may appear sad only because he is not getting everything he did when his master was there.

The psychologists are right when they say that animals can only howl, whereas human beings weep. Weeping and sorrow offer the strongest proof of the depth of the I within us, and the ability it gives us to connect with what is around us. In sorrow, the resulting compression or contraction of our I emerges as tears. And because this is so we can say that basically weeping and tears are connected with the inmost core of our human nature.

When we re-establish our inner footing, we can best express this condition through tears. In Goethe's *Faust*, when Faust decides against suicide and removes the cup of poison from his lips, the words that follow are most profound: 'My tears are flowing, the earth has me once more!'[39] The I is speaking at this moment, coming to expression in these words, 'My tears are flowing, the earth has me once more!'

The sorrowing sympathy we feel with our surroundings is connected with our inmost being. And what is connected with our inmost being requires us to pay serious heed to it. It is important that we can become sorrowful about the misery around us, though never through merely imagined misery. All the plays that portray human misery elicit only unnatural stirrings in the soul. All unreal misery on the stage can be connected with human dignity only insofar as the hero, the protagonist, emerges victorious even if he dies. The plays that present misery to us can only be endured if we witness the triumph of good. In that case they have a right to our sorrow and our tears for they embed in us fully the sense of sorrow we may feel in the face of reality.

But there is also an opposite I experience, which we can call by many names. We find it in laughter, joviality, pleasure, perhaps even in jokes; here we participate in a cosmic element. It would be inhuman to laugh at someone with an actual mental impairment, but to laugh at an imagined idiocy is very liberating. It is good to experience foolishness, idiocy, for it has a healing effect to do so. Circus clowns are a good remedy for the soul. This laughter, once again, leads us to our own I. If we are able to laugh, we raise ourselves above a situation, becoming conscious of our own inner worth and thus elevating ourselves. There is something wonderfully healthy and healing in the burlesque jokes of the Punchinello theatre, through to the tomfooleries and hilarious contradictions of comedians, whereas laughing at actual idiocy betrays a complete lack of humanity.

It is rather curious how the I comes to expression in its healthy relationship to our surroundings. In relation to sorrow—to real, not merely depicted sorrow—we feel the urge to cry. The reverse is true of laughter and jokery: we are inhuman if we laugh at the natural failings and foolishness of another person. But it is healthy and humanly educative if we take pleasure in the portrayal of comedy, for then it points us to the sound and healthy I that lives in us.

And so you see how this healing element can also be regarded in the world—when we become aware that we also possess an I. But now let us ask this: in our materialistic age, does this also become apparent in relation to art? Yes indeed, it comes to very characteristic expression. If people were actually to encounter situations such as those depicted in plays by Hauptmann or Sudermann,[40] a great many of them would be overcome entirely. They can endure a depiction of what, in actual life, would sadden them and move them to intervene. Of course they can't intervene when these things are portrayed on stage. How does such a reversal of reality come about? It is because, in our age of materialism, people live most outside themselves, in the periphery, where the I is not actually in play. The most terrible event in world evolution, the Mystery of Golgotha, can sadden us most of all—the suffering and whole tragedy of Christ Jesus. And then we can rejoice most greatly at the portrayal of the victory of eternal life over death in the Resurrection. There is no other victory in which such a sublime hallelujah is so closely related to such profound sorrow: all the suffering of the death on Golgotha and all the glorious rejoicing of Easter in the Resurrection. There is no other event in which the profoundest sorrow and the most sublime rejoicing come to expression in this way.

And for this reason there is no deeper wisdom than that of Paul in relation to this whole event: Not I but Christ in me![41] Here we see how we can find the right focus to make the I within us as stable as possible—when it imbues itself with the revelation of Christ. In pervading its teachings with Christ, anthroposophy enables this insight also to penetrate into our I, giving us the greatest possible certainty in life, the greatest strength for living. You see, it is only by understanding Christ, as we do in spiritual science, that we can gain the right vantage point and focus.

Thus if anthroposophy is to come into effect in the way I have suggested in my book *Occult Science, an Outline*, then we will seek to offer something that can endow people with the kind of stability found in the saying 'Not I but Christ in me'. By means of it, the human being can increasingly be transformed; we can find within us a resurgent awareness of eternity, discovering that what we thus assimilate can never again be taken from us.

And then we will sense what it means for Johann Gottlieb Fichte, a great forerunner of anthroposophy, to say, 'When I feel and grasp my connection with the eternal, I can look to you cliffs and to you mountains and say: you may fall down upon me and bury my body, and destroy its last solar particle, crush all my physical tools, yet I defy you, for you are not eternal. I, though, am connected with eternity, I am eternal!'[42] Anthroposophy can best of all convey to us this connection to the eternal. And then we can stand here on the earth and speak these words of Fichte with him.

Such words are those of someone who understands eternal wisdom. Thus speaks someone who absorbs anthroposophy, addressing their whole corporeal, astral, etheric being, elevating their existence, integrating themselves into worlds of spirit, knowing that they are spirit of that same spirit. The human being, you see, is not only flesh of flesh but spirit of the eternal spirit.

Lecture 8

OSSIAN AND FINGAL'S CAVE

ADDRESS AFTER A PERFORMANCE OF MENDELSSOHN'S
THE HEBRIDES OVERTURE

BERLIN, 3 MARCH 1911

The music of this overture has carried us in spirit to the coast of Scotland, and in our souls we have embarked upon a journey in which the mysteries of karma played a great part during human evolution. From very different regions of the West, peoples once migrated to regions close to those to which this music has led us, and to those regions themselves, where, as if drawn by karma, they settled. And we hear of mysterious destinies. We can gather, both from esoteric vision and from external, historical documents, what these peoples experienced on Scottish soil in long-gone antiquity.

In 1772, when Fingal's Cave,[43] the cave on the Isle of Staffa in the Hebrides, was rediscovered, it was like coming upon a memory of the mysterious destinies of those long-gone times, a reawakening. People were reminded of the mysterious destinies of that ancient race when they saw how nature, as it seemed, had constructed something resembling a wondrous cathedral: countless tall pillars, ranged in long, regular rows, and over them arching a ceiling of the same stonework; and below, the feet of those columns washed by the ocean's influx, continually surging and thundering in this great edifice; water falling in countless drops from the stone formations, making a never-ending magical, melodious music upon the stalagmite stumps below. Those who discovered the cave, or at least those who had a sense for the mysteries that had once unfolded there, were inevitably reminded of the famous hero of antiquity who once upon a time governed human destinies with a strong hand and whose deeds were sung by his son, blind Ossian, a kind of Western Homer, a blind singer.[44]

If we recall the impression that the news made upon people at the time, we can understand why people throughout Europe were so struck when, in the eighteenth century, MacPherson brought these ancient songs to life again.[45] They exerted an incomparable hold on the imagination. Goethe, Herder, Napoleon,[46] and everyone else, believed they were hearing something of the magic of ancient days. We have to realize that a world of culture still present to people at the time, a world of spirit rising in their hearts, was drawn toward the power of these ancient songs. What sounded forth from them?

We need to look back to times corresponding to the early impulses of Christianity and the first few centuries afterwards. What was happening then around the Hebrides, in Ireland, Scotland, in the Old Erin that encompassed all the neighbouring isles between Ireland and Scotland, and northern Scotland? We find here the core of those peoples of Celtic origin who best preserved ancient Atlantean clairvoyance in its full vitality. The others, those who had migrated eastward, had developed further, and no longer felt a connection with the ancient gods. These peoples, immersed entirely in personality, in individuality, retained the capacities of ancient seership. They were guided, as it were, to these regions as by a special mission, encountered the forms of Fingal's Cave that reflected their own musical inwardness, that seemed to have been formed architecturally entirely from the world of spirit itself, as I sought to describe just now in a few words. We imagine this in the right way if we conceive of the cave as a centre that reflected what lived in the souls of these people whose karma had brought them here as to a temple built by the gods themselves. Here were prepared those who would later receive the Christ impulse with their full humanity. Here they underwent something most singular in preparation for that event.

We can picture this if we consider that there was preserved here, specifically, the ancient institution by means of which clans were divided into small, family-like groups. People related by blood felt they belonged together, while all others were seen as 'other', as belonging to a different group I. But over each of these groups there poured, as it were, the harmonizing influence of the Druid priests who had remained behind during the eastward migration of peoples from Atlantis. What these priests could give still lived in the bardic tradition. But we can only properly conceive what worked through these bards if we recognize that the most elemental passions here coincided with the ancient power of vision of the world of spirit, and that those who led each group that battled sometimes furiously, passionately and vigorously with other groups, had vision of impulses working out of the world of spirit which they directed into these battles. Nowadays we can no longer imagine such a union of physical contest and soul apprehension. When the hero raised his sword, he believed that an airy spirit was guiding him, and in this spirit he saw an ancestor who had himself once fought on this battlefield, had ascended to the skies and was now his battle companion working from above. In their battle-lines they felt their forefathers at work, their forefathers from both sides: they not only felt their presence, but, by clairaudience, also heard them. This was a wonderful thought that lived in these ancient peoples: that heroes must fight on the field of battle, that their blood must run, but that after death they rose into the world of spirit and that their spirit would then reverberate onward as tone, resound through the air as spirit.

And those who were familiar with battle, but were primarily intent on hearkening to the voice of antiquity that resounded from the air, who, as they developed in this way, became blind for the physical world, no longer seeing the flashing of swords, growing blind to the physical plane: such figures were greatly revered. And one of these was Ossian. And as the heroes brandished their swords, they knew that their deeds would continue to resound in the world of spirit, and that bards would come who would celebrate their deeds in song. In these peoples all this was living vision.

But this also gives us a quite different picture of humanity altogether. It gives us a vision of the human being as connected with spiritual power that resounds from the whole of nature. With such vision one cannot see a storm or lightning, cannot hear thunder or the raging of the sea, without intimating that spirits are present in all natural phenomena, and that these spirits are allied to souls of antiquity, to the souls of one's own ancestors. With such an outlook, nature has a quite different countenance. This is why there was such potency and significance in the songs that resounded once more—that previously lived only in oral tradition and were then reinvigorated by the Scot, MacPherson, giving a sense of how people were connected with the souls of their ancestors and with all natural phenomena.

MacPherson describes how a battle phalanx storms onward, driving darkness before it, like the spirits who enter the fray. Such things could indeed make a powerful impression on the culture of Europe. And the whole style of the poetic work, albeit rendered somewhat freely, awakens in us a sense of the perceptions that lived in those ancient peoples. A living wisdom was at work in them, a living knowledge of the connection between the world of spirits and the natural world within which the world of spirits is active.

With this kind of wisdom, the best sons of the various clans—that is, those who maintained the closest connection with the spirits of antiquity, who were best able to embody the spirits of antiquity in their deeds— were chosen to form an elite band. And those who possessed the greatest clairvoyant powers were made leaders. The mission of this band or cohort was to defend the core of the Celtic peoples against surrounding clans. One of these leaders was the clairvoyant hero whose name has come down to us as Fingal.[47] The old songs, as these were heard and drawn from the spiritual world, told of how this figure, Fingal, defended the ancient gods against those who sought to endanger them: the old songs of the bard Ossian, Fingal's son, living on as living tradition until the sixteenth or seventeenth century. The deeds Fingal performed, and what Ossian heard once Fingal had risen into the realm of spirits, songs that were intended to drive on later generations to their great deeds, was something that still exerted a powerful effect in the eighteenth century. And we gain an idea of this when we hear how Ossian has his father Fingal's voice sing forth in these songs. In the passage I will read, the heroes are hard pressed, they have almost been defeated—and now suddenly new life fills their ranks.

> The king stood by the stone of Lubar. Thrice he reared his terrible voice. The deer started from the fountains of Cromla. The

rocks shook on all their hills. Like the noise of a hundred mountain-streams, that burst, and roar, and foam! Like the clouds, that gather to a tempest on the blue face of the sky! So met the sons of the desert round the terrible voice of Fingal. Pleasant was the voice of the king of Morven to the warriors of his land. Often had he led them to battle; often returned with the spoils of the foe. 'Come to battle,' said the king, 'ye children of echoing Selma! Come to the death of thousands. Comhal's son will see the fight. My sword shall wave on the hill, the defence of my people in war. But never may you need it, warriors; while the son of Morni fights, the chief of mighty men! He shall lead my battle, that his fame may rise in song! O ye ghosts of heroes dead! ye riders of the storm of Cromla! receive my falling people with joy, and bear them to your hills. And may the blast of Lena carry them over my seas, that they may come to my silent dreams, and delight my soul in rest.'

Now like a dark and stormy cloud, edged round with the red lightning of heaven, hying westward from the morning's gleam, the king of Selma removed. Terrible is the light of his armour; two spears are in his hand. His grey hair falls on the wind. He often looks back on the war. Three bards attend the son of fame, to bear his words to the chiefs. High on Cromla's side he sat, waving the lightning of his sword, and as he waved we moved.

Fingal at once arose in arms. Thrice he reared his dreadful voice. Cromla answered around. The sons of the desert stood still. They bent their blushing faces to earth, ashamed at the presence of the king. He came like a cloud of rain in the day of the sun, when slow it rolls on the hill, and fields expect the shower. Silence attends its slow progress aloft; but the tempest is soon to arise. Suaran beheld the terrible king of Morven. He stopped in the midst of his course. Dark he leaned on his spear, rolling his red eyes around.

Silent and tall, Fingal, like a beam from heaven, shone in the midst of his people. His heroes gather around him. He sends forth the voice of his power. 'Raise my standards on high: spread them on Lena's wind, like the flames of an hundred hills! Let them sound on the winds of Erin, and remind us of the fight. Ye sons of the roaring streams, that pour from a thousand hills, be near the king of Morven! attend to the words of his power. Gaul, strongest arm of death! O Oscar of the future fights ! Connal, son of the blue shields of Sora! Dermid, of the dark-brown hair! Ossian, king of many songs, be near your father's arm!' We reared the sun-beam of battle, the standard of the king ! Each hero exulted with joy, as, waving, it flew on the wind. It was studded with gold above, as the blue wide shell of the nightly sky. Each hero had his standard too, and each his gloomy men![48]

Thus Fingal stormed into battle; thus he is described by his son Ossian.

No wonder that this life, this awareness of a connection with the world of spirit which implants itself in the souls of these people, the souls of the ancient Celts, is the best preparation for the personal divine element to be disseminated later from those regions across the Western world. What they experienced in their own passionate way, what they heard resounding in melodies from the spiritual world, prepared them for the era when their descendants would later cleanse and purify those passions, bringing them to milder, more inward expression. We can say this: It seems to us as if Erin's best sons again discerned the tones of their ancient bards—those who had once heard these songs resounding from the spiritual world as the deeds of their ancestors—but as if now, in Erin's best sons, the old battle-cries, the din of battle, had become configured and clarified into the Word that must express humanity's greatest impulse.

From the deeds of the ancient Celts, who had fought in such fierce battles in order to prepare themselves for further, spiritual deeds, resounded a music that we can discern again in what the best sons of the Occident accomplished. These were the impulses that flowed then into the souls of people in the eighteenth century when these ancient songs reappeared in new form. And this was brought to mind, too, in those who saw the wonderful cathedral that nature herself had built. Here, they said, karma created a place, a shrine, where the bards' songs of the deeds of their forefathers, of what their ancestors needed to do to steel their powers, echo back to them from the cathedral they themselves did not need to build, from the sacred temple built for them by the spirits of nature, as a means of inspiration for all who saw it.

In the same way the tones of this overture we have heard can allow us, in our own way, to sense something of the deep, mysterious contexts that do indeed hold sway in the history of those who preceded us and lived almost in exactly the same region where we now live. And since we must delve deeply into what lives within us, and since what lives in us is only a further reverberation of what existed in antiquity, such intimation of what once existed and works on still in humanity, is of great significance for esoteric life.

Lecture 9

THE IMPORTANCE OF SPIRITUAL ENQUIRY FOR MORAL ACTION

BIELEFELD, 6 MARCH 1911

The accusation is often made that anthroposophy basically does not address the moral realm directly, and even that, in some of its teachings, it not only does not oppose egoism but cultivates it. Those who think this put it roughly as follows: anthroposophy teaches, they say, how a person develops through recurring lives and, whatever setbacks may occur, the principal thing is that people can evolve to ever higher stages, that they can use the fruits of whatever they learn in one life, as in a school, in a following life. Those who are wedded to this belief in people's capacity to perfect themselves will always strive to enhance and purify their I, to enrich it as far as possible, and thus to ascend to ever loftier heights. And so, say such opponents, this is really very egoistical. We anthroposophists seek to draw from the world of spirit teachings and powers that help raise our being to greater heights, and thus our motive is egoistic. Such people also say that we anthroposophists are convinced that imperfect actions will lead to bad karma, and that to evade this we avoid doing certain things we might otherwise have done. In other words, our actions or inactions are driven by fear of bad karma, and all this appears as egoistic motivations. Some say that teachings of karma and reincarnation, and all other striving for perfection arising from anthroposophy, lead people to seek a kind of refined or higher egoism. It would actually be a grave reproach if it could be said that anthroposophy induces people to act morally not through empathy and compassion but primarily out of fear of punishment. Let us ask ourselves if such a reproach has any justification. Here we must engage very deeply with esoteric enquiry if we are truly and fully to refute such an objection.

Someone might say that if we do not already have a striving to grow more perfect, anthroposophy will not move us to act more ethically. Yet delving deeper into the teachings of anthroposophy will show that we participate in the whole of humanity; thus immoral actions mean more than just doing something that might perhaps lead to our punishment. To think or act immorally is to do something nonsensical, something that cannot be reconciled with really sound or healthy thinking.

An immoral action not only opens the way to some karmic punishment but is, in the profoundest sense, an action that we ought not to commit. Let us imagine that someone commits a theft, and in consequence attracts a karmic retribution. If we wish to avoid this we do not steal. But the whole thing is more complex than that. Let us ask ourselves what someone who lies or steals actually intends. The liar or thief wishes to gain some advantage; the liar may wish to avoid an unpleasant situation. Such an action only has any meaning if we actually gain some advantage from lying or stealing. If we were to recognize that this is mistaken, that it will not give us what we want, but on the contrary that it will be to our disadvantage, then we would say it is nonsense to even think of doing such a thing. As anthroposophy becomes ever more part of human civilization, people will come to know that it is nonsensical, ridiculous, to believe that lies or stealing will get them what they think they might get by them. One thing in particular will become ever clearer to all people as they imbue themselves with anthroposophy: in a higher sense, from the perspective of higher causation, there is actually no such thing as separate human individualities. Alongside these separate individuals, the whole human race forms a unity. Increasingly people will come to see that, in terms of a true world outlook, the finger on our hand is actually more sensible than the whole human being, since it does not imagine itself to exist without the whole human organism to which it belongs. In its dull consciousness, the finger knows that it cannot exist without the rest of the organism.

People, on the other hand, continually succumb to illusions. They think that the fact they are enclosed in their skins means they are separate. But they are so as little as the finger exists separately from the rest of the organism. The reason for this illusion is that a person can walk around on their own while the finger cannot. But our place on the earth is really the same as that of the finger on our hand. The sort of science that holds our earth to be a molten ball surrounded by a hard shell upon which we human beings wander about, that thinks this is enough to explain the earth, is at roughly the same level as a science that imagines human beings are nothing but their skeletal system and no more than that. What we see physically of the earth is really nothing more than what the skeletal system is for the human being. The rest of the earth is actually supersensible in nature. The earth is an organism in fact, a living entity. If you imagine the human being as a living creature, you can picture the blood with its white and red corpuscles. These can only develop inside the whole human organism and be what they are there. What the red and white blood corpuscles are for the human being, we are for the earth organism. We certainly belong to this earth organism: we form a part of the whole living entity of the earth, and we only properly understand ourselves if we say that we are nothing as a single individual; we are only complete if we think of ourselves as part of the earth's body, of which we see only the skeleton, the physical, mineral shell—unless we acknowledge the spiritual aspects of this earth organism.

If an inflammatory process occurs in our human organism, the whole organism is seized by fever, by illness. If we transpose this to the earth organism, we can recognize the truth of what esotericism asserts: that an immoral action anywhere on the earth is the same for its whole organism as, say, a small abscess somewhere on the human body that makes the whole organism sick. In the same way, when someone steals something, the whole earth gets a kind of fever. This isn't just a metaphor; it has deep roots. The whole earth organism suffers from all immoral actions, and, as single individuals, we cannot do such an action without involving the whole earth organism, without sympathetic participation from it.

This is a very simple idea, of course, but people find it hard to grasp. Those who don't believe it to be true will have to wait and see. We should try to impress such ideas upon our culture, to appeal with such ideas to the human heart, the human conscience: if immoral actions are done somewhere, they are a kind of abscess for the whole earth, make it sick; and experience could show that realizations of this kind would produce a powerful moral impetus.

Moral sermons will never help us. Yet seeing the truth of what I have said would do more than increase our insight. If it really embedded itself in culture, if it impressed itself on the child's sensibility, it would also provide a huge moral impulse. Moral sermons never entirely persuade or reform people. As Schopenhauer said,[49] preaching morality is easy but establishing morality is hard. People have a certain antipathy to moral sermons. It calls forth an inner resistance from them when they think that someone else wants them to behave in a certain way, and they are just meant to go along with it! And such resistance will keep increasing as materialistic consciousness gains the upper hand.

The idea current today that it is right to impose a 'class morality' upon another class is one that has gained acceptance and will grow ever worse in future. At the same time people increasingly feel that they themselves wish to discover the right thing to do in this realm, and that their desire for objective knowledge should lead them to it. The human individual seeks ever greater self-assertion. But, to put it metaphorically, if the heart were to recognize that it will suffer illness when the whole organism to which it belongs falls ill, then this heart would do whatever is necessary to avoid such illness. And in the same way, when we recognize that we are embedded in the whole earth organism, and that the earth body should not suffer from an abscess, then we will find an objective reason to be good. We will see that in stealing we seek to gain an advantage, but that we must refrain from this because it will make the whole earth organism sick, and without the earth organism we ourselves cannot survive. People will come to see that acting morally therefore not only benefits the whole organism but also themselves.

This is more or less how moral consciousness will gradually shape itself in future. Someone who draws moral impulses from anthroposophy will say that it is an illusion to think you will gain advantage from an immoral action. If you do this you are like a squid that emits a cloud of dark fluid to envelope it: a dark aura of immoral impulses. Lying and stealing are the germs of an aura that will envelop you and will at the same time spread unhappiness through the world.

People say that we are surrounded by *maya*, illusion. But such truths must become living truths for us. Through anthroposophy we can show that humanity's moral evolution will in future encompass the realization that, in trying to gain an advantage for ourselves alone, we shroud ourselves in an aura of illusions. Then the idea that the world is *maya* will become a practical truth and reality. The finger already knows this in its dull awareness, its sleeping, dreaming consciousness: it is clever enough to know that without the hand and the rest of the body it isn't really worth anything—it isn't a finger at all any more. But human beings are not yet as clever as this. They have not yet accepted that they aren't anything really without the earth body. They need to realize it. The finger is ahead of the human being in this respect. It does not cut itself off. It does not say: 'I want to have the blood I contain for myself alone, so I will cut myself off from the flow.' It is in harmony with the whole organism to which it belongs. But to find harmony with the whole earth organism, the human being must develop a higher consciousness. People are as yet unaware of this in the moral precepts they embrace today. They might say to themselves if they wanted: we breathe in air; just now this air was outside me, now it is within my body: something outer becomes inner. And if I breathe the air out again, something inner becomes outer; and the same is true of the whole human being. But it does not dawn on people that, sundered from the air they breathe, they are nothing. They must seek to develop an awareness, therefore, of how they are integrated into the whole earth organism.

How can people recognize that they are a part of the whole earth organism? Anthroposophy enables them to become aware of it. It teaches that a Saturn condition first existed, then a Sun condition, followed by a Moon stage. The human being was always present in these conditions, albeit in a quite different form from today. Then the Earth arose from the Old Moon condition and slowly human beings evolved as earthly beings. We can look back on a long evolution, and in future further evolutionary stages await us. With the earth in its present form, we human beings evolved in our present form too. If we study anthroposophy and trace how the earth and the human being arose, it becomes apparent that we are indeed a part of the whole earth organism. Then we discover how earth and human beings gradually arose from spiritual existence, how the beings of the hierarchies formed the earth and the human being, how the latter belongs to the hierarchies, though standing at the lowest level. And then also anthroposophy teaches us about the being who stands at the midpoint of all earth evolution, the Christ as the great, archetypal exemplar of human existence. And from all these anthroposophic teachings we can come to see how our conduct must be, how we should act.

Spiritual science shows us how we can feel ourselves to be a part of all life on earth; it shows us that Christ is the spirit of the earth. Our fingers, toes, nose, all our limbs, have a dream sense that the heart supplies them with blood, and that they would be nothing without this central organ. And anthroposophy teaches us that it would be terrible foolishness in earth's future evolution not to take up the idea of Christ, since he is, for the earth body, what the heart is for our organism. And just as our blood supplies the whole organism with life and vigour through the heart, so the being of Christ must pervade every single earth soul, so that the Pauline phrase, Not I but Christ in me,[50] becomes truth for them. The Christ must have entered all human hearts. And if someone were to say that they can exist and survive without Christ, they would be as foolish as it would be for eyes and ears to say they could survive without the heart. If there's a difference it is this: the human heart must be present in us from the very beginning, whereas the heart of our earth organism entered it only with the advent of Christ. But for all succeeding ages, this heart's blood of Christ must have entered all human hearts, and those who do not inwardly unite with him will grow arid. Earth's evolution does not wait; it arrives at the point that it must. Only human beings can be left behind—and would be if they resist inward affirmation of Christ. In their last incarnation on earth a number of human beings would then stand there and have failed to attain the goal, have failed to recognize Christ, have failed to embrace Christ feeling, Christ knowledge in their souls. They will not be mature enough to progress to higher stages of evolution, and will sunder themselves from it.

But whereas nose or ears would be destroyed entirely if they sundered themselves from the rest of the human organism, such human beings will not suffer a fate so extreme. Esoteric enquiry shows that those who do not wish to imbue themselves with the Christ element, the life of Christ, as anthroposophy makes possible, will have absorbed substances of decline and decomposition instead of progressing on into new stages of planetary existence. Initially they will have to take different paths. Once human beings have absorbed the Christ into their perceptions, feelings and into their whole souls over successive incarnations, the earth will fall away from these souls as a corpse lapses from the human being at death. The earth corpse will fall away, and what remains as Christ-pervaded spirit and soul will develop into a new form of existence and reincarnate again on Jupiter.

And what will happen to those who have not taken up Christ into themselves? Spiritual science will offer them plenty of opportunities to perceive and absorb Christ. While people today are still resistant, they will become ever less so. But if we assume that at the end of earth's evolution there will be people who are still resistant to the Christ impulse, a number of human beings would remain who could not progress to the next planetary stage, who have failed to reach the real goal of earth existence. These people would greatly hamper the planet upon which the rest of humanity would continue to evolve, for they would not be able to co-exist with the Jupiter condition as it is meant to be, they would be unable to experience the developments occurring there, and yet they would be present on Jupiter. Everything that later becomes material has first existed spiritually. Thus the immorality, the opposition to absorbing Christ, that people develop spiritually during the earth condition, first exists in the soul and spirit. But this will later be materialized: it will surround and pervade

Jupiter as a neighbouring element. And this element will have issued from those human beings who did not integrate the Christ during earth evolution. The immorality and Christ-resistance that is now developing in the soul will then have become material, fully physical. And whereas the physical nature of those who have absorbed Christ will have refined itself on Jupiter, the physical nature of these others will be substantially coarsened. Esoteric enquiry conjures before us a picture of the future of those human beings who have not achieved maturity during earth's evolution.

Today we breathe air. On Jupiter, there will largely not be air but the atmosphere there will consist of a substance that is finer, more ethereal than our air. People who have achieved the ends of earth evolution will live in this element, while the others, those left behind, will have to breathe something like an unpleasantly hot, boiling fire-air, a sultry element containing unpleasant vapours. Thus those who failed to reach the goal of earth maturity will be a cross for the other Jupiter humans to bear, exerting a pestilent influence in the environment, in the swamps and the rest of the Jupiter soil. The fluid-physical nature of these people's bodies will be comparable to a fluid that keeps hardening into solid, that inwardly freezes and congeals; thus these beings will not only breathe this dire kind of air, but will have a bodily condition such that their blood continually congeals instead of flowing. The physical body of these beings will be of a mucilaginous substance, nastier than the substances of our slugs and snails today: endowed with these properties, they will secrete such substances like a kind of crust that surrounds them. These crusts will be softer than the skin of our snakes today: they will be a kind of soft scaly hide. And these beings will live a somewhat distasteful life within the elements of Jupiter.

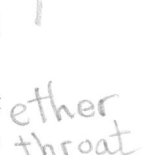

Images like this, which the esoteric investigator discerns as a prefiguring of the future, appear gruesome. But woe betide us if, like the ostrich, we refuse to contemplate such a danger, and close our eyes to the truth. For this is precisely what lulls us in error and illusion, whereas keen discernment of the truth gives us the greatest moral impulses. If people attend to what truth tells them, they will feel, when they lie, a picture arising in them of the effect of this lie upon human nature in the Jupiter condition: a sense that lies make you slimy, create a pestilential atmosphere for the future. And this ever-recurring picture will guide their soul impulses toward healing. You see, no one who knows the true consequences of immorality can actually be immoral. We should teach people the true effects of causes. Such guidance should already be given to children. Immorality exists only because people lack knowledge. Only the darkness of untruth makes immorality possible.

Yet let us remember that such connections between immorality and ignorance must be wisdom not mere rationality. Intellectual knowledge alone compounds immorality, and even, if it becomes subtle ingenuity, deceitfulness. Wisdom, on the other hand, acts upon the human soul so that truth and inmost morality emanate from it.

My dear friends, it really is true to say that moral sermons are easily come by while actually establishing morality is hard. Establishing morality means doing so in wisdom, and wisdom is first necessary for this. You can see that Schopenhauer was absolutely correct when he coined this phrase.

And so we can see how unfounded it is for people, who do not know anything, really, about spiritual science, to accuse it of being devoid of moral impulses. Anthroposophy shows us what we engender in the world when we fail to act morally. It offers wisdom from which morality itself issues. There is nothing more arrogant than saying we need only be good people and everything will be fine. We first have to know how to actually be a good person. Modern consciousness is very arrogant in rejecting all wisdom. True perception of the good requires us to delve deep into the mysteries of wisdom, and this is inconvenient for it necessitates us learning a great deal.

And so when people come and tell us that teachings about reincarnation and karma are the basis for egoism rather than morality, we can reply: No! True spiritual science shows us that if we act immorally this is roughly tantamount to taking a piece of paper to write a letter, and then instead lighting a match and burning it. This would be grotesque and nonsensical. But this is what we do if we act wrongly or harbour an immoral outlook.

For our true, deeper human nature, stealing signifies the same as lying. If we steal we plant in ourselves the seed for the growth of a slimy, nasty substance in future, for the spreading of pestilential smells around us. Only by clinging to the illusion that the present moment is something intrinsically true and sufficient unto itself can we undertake such an action. By stealing, a person incorporates into themselves something that equates to a flaying of our human nature. And if we know this, we will be unable to commit immoral actions any more; we will be unable to steal. Just as a plant seed will sprout in future into a blossom, so spiritual science, if implanted in the human soul, will sprout into human blossoms, that is, human morality. Anthroposophy is the seed, the soul is the good soil for it, and morality is the blossom and fruit of the plant of the evolving human being.

Lecture 10

APHORISMS ON THE RELATIONSHIP BETWEEN SPIRITUAL SCIENCE AND PHILOSOPHY

REFLECTIONS TO COMPLEMENT THE LECTURES ON *OCCULT PHYSIOLOGY*[51]

PRAGUE, 28 MARCH 1911

FOLLOWING the public lectures on 'How to Refute Spiritual Science', and 'How to Defend Spiritual Science',[52] as well as the reflections I offered over the past few days in the lecture cycle on 'Occult Physiology', a range of questions can emerge, and the need to discuss these questions a little with my listeners. The two public lectures aimed above all to highlight the need for awareness of the possible objections that may be raised against spiritual science. The occult investigator can fully acknowledge the justification of such objections, but on the other hand, as you will have seen from these lectures, a very particular, sharply delineated position can be adopted when it comes to defending the truths of spiritual science against them.

With insight into the difficulties that arise for spiritual science, every anthroposophist should feel the need to represent the truths of spiritual science with the greatest possible accuracy and precision. This is something of which those representing these matters, with knowledge of all the relevant circumstances, will be very aware, and yet—despite everything I emphasized in the public lectures—they will still inevitably collide with people who adhere to the position of modern science. And for this reason, however curious it may seem, anthroposophy requires us to clothe in words truths drawn down from higher worlds but at the same time to use the most precise, logical formulations couched in the forms of ordinary rational discourse. Those who set themselves this task, to formulate things in a precise and logical way, and in doing so to avoid everything that might be word-padding or rhetorical glossing, will often feel how easily they can be misunderstood, simply because, in our time, there is not a universal need to accept truths thus expressed in as exact and precise a way as they are uttered. In our era, even where people engage in the activity of science, they are not accustomed to taking things exactly as intended. If you very precisely assimilate what is said in this way, not only should you not alter anything in the phrases used but you should also attend very carefully to the limits that are included in such formulations.

Here's a simple example that recently arose during questions and answers. Someone asked,[53] If dream consciousness is only a kind of picture consciousness, how does it happen that a sleeper can perform certain subconscious actions such as sleepwalking? The questioner had not noticed that when I said the contents of dream consciousness are pictorial in nature, this did not mean they were *only* pictorial. Since the scope of dream consciousness was described only from one angle, the very nature of this characterization allowed for the fact that, just as our actions in waking life follow from our waking consciousness, so certain actions of a less conscious nature can also follow from the picture consciousness of dream.

I am not in the least complaining when I say that imprecise listening is one of the chief reasons why anthroposophy and those who represent it meet with so many misunderstandings today. Such misunderstandings do not come only from opponents of anthroposophy but to a great degree also from its adherents. And perhaps a great part of the blame for misunderstandings that arise in the wider world toward spiritual science lies with those who stand within the movement.

If we survey the disciplines that are held in due regard today, we might gain a general sense that anthroposophy is most closely related to the various branches of philosophy. This is certainly correct; and because of this it might easily be supposed that the best means of meeting with understanding for anthroposophic insights would be in the field of philosophy. But it is precisely here that we encounter other difficulties.

Philosophy as it is cultivated everywhere today has become a specialized discipline to a far greater extent than it was only a relatively short time ago. It has become a specialized field, and, if we consider what it actually practises today, and not its various theories, we find that its activity is focused upon abstract regions. Philosophers show little inclination to apply philosophy to a specific or tangible apprehension of realities. Indeed, difficulties arise in modern philosophical discourse if you try to apply philosophical endeavours to the real world. The theory of knowledge that was developed with great acuity in various directions in the second half of the nineteenth century, and through into our own time, arose in the form it now exists largely because people sensed these difficulties in drawing concepts down from the abstract heights of thinking and applying them to facts and realities.

Now it can be felt, especially in lectures such as this cycle on 'Occult Physiology', how anthroposophy must seek everywhere to bring the supersensible contents of consciousness to bear on our actual world. To put it somewhat trivially, anthroposophy is not as well off as modern philosophy, which remains in abstract regions and has little inclination to encompass in its reflections concepts such as the blood, the liver or the pancreas, thus terms that apply to reality. Philosophy would take fright at the thought of having to build a bridge from its abstract formulations to tangible, immediate realities as we encounter them in things and occurrences. In this respect, anthroposophy is more reckless and, from a philosophical perspective, can easily be seen as an activity of the mind which audaciously and unjustifiably builds bridges from the most rarefied spirit to the lowliest mundanities.

Now it is surely interesting to ask why philosophy finds it so difficult to approach anthroposophy. Perhaps it is precisely because philosophy refrains from such bridge-building.

But for spiritual science this fact is in certain respects disastrous, for our anthroposophic insights, especially when we seek to lead them down as far as logical discourse, very frequently meet with resistance. Especially from philosophers we encounter resistance in this respect. In fact, you meet less resistance by throwing caution to the winds, as it were, and recounting more sensational observations from higher worlds. People often seem to forgive this relatively more easily, for such things are, firstly, 'interesting', and secondly people think that because they themselves cannot perceive these worlds there is therefore no requirement for them to make any judgement about them.

But anthroposophy endeavours to bring down into rational understanding everything that can be discovered in higher worlds. Such realities are discovered through supersensible enquiry in supersensible worlds. But in our modern era, the presentation and description of such realities should be clothed in rigorously logical forms. Wherever this is already possible today, we should show how the most tangible of outward processes can everywhere confirm what we assert on the basis of spiritual enquiry. In this whole process of drawing insights down from the world of spirit and clothing them in logical or other rational formulations, and presenting them in a way that satisfies the logical needs of our age, there exists, it has to be said, a really very understandable source of the most numerous misunderstandings.

Consider for a moment the complex nature of what has been said in these lectures on 'Occult Physiology', presentations that must be taken everywhere with qualifications, with precise acknowledgement of their due scope and limits; consider the very complex nature of the mobile, fluctuating world of spirit, and compare this world of spirit, in all its variability, in the difficulty one has in encompassing what descends from spiritual worlds in coarse concepts, compare this with the ease with which one can characterize any outward fact by means of an experiment or by sense observation, and describing it in logical terms.

Now the tendency exists everywhere in philosophy, wherever concepts are explained and described, to take account of nothing other than ideas gained from the world, the sensory world spread before us. This becomes especially apparent in philosophy when it is obliged, in the field of ethics, say, to discover a source for its fundamental concepts other than those that can be derived from the physical world. We find—and this would not be hard to demonstrate, but of course only by citing extensive passages from contemporary philosophical literature—that in philosophical arguments the concepts used are coarse in nature because they basically take account only of the world of sense perception that surrounds us, from which these philosophical concepts are formulated.

Is there anything to suggest that, in formulating the most primary concepts in philosophy, contents of consciousness could be drawn from anywhere other than the sense-perceptible world? In a nutshell, modern philosophy lacks the means to understand anthroposophy since its theories cannot relate to concepts such as those we cultivate in our anthroposophic discourses. In philosophical literature the mind's scope is determined by formulating concepts only by reference to the outward, sense-perceptible world, rather than to contents that originate other than in sense perceptions.

Spiritual science has to obtain its concepts by quite different means: it has to rise to supersensible perception and draw its concepts down from the supersensible realm. But it also has to immerse itself in reality, and master philosophical concepts gained through observation of the sense world. If we picture the world schematically for a moment, on the one hand we have in philosophy concepts gained through outward perception, and, on the other, concepts gained from the supersensible realm through spiritual perception. And if we survey the field of concepts we use to communicate, we must say this: if anthroposophy is to be regarded as justified, then our concepts must be drawn from both sides: on the one hand from sense perception, and on the other from spiritual perception; and these two sides have to meet each other within our conceptual field.

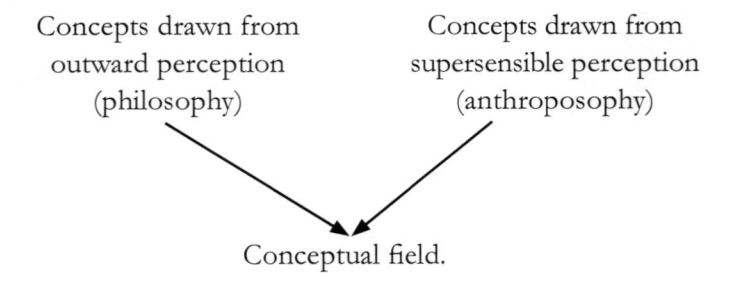

Concepts drawn from   Concepts drawn from
outward perception   supersensible perception
(philosophy)   (anthroposophy)

Conceptual field.

We must acknowledge the need, in anthroposophic accounts specifically, to reconcile concepts drawn from the world of spirit with philosophical concepts, that is, to enable our terms and concepts to relate everywhere to those gained from the outer sense world.

Our modern theories of knowledge are more or less exclusively founded on concepts gained from only one direction. I do not mean to say that there are not also theories of knowledge that allow for a supersensible element as origin of their concepts. But wherever something is to be positively proven, examples are characterized by the fact that the terms employed are drawn only from the left-hand side of the schema, that is, from the world of sensory, physical perceptions. This is also perfectly natural since philosophy does not as such acknowledge spiritual realities. No account is taken of the possibility of rendering spiritual realities in concepts in the same way as realities of the physical world. This fact means that anthroposophy finds no common, prepared ground in philosophy when it seeks dialogue with it. And philosophers cannot easily understand the way in which terms and concepts are employed in anthroposophy.

It's like this: in relation to the outer world of sense perception, it is easy to give concepts clear, sharp outlines. Things themselves have these clear outlines, sharp delineations, and we can easily offer clear concepts for them. But in relation to the mobile, fluctuating world of spirit, much has first to be united and reconciled, and concepts must be carefully limited or enlarged in order to formulate and characterize. The modern theory of knowledge is most unfit for encompassing concepts such as those employed in spiritual science. When defining concepts, and taking the foundations for such definition—whether consciously or unconsciously—from one side only, all the concepts we formulate are tinged, without our knowledge, by something that gives rise to epistemological terms that are of no use at all for explaining or elucidating anything in anthroposophy. The concept supplied by, as it were, the non-anthroposophic world, is simply an unfit tool for characterizing what spiritual science draws down from the world of spirit.

Now there is one term, in particular, which has proven terribly disruptive in the field of epistemology. I'm well aware that this is not acknowledged, and yet it is so. And this concerns the point—if we disregard all finer points that have been ingeniously elaborated during the nineteenth century—where the problem of epistemology is formulated as follows: How does the I, with its content of consciousness... or to avoid speaking of the 'I' we can say, How do *we* succeed in relating our content of consciousness to any reality? These trains of thought, with the exception of certain epistemological schools in the nineteenth century, led to a theory of knowledge which repeatedly stumbles when it tries to explain how the trans-subjective or transcendent element—that is, what lies beyond our consciousness—manages to enter our mind. Admittedly, this is only a rough-and-ready account of this problem of knowledge, but it does more or less cover the difficulties involved if we ask how the subjective content of our consciousness approaches the reality of existence. How can it relate itself to reality? You see, we have to recognize that even if we assume the existence of a trans-subjective reality lying outside our consciousness, what is contained in our consciousness cannot directly approach it. A content of the mind is posited within us and we must then ask how it is possible to emerge from this content of consciousness into a reality that is independent of our mind.

An important modern epistemologist[54] characterized this problem in telling terms: the human I, in so far as it comprises the scope of consciousness, cannot, he said, overleap itself, and it would have to leap beyond itself if it were to succeed in leaping into reality. But then it would exist within reality and not within the mind. For this epistemologist, therefore, it seems clear that we can deduce nothing at all about how the content of our mind relates to actual reality.

Many years ago, in my epistemological writings,[55] I was concerned to formulate this epistemological problem—which is also fundamental to anthroposophy—and then to surmount the difficulties that arise from a formulation such as I have now given. In the process, though, curious things occurred. At the time I am speaking of, for example, there were philosophers who assumed, very much like Schopenhauer, that 'the world is my idea'. That is, what is present in the mind is initially only the content of my thought; and then one must see how to build a bridge from this thought content to what lies outside of what is thought or conceived, to trans-subjective reality. Now anyone not daunted and over-impressed by assertions that philosophers make in this realm—especially in epistemological writings from the seventies and the first half of the eighties of the last [nineteenth] century—but instead approaching these issues with an open mind, will immediately ask this: If something is 'my idea' and if this idea or mental picture of mine is meant to be more than merely the content of my mind, if it is to have self-founded validity, this points to something that basically cannot lie *before* the point at which epistemological theory sets to work but can only be ascertained *after* these far more important epistemological principles have been examined. We first have to ask, you see, why we should be permitted to regard something appearing as the content of my mind as 'my idea'. Do we have the right to say that what appears within my mind is *my* idea? Epistemology has no right at all to start from the judgement that this given is my own thought, but it is obliged, rather, if it really seeks to start from an a priori position, to first prove the fact that what appears in my mind is only its subjective content.

Naturally there are hundreds of possible objections to what I have just said, but I do not think it is possible to maintain a single one of them on closer scrutiny. A well-known and important philosopher[56] once gave me a curious answer when I drew his attention to this dilemma, and tried to explain to him that one should first check whether it was justified, in epistemological terms, to describe a thought or mental picture as something not real. He said this: 'But it's self-evident, the very definition of the word "mental picture" already tells us that we are picturing something in our minds, and therefore it isn't real.' So firmly were such ideas rooted in him from centuries of philosophical discourse, that he could not grasp the fact that such a definition is as yet entirely unsubstantiated.

If we wish to ascertain anything within the scope of the world around us (and by the phrase 'world around us' I mean the world we have around us in ordinary daily life)—for instance that the world we see is a 'mental picture'—then we must be clear that we cannot ascertain such a thing at all without what we call our thinking activity, without thoughts and concepts. At present I am not saying anything about such a statement being, in formal logical terms, already a 'judgement'. But the moment we in any way begin not to allow something simply to be as it appears before us, but instead take a view of it, ascertain it in some manner, make a statement about it, we intervene in the world around us with our thinking. And if we are to have any right to intervene in the world such that we determine something to be 'subjective', then we must be aware that the defining and determining activity that calls something subjective *cannot* itself be subjective.

You see, if we assume that this is the sphere of subjectivity (*draws a circle on the board and above it writes the word 'subjectivity'*), and from this sphere issues, say, the statement that A is subjective, is my 'mental picture' or whatever we call it, then this statement is itself subjective.

Subjectivity

⊙⟶   A   mental picture

We must deduce from this not that we should allow this statement to be valid, but rather that such a conclusion should not be made, for it would cancel itself out. If a subjectivity can only be ascertained out of itself, this would be a self-cancelling conclusion. If the statement 'A is subjective' is to have any meaning, it cannot issue from the sphere of subjectivity but from a reality that lies outside this subjectivity. This means that if the 'I' is to be in any position at all to say that something possesses a subjective character, for instance that it is my 'mental picture', if the 'I' is to have the right to define something as subjective, then it cannot itself reside within the subjective sphere but must make such a conclusion from outside the sphere of subjectivity. In other words, we should not attribute the statement that something is 'subjective' to the 'I' that is itself subjective.[57]

And this gives us a way out of the sphere of subjectivity: we recognize that we could not determine what is subjective and objective, and would have to relinquish the very first steps in thinking about this altogether if we did not possess a relationship to both subjectivity and objectivity in which both have an equal share in us. This leads us to see—though I cannot elaborate on this further here— that our I should not only be regarded as subjective but is in fact more comprehensive than our subjectivity. We have a right to exclude from any given content, thus from something objective, what pertains subjectively to it.

Initially we encounter the various terms 'objective', 'subjective' and 'trans-subjective'. 'Objective' is of course different from 'trans-subjective' [gap in the transcript here].

Now, with these provisos, we need to see whether we are able to remove the stumbling block that is one of the most significant obstacles in epistemology—the question as to whether the whole scope of our I can be found within subjectivity or not. You see, if the I must also share in objectivity, the question 'Can something enter the subjective sphere?' acquires a quite different form. As soon as we can assign the I a participation in the sphere of objectivity, the I must possess qualities that are of the same kind as objectivity. That is, it must be possible to discover something of the sphere of objectivity in the I. And so we may now assume a relationship between objective and subjective that deviates considerably from the view that nothing can filter through from trans-subjectivity into the subjective sphere.

In saying that nothing can filter through into the subjective domain, we have, firstly, defined the subjective in epistemological terms as being self-enclosed, self-contained; and secondly, we have employed a term that is only justified for a certain sphere of reality, but cannot have validity for the whole scope of reality. This term is the 'thing-in-itself', a concept that plays a significant role in the works of many epistemologists: it is like a net in which philosophical thinking traps itself. But people fail to notice here that this concept only applies to a certain sphere of reality and that it ceases to be valid where this sphere ceases.

The concept is valid, for instance, in the material realm. I'll cite the example of a signet and sealing wax. If you take a signet with the name 'Smith' on it and press it into hot sealing wax, you can rightly say that nothing of the signet ring can filter through into the sealing wax. So here you have something where this 'not filtering through' applies. But the name 'Smith' itself can flow entirely into the sealing wax and be captured there. And if the sealing wax could speak and wished to make clear that nothing of the substance of the signet had transferred to it, it would nevertheless have to accept that the name 'Smith' had been transferred to it in full. So here we have already passed beyond the realm where the concept of 'thing-in-itself' remains valid.

What caused this concept—which appears in subtler form in Kant, then rather ham-fistedly in Schopenhauer, but was later described with great acuity by the most varied epistemologists of the nineteenth century—to acquire such importance?

If we examine this more closely, we see that it was because what people elaborate in concepts does after all depend on their whole manner of thinking. Only in an age in which all concepts must be described as developing in response and in relation to outward perception was it possible for a term such as 'thing-in-itself' to develop.

But concepts acquired only from outward perception are not suited for characterizing spiritual realities. If epistemology had not been invested with such a concealed, and thoroughly masked materialism—for this is the salient fact here: there really is an easily recognizable materialism inhabiting epistemology—then people would see that an epistemology that is to apply to the spiritual realm must also possess concepts that are not so roughly hewn as that of the 'thing-in-itself'. For the realm of spirit, where we cannot actually speak of 'outside' and 'inside' in the same sense, it must be apparent that we need subtler concepts.

I would have to write a whole book to do this justice, and have only touched on it briefly here. Such a book would have to have several volumes, since it would need to cover metaphysical considerations as well as the history of philosophy and epistemology. But you can see from what I have said that this kind of thinking, springing from deep, concealed preconceptions, is of no use for everything that extends into the world of spirit.

I have now been talking for an hour about this most abstract concept. I have tried to make it comprehensible, and I fully recognize that possible objections to what I have said, of which I am very much aware, may of course have arisen in some of my listeners. If this were a different kind of gathering I might have been obliged to give special grounds for burdening my listeners, if you like, by speaking in the most abstract, and as many may think, convoluted terms instead of offering the usual and expected subject matter. But in the course of our studies we have repeatedly seen that one of the qualities of anthroposophy is our obligation to develop knowledge in this movement, and gradually, by so doing to overcome an errant concept that exists everywhere, a very misleading one that suggests these things are beyond our scope, that we should not preoccupy ourselves with them, and that they cannot interest us.

Those who concern themselves with philosophical questions, and who may be familiar at first hand with rather poorly attended conferences on epistemology, may be surprised that there are here, in our movement, so many people—who after all might be seen as complete epistemological 'dilettantes' in the view of this or that philosopher—who nevertheless attend a gathering on such a theme in large numbers. In fact, in some places we have had larger audiences for lectures on philosophical matters, inserted between others on anthroposophy. But if we consider this more carefully, we can say that it is actually one of the best testimonies to anthroposophists. They know that they should listen with an open mind to all objections that are presented. They can do so calmly, for they know very well that, while objections to the results of enquiry into supersensible worlds are possible and justified, nevertheless much that has been dismissed as illogical can ultimately turn out, after all, to be perfectly logical. Anthroposophists also learn to feel obliged to acquire knowledge even if this is arduous, to make it their own: to concern themselves with epistemology and logic. And in this way they will become ever more able not only to engage with presentations on general anthroposophic themes but also to undertake serious work with logical concepts and categories. The world will have to come to see that philosophy in its broadest sense can be reborn within the anthroposophic movement. Enthusiasm for philosophical rigour, for the thorough, logical forming of concepts, will gradually make itself at home within the anthroposophic movement. This is not to say that the results, on closer inspection, are already fully satisfactory. We need to be modest about our achievements so far, but we are on the way to this goal.

The more we develop good will for conscientious thought and science, for philosophical rigour, the more our anthroposophic work will not only pursue transient personal aims but also ones that sustain and advance humanity. Much is so far only a first budding of will. But it becomes apparent that in the will that is applied to knowledge there already lies something like an ethical self-education, achieved by the interest we bring to bear upon anthroposophy. If no other obstacles arise than those already present, the world at large will not be able to withhold its acknowledgement that anthroposophists do not seek for easy fulfilment of their inner longings, but that, in anthroposophy, there exists an earnest striving for philosophical rigour and conscientiousness, rather than mere dilettantism. This striving will be well suited to honing people's philosophical conscience. If we regard anthroposophic teachings not as dogmas but understand, rather, what anthroposophy can be as a real power in the soul, this can be a fuel for this human soul to kindle hidden powers within it and to come increasingly to consciousness of its destiny. Within our movement, therefore, let us nurture this enthusiasm for rigorous logic and epistemology and in this way, standing ever more firmly on the ground of our physical world, we can learn to look up to worlds of spirit with ever greater clarity and without sentimentality or nebulous mysticism; we can learn to draw down the content of that world and integrate it into our physical worldview.

Whether or not we wish to do so is the sole deciding factor in whether we can give anthroposophy a real mission in humanity's earth existence.

Lecture 11

ORIGINAL SIN AND GRACE

MUNICH, 3 MAY 1911

Since karma has determined we should meet here instead of in Helsingfors (Helsinki)[58] where the course was supposed to begin, let us start with a brief reflection on spiritual-scientific themes, and then perhaps members of the audience can ask any questions which arise for them and so extend this improvised evening event.

Let us perhaps first consider a few little gleams that illumine our spiritual movement if we consider our human evolution in connection with the earth's evolution. As we have sometimes done, let us shed a particular and different light on various things that we know already. It is possible that things that have made a deeper impression on you in the religious sensibility of humanity may have elicited questions in you. You may have asked yourselves how themes in humanity's religious feelings, or the themes apparent in other kinds of worldviews, relate to our own deeper views as expounded in spiritual science.

I want to point at the outset to two important concepts, despite the fact that modern people today believe such things to be very outmoded: to the two terms 'sin' and 'grace'.

We all know that these words, 'sin' and 'grace' are hugely significant for the Christian worldview, that they play the greatest role there. However, certain anthroposophists have become accustomed—from, as they believe, the perspective of karma—to not reflecting very much upon such ideas, especially not reflecting upon these terms in their broader sense. Now this disregard of such reflection leads to less than beneficial consequences since it hinders them from discerning, say, the profounder aspects of Christianity, indeed the profounder aspects of worldviews in general. These terms, 'sin', 'original sin', 'grace', actually have a much deeper background than people usually think. This is no longer discerned today simply because almost all traditional religions in the world—almost all, more or less, in the outward forms in which they now exist—have erased their true depths so that scarcely anything that is now promulgated in any particular religion bears a resemblance any more to what actually underlies the terms employed. Behind the words 'sin', 'original sin' and 'grace', the whole evolution of the human race in fact lies hidden.

We have become accustomed to dividing this evolution into two parts: a descending trajectory from the most ancient times of human evolution up to the appearance of Christ on earth, and an ascending one, beginning with the advent of Christ and passing on into the most far-distant future. Thus we see the coming of Christ as the greatest event not only in our human evolution but in our whole planetary evolution altogether. Why must we place this Christ event at the very midpoint of world evolution, as something so extraordinarily significant? We must do so for the simple reason that the human being, as we know, has descended from spiritual heights into material, physical depths, and because he must again rise in turn from material, physical depths to spiritual heights. Thus we are concerned with the human being's descent and re-ascent. And in regard to our soul life, we characterize this descent of the human being in more detail by saying this: when we look back to very ancient times, we find that in those eras human beings were able to lead a life of spirit that basically had far greater affinity with the divine than nowadays; that human beings stood closer in a sense to the divine, spiritual world; that more divine, spiritual life shone into the human soul.

We should not forget that it became necessary for humanity to descend into the material, physical world because, in those ancient times when people stood closer to the divine, spiritual realm, at the same time the whole awareness of our soul was a duller and more dreamlike one. It was a less sharp, focused consciousness, but pervaded more by divine-spiritual thoughts, feelings and will impulses. Our closeness to divine, spiritual reality at the same time means we were less clear, more like a dreaming child. We descended as we acquired the power of judgement necessary for physical life, the power of reason. And in doing so we distanced ourselves from divine, spiritual heights, and instead became inwardly clearer, found a more stable point of reference within ourselves. And now, in order to work our way upward again with this inner anchorage of our soul life, we must fill it with what occurred through the Christ impulse. The more we do so, the more we will ascend again into the divine, spiritual world—not now arriving there as a dreaming being with dull awareness, but as one whose consciousness can look with clear focus into the world. We have often spoken of this from various angles.

Now if we examine human evolution in more detail, we also know that we became able to look into the physical sense world with a clear, bright, rational gaze solely because of the human I. This, though, was the last aspect to develop in the course of human evolution, following previous evolution of the astral body, before that the etheric body, and still longer ago the first rudiments of the physical body. Today therefore we will recall that a first evolution of the astral body preceded actual I evolution as such. If we survey various things that we have heard over some time, though, we must be clear that before we could pass through our I evolution, we underwent an evolution in which we possessed only these three aspects: physical body, etheric body, astral body. Nevertheless, human beings were already heading toward I evolution. They lived within this evolutionary trajectory, were waiting in a sense for the later addition of the I. If we keep this in mind, we can gain an idea that preparatory developments must have occurred with human beings and their whole evolution before they could actually assimilate the I—as it were, evolutionary developments preceding the I. This is very important, for if human beings already underwent an evolutionary process before assimilating the I, we cannot ascribe to them the evolution they passed through then in the same way as we must ascribe to them what they subsequently underwent in possession of the I.

After all, we know of creatures who do not possess an I in the human sense—the animals. They possess only a physical body, etheric body and astral body. Because of this nature of theirs, the animals compel us to recognize something very particular about them, which we all do recognize, indisputably, if we think at all rationally. However angrily a lion attacks us, say, we cannot say, as we can of a human being, that the lion is wicked. We can be wicked, we can commit crimes, can act immorally. But we cannot say this of any animal. No animal acts immorally. This is very important. Even if we do not reflect upon this, we can see that the difference between human beings and animals is due to the fact that the latter possess only the physical, etheric and astral body, while the human being also possesses an I.

Now before we assimilated the I, we passed through a process of evolution in which our highest aspect was the astral body. Did something occur here with humankind that we should regard in a different light from what we presently see in the animal kingdom? Yes. We must recognize that even though we once were constituted of physical body, etheric body and astral body, we were certainly not like the animals of today. We were never animals but passed through this stage at other periods when we were constituted of physical, etheric and astral body, in periods when the animals in their present form did not yet exist—when quite different conditions existed on the earth. What occurred at that time with the human being? We can characterize it by saying that human beings did not yet possess the I, and so we cannot assign to them properties we assign to ourselves in distinction to the animals. We must judge the realities that issued from them differently from the way we judge such things today now that we possess an I. In this last transitional stage of evolution where humankind stood at the threshold of receiving the I, the luciferic influence was still at work. While we cannot judge the humankind of those times as we would today, we must nevertheless see them differently from the animal kingdom. Lucifer was urging himself upon humankind. As yet, without full moral responsibility, the human being could not choose either to follow Lucifer or not, but Lucifer was still able to draw human beings into his net, as it were, in a way that differs from the nature of our animals today. Thus the temptation of Lucifer falls precisely at the time when humankind stood at the threshold of receiving the I. Thus a mode of human action predating our current I evolution nevertheless casts its shadow over this whole I evolution. So who really lapsed into sin? Not human beings in so far as they are I beings. Through Lucifer, human beings became sinners with a part of their being with which, basically, they can no longer be a sinner nowadays. Today we possess our I. Thus, back then, the human being became a sinner with his astral body. This is the radical difference between any crime we may sully ourselves with nowadays, and the sin that entered human nature in those ancient times. In succumbing to the temptation of Lucifer back then, it was the human being's astral body that succumbed. This was, therefore, a deed of pre-I evolution, a quite different kind of deed from all those we could have done once the I, even in its very first intimations, had entered our nature. Thus human beings committed a deed before the I entered their nature, and yet this deed casts its shadow upon all subsequent times. Human beings were able to commit this deed of hearkening to the temptation of Lucifer before they assimilated the I, but the influence of this deed would continue to affect them for all subsequent times. Why? Because our astral body became culpable before our I evolution began, this created conditions where, in succeeding incarnations, in each one really, we had to sink lower into the physical world. This deed, unfolding still at the astral level, was the impetus for our descent. In consequence, human beings were set upon a declining path, and with their I followed forces in their nature that originate from their pre-I evolution.

How did these forces now express themselves in human evolution? We know from previous lectures that we develop our physical body until roughly the age of six or seven, then the etheric body from seven to fourteen, and our astral body from the age of fourteen to twenty-one, and so forth. We know that with development of our etheric body we enter upon a stage where we can reproduce our own kind. Let us leave aside entirely the same phenomenon in the animal world at present. We know that, having developed our etheric body, we can then reproduce our own kind. This is connected with the fact that we have fully developed the etheric body. If you reflect on this a little—and you don't need to be clairvoyant to understand this—you can see that this full development of the etheric body must at the same time bring with it the full capacity for us to bring forth our own human kind. In other words, as we continue to develop into our twenties, we will not acquire new or further capacities to reproduce our own kind. It cannot be said that at the age of 30 we will in any way augment or add to this ability to reproduce our own kind. Once the etheric body has been fully developed, we possess all the capacities we need to reproduce. So what is added later? Through what we later assimilate, nothing more of our human nature is added, for we must already possess the full capacity to bring forth our own kind. Nothing more can be acquired or achieved in this way once we have fully developed the etheric body. So what is added? Yes, the only capacity we later acquire in relation to our reproductive powers is that we mar the full scope of our ability to bring forth our own kind. Whatever we can still acquire after the full development of the etheric body cannot enhance the power to bring forth our own kind but only diminish it. Qualities, powers, we acquire after sexual maturity has been attained, do not in any way help to improve the human race but only degrade it. This is due to the effect of the impulse I described, that originates in the astral body's culpability. Once the etheric body is fully developed, thus roughly from the age of 14, the astral body continues to develop. But it harbours the influence of Lucifer! And what passes back into the development of the etheric body can only induce a decline in etheric forces that involve the ability to reproduce. And this means that what the astral body became through the temptation of Lucifer is an ongoing reason for the degeneration of the human race, for our decline.

In succeeding incarnations, therefore, the human being continually declined. And the further back we go into Atlantean times, the more we would find higher forces of the human physical matrix than in later eras. This impulse produced in the astral body by the temptation of Lucifer therefore came to inform heredity, to which it brought increasing degeneration. The sin we acquire with our I may work back upon the astral body but can only come to manifestation in karma. The sin we brought upon ourselves before we possessed an I, contributes to the continual decline and degeneration of the whole human race. This sin became an inherited attribute. And just as it is true that no one can inherit a higher spiritual quality from their forefathers, cannot inherit attributes but must gain them through education—since no one is clever by virtue of having a clever father, but only by developing their own abilities; no one has yet inherited a gift for mathematics from their ancestors, nor other kinds of thought—so likewise it is true that the influence passing back to the etheric body from the astral body, all that we acquire in such a way that it works back upon the etheric body, contributes only to an erosion of the capacities of the human race. And this is the true meaning of original sin. This original sin, persisting still in the astral body, gradually reproduced itself and came to inform human inherited attributes which at that time were already rooted in human physical degeneration, leading to the human being's descent and decline from spiritual heights. Thus the influence of Lucifer brought a continuing impulse that can indeed be correctly termed original sin.[59] What entered the astral body through Lucifer is passed on from generation to generation. And there is no more apt term than 'original' or 'inherited' sin for what truly underlay the descent of humanity into the material, physical world. But we should not regard this inherited sin in the same way as other sins in ordinary life, which we attribute entirely to ourselves, but as a human destiny; as something which cosmic dispensation inevitably laid upon us since we had to be led downward—not only to make us worse than we were, but to awaken in us forces to work our way upward again, to find these powers within our own being. We must therefore regard the Fall of humanity as something intrinsic to human destiny. We could never have become free beings if we had not been pushed downward. We would instead have had to blindly follow the cosmic order, harnessed by it. And we must now, in turn, work our way upward again.

Now nothing is ever without its opposite pole. We wouldn't have a North Pole if we didn't have a South Pole; and likewise, this sin in the astral body inevitably has its complementary pole. Though we cannot ascribe this to ourselves in the modern sense, cannot speak of any moral failings on our part, it is our destiny to be filled with Lucifer. In a sense we can do nothing about this, and must even be grateful for this dispensation. On the one hand this is right. We can do nothing about it. We had to lay upon ourselves something for which we cannot bear full responsibility.

This contrasts with something in human evolution that relates to it like the North Pole to the South. This sin passed down through generations, an influx of culpability in us for which we are not truly to blame, must be complemented by the potential to ascend again, again without our culpability. Just as we had to fall without culpability, so we must also be able to ascend again without our culpability, or, in this case, without fully meriting it. We fell but it was not our fault. And so we must likewise rise again, now without deserving it. This is the necessary counterpole. Otherwise we would have to remain below in the physical, material world. Thus in the same way that a culpability necessarily marks the outset of our evolution, so the end of our evolution must be marked by a gift that we receive without deserving it. These two things inevitably belong together. Why this is so can best be understood in the following terms.

What we do in ordinary life proceeds from the impulses of our feelings, our emotions, drives and desires. Someone gets angry, say, and acts out of anger; or feels love and acts out of this sentiment of ordinary love. There is only one word that can describe everything that we do in this way. You will all acknowledge, I am sure, that what a person does when he feels passion or anger, when he loves ordinarily, cannot be captured in abstract concepts, cannot be defined. You would have to be a very dry scholar to wish to define in words what underlies any human action. Yet we do have a word that describes what is going on in us when we do something in ordinary life, and that is the word 'personality'. This is a word that encompasses at once all those undefined things I'm referring to. Once we have grasped a person's personality, then we may also be able to judge why he felt this or that passion, this or that desire and so on. All these things have a personal character, arising from our drives, desires, passions and so on. But in living and acting out of these drives, desires and passions, we so easily get entangled in physical, material life: our I here immerses itself in the seething flux of the physical, material world. It is unfree when it follows the dictates of anger, desire, passion, and love too in the ordinary sense. It is unfree because it is bound by these emotions. But if we consider our modern era, we will acknowledge that there is something different now which did not exist really in older times.

Only those who have no knowledge of history and judge everything by a measure that goes no further than their own noses, can claim that in ancient Greece, for instance, qualities were already present that have been prized for the past century and more, such as freedom, equality and fraternity—moral ideals framed in words that underpin our principles and statutes. For instance, in its guiding principles the Theosophical Society* upholds 'a common bond of fraternity without distinctions of faith, nation, class or gender'. These ideals are ones we pursue in the modern era, but this was not the case in ancient Egypt, Persia, or anywhere in the ancient world in the sense in which we speak today. In our modern age, we feel it is beholden upon us to follow such ideals; and yet our enactment of these principles of freedom, equality, fraternity and so on has a rather abstract character for most people. Most people's grasp of freedom, equality, fraternity and so forth is couched only in abstract definitions since these ideals do not affect them personally very much. Though these ideals can be used to appeal to human passions, they can easily awaken in us a sense of aridity. These abstract ideas do not yet touch us personally: they do not yet possess the full-blooded feeling of personal life. And we have high regard for individuals in whom the idea of freedom does emerge and pour forth with primary elemental power in the way we know from anger, passions or worldly love. The ideas that we regard as the greatest moral ideals leave most people more or less untouched. And nevertheless this marks the beginning of a great development. Just as we gradually immersed ourselves in the ocean of physical materiality, developing what we call personality and acting under the influences of passions, drives and desires, so likewise we must begin to live our way upward into these abstract ideas with our personality, not merely relate to them in the abstract as we do at present. With the primary elemental power with which

---

* See footnote on page 4.

we see that some action or other erupts from hatred or love in the mundane sense, the most spiritual ideals will also spring forth.

Human beings will work their way upward to higher spheres with their personality. But this requires something else. In immersing ourselves with our I in the surging flux of physical, material life, we discover our personality, we find our hot blood, our surging drives and desires in the astral body, we immerse ourselves in our personality. But now we must raise ourselves into the realm of moral ideals, without this being abstract. We must ascend to the spirit, and in doing so something personal must pulse toward us in the same way as happens when we immerse our I in our hot blood, our drives and passions. We must ascend without succumbing to the abstract. In ascending to the spirit in this way, how do we embrace something personal at the same time? How can we develop these ideals in such a way that they acquire personal character? There is only one means to do so. In spiritual heights we must be able to draw toward us a personality that is inwardly personal as the personality below in the flesh is. What personality is this that we must attract to us as we seek to ascend into the realm of spirit? It is Christ. Just as someone might say, in the obverse of the Pauline phrase, 'Not I but my astral body', so Paul says: 'Not I but Christ in me';[60] and in this way shows that by virtue of Christ living within us, abstract ideas acquire a very personal character. This, you see, is the significance of the Christ impulse. Without it we would arrive at abstract ideals, all kinds of ideals of moral powers and suchlike, would come to what many historians describe as 'historical ideas', which can neither live nor die because they possess no creative power. In speaking of 'ideas' in history, we should be aware that these are dead, abstract concepts which really are not equal to actual periods in history. Only life itself is. And we need now to develop and work our way toward a higher personality. This is the Christ personality which draws us toward it, and which we take up and assimilate into ourselves.

Thus we re-ascend to the spirit, not only speaking of the spirit but assimilating the spirit in the living, personal form that we encounter in the events of Palestine, in the Mystery of Golgotha. Under the influence of the Christ impulse we re-ascend. The only way in which we can come to invest abstract ideals with ever more of a personal character is to allow our whole life of spirit to be pervaded by the Christ impulse. But just as we took upon ourselves the culpability we call 'original sin' before the I evolved, and thus possess something that cannot be laid entirely at our door, so the fact of Christ's entry into the world and the capacity to draw Christ toward us cannot be celebrated as ours either. What we do, what we try to do, to come closer to the Christ, is already implicit in our I, is something we have merited. But that Christ is there, that we live upon a planet where Christ walked abroad, that we live in an era after these events occurred, is not something we have earned or merited. Thus what flows out from the positive, the living Christ to bring us back up again into the world of spirit, is outside and beyond our I. It draws us upward to it without any ability on our part to achieve it, as little as we can do anything about the guilt that, we might say, accrued to us without our culpability. Through the fact that Christ lived on earth, we gain the strength to re-ascend again, as little merited as the culpability that burdened us without our guilt. Neither of these, you see, have anything to do with the personal realm in which the I lives, but instead with what precedes and succeeds the I. We have often stressed that humankind evolved from a condition in which it possessed only a physical, etheric and astral body; and that we evolve further by transforming our astral body, thereby making this astral body into manas. Just as we harmed our astral body through original sin, we remedy it again through the Christ impulse. Something flows into it that heals it as much as it was harmed before. This is the equivalence, which we can truly call 'grace'. Grace is a term equivalent to original sin, the redress for it. Thus the influx of Christ into the human being, the possibility of becoming one with Christ, the capacity to say, like Paul, 'Not I but Christ in me', at the same time expresses everything we understand by the term 'grace'.

And so we can say that we do not misconceive the idea of karma if we acknowledge both original sin and grace. In so far as we speak of the idea of karma, we are speaking of the reincarnation of the I in various lives on earth. Karma is inconceivable without the presence of the I. In speaking of original sin and grace, we are speaking of impulses that underlie the surface of karma, that lie within the astral body. Indeed, we can say that the nature of human karma only arose because we brought original sin upon ourselves. Karma runs through many incarnations, and preceding and succeeding it are things that initiate it and redress it once again: beforehand, original sin, and afterwards the full success of the Christ impulse, the arrival of complete grace.

And so we can say that, from this perspective too, spiritual science does indeed have a great and significant mission in the present age particularly. For as true as it is that humanity has only recently come to acknowledge abstract ideals at all, as true as it is that we can develop what we may call the abstract ideals of freedom and fraternity, it is equally true that a time must soon come when these ideas are no longer merely abstract ideals but approach us as living powers. Humankind has passed through a point of transition in which it could encompass and formulate abstract ideals, but now it must progress to a stage where these ideals can come to personal expression: it must move onward to enter the new temple. We stand at its threshold. And people will be taught that what works downward from spiritual heights are not mere abstracts but living powers. When they begin to recognize what awaits their vision in the next epoch of evolution, when they cease thinking 'How good I am!' but when instead they begin to discern the Christ as a living being, when their etheric vision reveals to them the living power of Christ, whom they will perceive in the etheric body—as we know, from the middle of this century [the twentieth century] certain people will gain this capacity of vision—then they will know that what they perceived for a period in the form of abstract ideas are in fact living beings: living beings alive within our evolution. The living Christ, who first appeared in physical form, and who at that time could only impart himself to people in this form so that they could believe in him, even if they were not his contemporaries, will reappear in renewed form. Then no proof will be needed that he lives, for those who can prove it will be present: those who can themselves experience in a kind of mature beholding—even without special schooling—that the moral powers of the world are living realities, not merely abstract ideas.

And so we see that our thoughts cannot lead us upward into real worlds of spirit because they are devoid of life. Only when these thoughts no longer appear to us as *our* thoughts, but as testimonies to the living Christ who will appear to humankind, will we properly understand these thoughts. Then, as we became a personality through submerging ourselves with the I in lower spheres, we will likewise become a personality by ascending to spiritual heights. Modern materialism fails to discern this. It can only grasp the existence of abstract ideals of goodness, of beauty and so on. That living powers exist that raise us through their grace, is something that still awaits comprehension. We discern this through spiritual-scientific schooling, as the renewed impulse of Christ. If we no longer regard our ideals only as ideals but through them find the path to Christ, then we uphold and continue Christianity in accord with spiritual science. Christianity then enters a new stage and ceases to be mere preparation. It will show that it contains the very greatest riches for all coming eras. And those who think that Christianity is always endangered when it develops and changes will see how wrong they are.

They are those of little faith, who grow anxious if they are told that Christianity contains still greater glories than have yet been conveyed. Those on the other hand whose ideas of Christianity have grandeur are the ones who know that Christ is indeed with us always[61]—that is, that he continually reveals new things to us; and that it is right to return to the source of Christ. In this way Christianity lives as something greater than people realize, bringing forth from itself ever new and more living creative realities. Those who keep saying this is not true Christianity because it cannot be found in the Bible, that those who claim anything different are heretics, should be referred to the passage where Christ says, 'I have much more to say to you, more than you can now bear.'[62] He did not say this to show that he was withholding something from them, but that he will reveal himself from era to era in ever new forms. And he will reveal himself through those who seek to understand him. Those who deny this, themselves fail to understand the Bible or Christianity. They fail to understand how to hearken to the Christian admonition in these words, 'I have much more to say to you, but prepare yourselves so as to learn to bear it, thus to gain understanding of it.'

True Christians will in future be those who hear what the first Christians, the contemporaries of Christ were not yet able to bear. The true Christians will be those who have the will to let ever more of Christ's grace flow into their hearts. Those who obstinately defend themselves against this grace will say, 'No, go back to the Bible, only the letter is true.' And in saying this they will deny the words that kindle a bright light within Christianity itself, the words that we should take properly to heart: 'I have much more to say to you, more than you can now bear.' Things will go well for humanity if it can bear to hear more and more of such things. Then it will become ever riper for the ascent into spiritual heights. And Christianity exists to pave the way for that.

Lecture 12

THE MISSION OF THE NEW SPIRIT REVELATION

INTRODUCTORY WORDS FOR THE CYCLE 'SPIRITUAL GUIDANCE OF THE HUMAN BEING AND HUMANITY'

COPENHAGEN, 5 JUNE 1911[63]

Over the next few days I will have the privilege of speaking about a theme that I consider important: the spiritual guidance of the human being and humanity. At the request of our friends, I will preface these lectures with a few words that may be taken as a kind of introduction to this theme.

Anthroposophists inevitably feel what we may call a longing for true self-knowledge in the broadest sense. Those who have delved even a little into anthroposophical life will feel that this self-knowledge must give birth to a comprehensive understanding of all human feeling and thinking, of every other being; and that such understanding must be indivisibly connected with our whole anthroposophic movement.

The fact that the symbol you know as the cross with roses has such pride of place within our anthroposophic movement is something so easily misunderstood. It is especially easy to harbour misunderstandings about the spiritual movement which, under the sign of the Rose Cross, seeks to find its way into the culture of our day, to find its way into human hearts and their feelings, to find its way into human will and its deeds. It is easy for misunderstandings to arise here since for many, also well-meaning souls of the present day, it is extraordinarily difficult to recognize that the spiritual movement seeking to work in harmony with this symbol is entirely governed by principles and by feelings of universal tolerance for all human striving and outlooks. This lies deep in the foundations of the Rose Cross movement, and is something that may be less immediately noticeable but it is still intrinsic to it. And so you will easily find that this movement is misunderstood in those quarters where real tolerance is confused with a narrower tolerance only for one's own opinion, one's own principles and approaches.

People imagine tolerance to be a very easy thing and yet tolerance of the very highest kind is one of the most difficult things to achieve. It is easy to think that someone who says something other than we do is our opponent. We can also easily confuse our own opinion with what is generally propounded as truth. But anthroposophic life will flourish and bear the right fruits for the culture and spiritual life of the future if it becomes an inclusive soil upon which we meet each other, meeting in inward understanding not only those who believe what we ourselves believe but those too who, through their own experiences, their own path in life, feel it necessary to assert what seems to be the opposite of what we ourselves assert. An old form of morality, which is now waning, taught that love and tolerance should be practised amongst those who hold the same thoughts and feelings as we do ourselves. But anthroposophic life, in its true form, will increasingly imbue human hearts with that much deeper form of tolerance that enables us to find mutual understanding, mutual stimulus, human community even with those with whom our thoughts and feelings are not initially in accord. This touches on an important point, for what do people first encounter when they turn their attention to our anthroposophic movement? What do they first find necessary to acknowledge? Even though this central insight does not have to be a dogma, and though there can be differences of opinion even here, a universal insight that people first encounter when they approach our movement is the idea of reincarnation, teachings about the causes in one life that lead to circumstances in another. Reincarnation and karma are convictions that appear paramount from the very beginning. But we travel a long way between the first moment when these truths become our conviction to the day when, in a sense, we place our whole life, our whole existence into the light of these ideas, these truths. A long time may pass between the day when this conviction dawns on us and the day when it can come to full life within our soul.

Let us imagine that we face someone who meets us with disparagement and insult. If we have dwelt long enough upon the teachings of reincarnation and karma, we will be able to ask who it is who has uttered injurious or insulting words that have penetrated our ears and overwhelmed us with their scorn, and may even have raised their hand to strike the other. And we will be able to reply: We ourselves! The hand is only seemingly that of the other person, for I am myself the person who, through my past karma, solicited the blow that the other has given me.

This is just to give a sense of the length of road we must travel from an abstract, theoretical conviction about karma and reincarnation to the point where we can place the whole of our life into the light of this thought. Then besides feeling the God within as an experience of our own higher self, teaching us how we participate in the divine with a spark of our own being, we also in particular learn this: that there is implicit in our higher self a sense of unbounded responsibility not only for the actions we ourselves take but also for what we suffer; and this is simply because what we currently suffer is only the necessary consequence of what we ourselves did long ago.

And now let us feel such an outlook penetrating our soul like the warm spiritual lifeblood of a new culture. Let us feel how new ideas of responsibility, new ideas also of loving kindness towards others arise and take root in our soul through anthroposophic life. Let us feel it to be more than an empty phrase to say that the anthroposophic movement emerged in our era because humanity needs new moral impulses, new intellectual and spiritual impulses. And let us feel that it is not merely arbitrary that a new revelation in the spiritual domain is arising for humanity, and must flow into our hearts, into our convictions, but that this new spirit revelation is necessary for these new moral impulses, these new ideas of responsibility; that, indeed, human destiny requires this. Then we can have a direct and vivid sense of the coherent meaning it has for the world that these same souls sitting in bodies gathered here today were previously incarnated so many times upon this earth. And we have to ask accordingly, why so many times? This gains meaning by virtue of the fact that we come to understand, through anthroposophy, that each time we inhabit a new body and look out through new eyes upon the glories of the world, we can intimate divine revelations behind the veil of the sensory world; or can hearken through new ears to the divine realities revealed to us in the world of tones. And through this we learn to see that in each new incarnation we can and should experience new and different things. Then we will also feel that there must be people whose karma destines them to prefigure and prophecy what will slowly and gradually become apparent to all humanity as the meaning of a particular era.

What can first be grasped and understood by members of this spiritual movement through revelations from the world of spirit must flow into all human culture. The souls who live their way into the world through the bodies they now have, feel themselves drawn so strongly to anthroposophy because they sense the need to add this new element to what human beings have previously succeeded in wresting from the world of spirit in past eras. But here we must acknowledge that in every epoch we must again come to understand anew the whole meaning of the enigma of the cosmos, that in every epoch we must meet in a new way what can flow down to us through revelations from worlds of spirit.

Our era is a very distinctive one. Although every period can easily be called one of 'transition', this term does truly apply to our present age. An era is in fact dawning when people must experience many new things relating to our whole evolution on earth. People will need to think differently about many things. And much that is new today is still being regarded and interpreted in an old light, an old style. It is still impossible for many people to really embrace and understand this new element in a new way. Often our ideas and concepts lag a long way behind new revelations.

Let me just remark upon one thing by way of example. People have repeatedly and rightly stressed the huge advances in human thinking that have led, over the past four centuries, to our ever greater understanding of the physical structure of the cosmos. The great achievements of figures such as Copernicus, Kepler, Galilei, Giordano Bruno and so on have been rightly acclaimed. But on the other hand I'd like to recall here a thought that sounds very clever, and runs roughly as follows: The ideas of Copernicus and Giordano Bruno have given us an understanding of space, and taught us that our small planet exists alongside countless other planets in the cosmos. Yet we say that the earth is supposed to be the place where the greatest drama was played out, the midpoint of evolution, and that the story of Christ Jesus should be seen as this midpoint of our whole evolution. How then should an occurrence of such cosmic significance happen to take place upon this little planet earth of ours, since we now know it to be just one among countless planets?

This thought, a very understandable one, appears to be very clever and astute if we regard things only intellectually; yet it is an idea that takes no account of the depths of spiritual feeling, the latter also embodied in the fact that, at the very beginning of Christianity, this event on earth did not even occur in a royal palace or in some grandiose setting, but in a stable with poor shepherds. In other words, placing this occurrence on the earth was not enough for spiritual feeling, but it insisted even on its being a small, disregarded corner of the earth as well. Someone has even, very curiously, compared this to 'performing the greatest drama of world events in a provincial theatre'. In fact it lies in the very nature of Christianity not even to present this great drama in a provincial theatre, but somewhere else altogether.

We can see therefore how difficult it is to bring right feelings, true feelings, to bear on things, and how much people still need to learn to recognize what the right thoughts and feelings are toward human evolution. We are approaching tumultuous times and it can be said that much of the old is no longer of use. A new element is flowing into humanity from the world of spirit. It is not because those who know something about human evolution wish it, but because the history of humanity compels them to state that our whole inner life will change in the course of the next centuries, and that the anthroposophic movement, if aware of its true mission, must stand at the outset of these changes, in all humility, but with real understanding of what must occur for humanity over the coming centuries. For however true it is that people have only learned over the course of time to regard the structure of the cosmos intellectually, as taught by Copernicus, Giordano Bruno, Kepler or Galilei; that they have only learned over the last few centuries to interpret the world through their intellect, compared to former times when human souls arrived at their knowledge in quite different ways, so it is equally true that in our era intellectual knowledge will be succeeded by a new form of spiritual discernment. Already human souls in their bodies are seeking urgently to regard the world in more than merely intellectual ways. And if materialism had not set in motion so much that suppresses spiritual stirrings, such souls—whom one can feel tempestuously desiring spirituality—would have given far more expression to these stirrings. They are waiting only to look upon the cosmos in a different way from previously, to look upon existence differently.

Those favoured spirits who have received the 'grace', as we can call it, of looking centuries into the future, can see what will later become a general vision in humanity. I have often spoken of how a figure filled with such grace, the figure of Paul—who, at Damascus, was alone in experiencing the impulse of the Christ event—prefigured what will gradually become common knowledge in humanity. Just as Paul knew, through a spiritual revelation, who Christ is, what Christ has done, so human beings will once more experience such knowledge, such vision. The time is fast approaching when a number of people will experience something like a renewal of the Pauline Christ event. This belongs to our earth's evolution: the spiritual gaze that opened in Paul outside Damascus, that can see into worlds of spirit and can draw from there the truth that Paul himself would never have believed when he was told of the Christ event in Jerusalem. This spiritual vision is something many people will experience. And its arrival—which has been referred to as the reappearance of Christ in the twentieth century—is a historical necessity. Christ as individuality will be recognized, as he revealed himself in his ever closer approach to the physical plane, from the moment onward when he appeared to Moses in the burning thorn bush,[64] as if in a reflection, to the point when he lived for three years in a human body. Such vision will discern in him the pivotal point of all earthly evolution.

Any system has only *one* point of focus: a pair of scales has only one balancing point. If you were to support the scales at several different places, you would violate the spatial laws of gravity. You need only one point of balance, one pivotal point for a system. For this reason, when speaking of the pivotal point of earth evolution in the true sense, the esotericists of all periods, both of ancient times and the modern era, acknowledge this emphasis, this single point of balance of evolution, as being the Mystery of Golgotha, from which humanity's evolution ascends again. It is extraordinarily difficult to recognize the true meaning of the Christ event, of the Mystery of Golgotha for the spiritual guidance of humanity. You see, to do so we have to silence all the feelings and judgements that we bring with us from this or that belief system. If we wish to recognize the true spiritual focus of earth's evolution, we have to regard the Christian schooling methods that prevailed in the West for many centuries with as cold and objective an eye as we regard other religious schooling methods in the world. You will find over the coming decades that those who most keenly proclaim this spiritual balancing point of humanity's evolution will be seen as 'bad Christians', and their very Christianity may even be denied.

It is already very difficult to grasp that Christ could be incarnated in a human body only once, as it were in passing, for three years. Those who have acquainted themselves more closely with what Rosicrucian anthroposophy has to say about these things know how complex the physical body of Jesus of Nazareth had to be in order to take up the mighty individuality of the Christ. We know that not one person but two had to be born to enable this to happen. The St Matthew Gospel tells us of one of them, and the Gospel of St Luke of the other. We know that the individuality who was incarnated in the body of the Jesus boy of whom Matthew speaks had previously achieved magnificent things in former lives on earth; that this individuality departed from his body at the age of 12 to assume a different earthly body until the age of 30, and to evolve further in this body, developing other capacities. In this way everything of magnificence and grandeur, on the one hand, and on the other the deepest humility that had been experienced previously in humanity, had to merge and work together to form the personality we refer to as Jesus of Nazareth in order to render a body capable of assimilating the being who can be called the true Christ. Deep understanding will be necessary to understand the unique nature of Christ; to understand what the occultists mean when they say that just as only one fulcrum can exist in mechanics, so only one event of Golgotha can take place.

In a time facing such mighty inner upheavals as I briefly intimated today, it is particularly apt to look inward. And amongst many tasks that the true anthroposophist has within this spiritual movement, this is certainly one of them: to look inward into one's own soul, into one's own heart, so as to recognize that renunciation is inevitably involved in the path we pursue to understand this unique truth, of which esotericism of all eras clearly teaches.

Eras in which the brilliant light of wisdom and warm gifts of love are to be poured out over humanity inevitably also bring with them something that confirms the truth of the saying, Where there is much light, there too are dark shadows. The black shadows that accompany the gifts I have referred to are the capacities for error. The great gifts of wisdom that are to flow into human evolution are necessarily bound up with the fact that the human heart can easily be exposed to error in such times. Let us not think, therefore, that the errant human soul will be less infallible in the times that are coming. We must understand that the human soul will be more exposed to errors and failings that at any other time. The occultists of all ages have prophesied this out of dim inklings. It is certainly true that in the days of illumination we have only been able to mention in passing, it will easily happen that errors, and indeed the greatest confusion, will take hold. It is all the more necessary therefore to look clearly at this capacity for error, to be clear that in anticipating great things it is all the easier for error to occupy the frail human heart.

If we now consider the spiritual guidance of humanity, this capacity for error—of which the prophesying occultists of all ages have warned us—should teach us this: to practise the very greatest tolerance, of which I spoke today at the beginning, and to relinquish everything that belongs to a blind belief in authority. Such faith in authority can seduce us, can lead directly to errors. On the other hand we must open our heart with warmth to all that now seeks to flow down to humanity in a new way from worlds of spirit. For this reason, an anthroposophist worthy of the name will be someone who knows that if, within this movement, we are to cultivate the light that seeks to enter human evolution, we must at the same time become guardians against the errors that can also insinuate themselves. Let us feel the full responsibility this implies, and let us have the open hearts we need to understand that there has never previously been a movement upon our earth in which hearts could be cultivated in such a warm, open and inclusive way. Let us learn to understand that it is better to be attacked by those who think that their own opinion is the be-all and end-all than for us to attack these others ourselves. A long road must be travelled between these two extremes. But those who encompass the spirit of the anthroposophic movement will know how to live with something that has rightly existed in all ages as a central motto for all spirituality. You may sometimes be overwhelmed by doubt at the thought that, though strong light is present, this brings with it the grave possibility of error, and how are you, as a frail person to orientate yourself? How are you to decide what originates in truth and what does not? If this thought rises in you, the following maxim can bring you strength and reassurance: truth will always bring the highest impulses for humanity's evolution, and this truth should be dearer to me than myself. If I have this stance toward truth yet go awry in this incarnation, then truth will have the power to draw me to itself in the next. If I am honestly mistaken in this incarnation, this error will be balanced out in the next. It is better to make honest mistakes than to adhere to dishonest dogmas. And before us will shine the thought that not through our will but through the divine power of the truth itself, this truth will be victorious. But if what we are compelled to embrace in this incarnation is not the truth, if it is error, and if we are too weak to be drawn toward the truth, then let what we profess lapse since it will not have the strength to live, and should not have the strength to do so. If we honestly seek the truth, it will be the victorious impulse in the world. And if what we already possess is a portion of the truth, this will not conquer within us through proofs we can offer for it, but through the power that indwells it. But if it is error, then we will also have the strength to say, Let this error lapse and perish.

If we make this into our guiding maxim, we will find the right perspective to say that we can always gain what we need within a spiritual movement, and that is trust. If what this trust offers us is truth, this truth will conquer however much its opponents attack it.

This sense of things can live in every anthroposophist. And if we are to mediate to others what flows down to us from the world of spirit, and awakens in human hearts feelings that give assurance and strength for life, then the mission of the new spiritual revelation will be fulfilled, entering humanity as what we call anthroposophy; and increasingly it will bear human souls into a more spiritual future.

Lecture 13

FAITH, LOVE, HOPE

VIENNA, 14 JUNE 1911

It is a great pleasure to me that, on my brief stop here, I can welcome you today again and speak of some anthroposophic matters. Over a year ago[65] we spoke at some length here about a theme of anthroposophic life and enquiry, and absorbed various ideas. So it is fitting that we now touch here on a theme that is closer to our inner life, our soul and sensibility, but that also in turn points us to perspectives relating to the connection of the human being with the great worlds of the stars, with what we call the macrocosm.

Today my point of departure is a saying that has accompanied us through human history and which expresses, on the one hand, the human yearning to come closer to our higher self, but on the other hand tells us how far short we fall of our divine self. In ancient Greece, Socrates[66] went around teaching people, using simple concepts to point them toward virtue,[67] to everything that concerns our human soul. Socrates, the Greek scholar and man of wisdom, wished to divert the gaze of his contemporaries away from outward nature. Whereas his predecessors considered what underlies great natural phenomena and sought to explain them, Socrates supposedly said, 'What's interesting about nature, about the trees and the birds? They cannot teach us how to be better human beings.' This saying is mistaken. But at this moment I am not concerned with his mistake but with his intent. He was one of the wisest people in the world, and even paid with his life for what he sought.

One of Socrates' sayings has been preserved, and it is instructive for all human souls who wish to know themselves. It concerns virtue, morality, and states that if we really knew what was right we would act accordingly. If we deviate from morality, says Socrates, this is only because we do not yet understand or acknowledge it fully. Thus virtue can be taught. But the human heart objects that human nature is frail, and often errs when it should be virtuous. Another figure, who coined this idea in a form in which it lives in many hearts, and there becomes an expression of the deepest regret, or apology, is Paul, who said: 'The spirit is willing but the flesh is weak.'[68] Many recognize what would be virtuous action but cannot adhere to it. This split runs through our whole human nature. We need only inscribe this saying of Paul in our souls and will have inscribed there also our ambivalent human nature. There is something in us that rises higher than we ourselves: our higher human nature surpasses our lower nature.

Anthroposophy teaches us to see human nature not in merely simple terms. The human soul, in our view, is threefold. Here we must recall the evolution of our planet, the former embodiments or stages it passed through, during which the human being also evolved. Our planet's first incarnation was the Saturn condition. Here the seed was laid for the human being's physical body. After a long duration of this condition, the planet dissolved and reappeared again, now as the Sun with the powers of the life ether. In this condition the physical body then acquired the etheric or life body. Again after a long time the planet dissolved and reappeared, now in the Moon condition. Here the astral body was added to the human physical and etheric body. And when this condition too had passed through dissolution, the earth was again embodied in the form that it now possesses. As fourth principle, the germ of the I was now integrated into the human being.

Saturn, Sun and Moon are a triad: the past of the earth. During this past, the human triad developed: physical body, etheric body and astral body. These are past human conditions. Our I is the present. Our future lies in what it elaborates from the lower triad, the spiritualization this achieves. As the I penetrates the astral body and learns to master it, it transforms it into spirit self or manas. As the I penetrates the etheric body, it transforms it into life spirit or buddhi. As it penetrates the physical body, it transforms it into spirit man or atman. These are the upper triad, the future of the human being.

Now the I is also threefold, for the soul possesses three aspects, three fundamental powers of which it consists, that can never be sundered from it. These three powers are what we have called the sentient soul, the mind soul and the consciousness soul. They are aspects of the individuality that gradually work their way through to consciousness. In the words of our language we could also describe them as cleverness, individuality and morality. In the sentient soul we experience our inner soul nature; the astral body can be regarded as the exterior of the sentient soul. The increasingly conscious I works its way out of the mind soul. Within these growing I forces the consciousness soul is experienced as the interior, the spirit self as the exterior aspect.[69]

Is there anything that can indicate that what I have just said is true? To answer this question, we take account of what we have become through humanity's evolutionary stages. We stand midway between the past, lower triad, and the beacon of the soul-spiritual triad that is to come. Today, in words taken directly from life, I want to characterize this latter triad, not as I did in the book *Theosophy*, where it is set out in more academic fashion. What is it that can signify for us our deepest inner deficiencies when we consider our cleverness, individuality and virtue, all the striving in us that can fill us equally with bliss and disharmony? This is the triad we can call faith, hope and love. These are the three fundamental powers of the soul that can never be taken from it.

Faith—what is faith? Faith is a power of the soul of which this soul can never be entirely deprived, and it lives in each and every person. There has never been a people devoid of it and no religion has been denied the capacity to speak of it. The longing for faith permeates the world. The soul always seeks to have something that it can cling to. If this longing for faith is not satisfied, the tormented soul will be in a bad predicament. If what it can believe in is taken from it—as happens through materialism—it is like depriving the human body of air to breathe, except that the body's suffocation happens quickly while that of the soul takes a very long time.

Often you can read proverbs such as 'knowledge is power' and so forth. Now at the beginning of the Bible, we can find a singular saying that has never yet been properly valued. In reference to the Tree of Knowledge and eating the fruit of the Tree of Knowledge, we should take very literally the thought that knowledge is food, that knowledge is sustenance for the soul. The soul eats or consumes the ideas of anthroposophy. It feeds upon what it believes, and only has healthy nourishment from what anthroposophy supplies it.

Faith, say academics and materialists, is a perspective that we have now overcome. The modern human being says, 'I only believe what I know.' This is an error. Faith is not a lapse into the past, for faith and knowledge are not in opposition to one another. But knowledge is mutable and cannot satisfy the need of faith in the human heart. When material science asserts that the world is composed of atoms, and arose by random chance, the human heart quite rightly says, 'I cannot believe that, I find no satisfaction in this hypothesis.' And since human beings cannot believe it because they have nothing that their feelings of faith and believe can cling to, the human soul is unhealthy and this unhealthy soul makes the body sick in turn. Nervousness develops in consequence, as we see it today, and grows ever more severe. Thus the soul works upon the body, and those who have become like this act in turn upon their surroundings, which they drag down and render unhealthy, and pass this onto their descendants. This is why humanity increasingly degenerates, and this situation will, unfortunately, grow ever worse. Materialistic science is what gives human beings 'stones instead of bread'. The soul has no sustenance despite the intellect being crammed with knowledge. And someone like this walks around and does not know what can sustain them, and just as when someone suffocates when deprived of air, so the human soul suffocates from lack of food, from lack of spiritual sustenance in life. Anthroposophy has arrived in the world to provide humanity with food.

When we gather to pursue anthroposophy together, we are not like other associations that concern themselves, say, with literature, the fine arts, social problems or suchlike. We do not pursue anthroposophy out of curiosity but in order to satisfy the urge for faith, to give the soul sustenance. And for this reason we allow anthroposophic ideas, thoughts and feelings to work upon our souls.

If we now consider this in relation to the evolution of the world and humanity, we must remember that during the earth's Moon condition, the astral body was added to the human configuration. What is the nature of this astral body? It consists of forces that must always encompass something, that must always find purchase somewhere. In their effect these forces are what we experience as faith, as the power of faith. The astral body is the very source and fount of faith. It has to be fed if it is to develop and live. The desire for sustenance is the yearning for faith. If this power of faith cannot be satisfied, if it is deprived of one thing after another that it might otherwise adhere to, the food supplied to it is poor and then the astral body falls sick, and consequently also the physical human being. But if we find satisfaction, if our hunger is stilled by ideas, thoughts and feelings that anthroposophy draws from truth, from the depths of world knowledge, then it has food that agrees with it and nourishes it. It is satisfied. It grows strong, healthy, and the human being himself grows healthy.

For the past century or so, views have changed, as has the world itself. Roughly a hundred and thirty years ago a person was called *nervous* if he was a solid fellow, with strong muscles and full vigour. Nowadays a nervous person is dissatisfied, weak and sickly, someone whose soul unhappily seeks something from which it can draw nourishment. It follows from all this that we can rightly call the astral body the 'faith body'.

A second fundamental power is that of love. No one lacks this, it is always present and cannot be eradicated. If you were to think that the person who hates most strongly, the greatest egoist, has no love in them, you would be wrong. The yearning for love is always present—whether this is sexual love or love of a child, or of a friend, or love of something else, of work or an ideal, it is always there. It cannot be torn from the soul because it is a primal power in the soul. But just as we need air to breathe, so we need the work of love, the activity of love for our soul. Egoism is its adversary, its hindrance. But what does egoism do? It prevents love working outward, it invariably and always compresses it into the soul. And just as air must stream outward when we breathe so that we do not suffocate, so love must stream outward to prevent the soul suffocating from what is so vehemently compressed within it. Or rather, the soul would otherwise be consumed by its own fire of life within it, and would be destroyed.

Let us now recall that on Old Sun the human being acquired the germ or rudiments of the etheric body; that this fiery, shining brilliance of the sun is the matrix of the etheric body. This reveals only another aspect of love, love in the spirit: light is love. In the etheric body therefore we are endowed with love and the longing for love, and we can rightly and truly call the etheric body the love body: light and love.

It truly can be said that love is the highest good.[70] But it can also have the most disastrous consequences. We see this in daily life, and I will recount an instance from actual experience. A mother loved her little daughter very much, and out of love she let her do everything she wished: she never punished her, fulfilled her every whim. And this little daughter became a toxic character, and this was because of love. Love has to be paired with wisdom, it must be illumined love, and only then can it really work for the good. Anthroposophy is called upon to bring wisdom to bear on love, to endow it with this illumination. And if we absorb and assimilate what is said and taught here about world evolution, about matters seemingly so remote, about the human being's connection with the macrocosm, then people will regard their fellow human beings with an illumined love, will gain insight into them, will be able to understand them, and so their love will become illumined love of others.

We often hear it said that life is arid and empty. This feeling about life spreads a kind of unease that extends even into the body. It is the unsatisfied power of love that causes this. If the world repudiates our love, we feel pain. If we do something out of love, we have to do it because the soul needs this, in the same way our lungs need air. Anthroposophy has arrived in the world not to satisfy academic curiosity or to present a theoretical view of things to the world—we have more than enough of such views, and still thousands of real issues await a solution—but to bring humanity fulfilment in life. As yet we still meet in small circles, but these circles will soon grow ever larger, and eventually we will be able to resolve the thousands of pressing questions that beset us today.

Who will solve our social problems? Those who debate them in theoretical terms? No, never. The anthroposophic outlook, and love, will solve them. And however paradoxical this may sounds, humanity will soon not even be able to cultivate potatoes—potato quality is getting worse and worse—without anthroposophy. How can this be? Today humanity does many things instinctively, but such instincts will increasingly fade. Why? Because a time has now come when instinct must become conscious. And because of this people will not know how to grow crops any more without acquainting themselves with anthroposophic truths about the nature of the soil, the forces active in it and so on.

The third fundamental power of the soul is hope. The human soul must hope, everyone knows this. There are many dissatisfied people who go searching through the world, and all too often we can meet those to whom all seems empty, whom nothing satisfies, through whose fingers life seems to keep draining away. They say that everything is dark around them, they have no hopeful prospects.

A great man once said that virtue without hope is the greatest crime, and eternity without hope the greatest lie! And yet the power of hope is inscribed in the soul, is an ineradicable force, and nothing can ever deprive us of it. But if humanity is not endowed with, but deprived of what it can hold fast to so as to climb aloft, the souls thus robbed will lose their certainty, their support, their stability. People will collapse in uncertainty, becoming dull-witted and senseless. The fundamental anthroposophic teachings of karma and reincarnation satisfy the human soul's power of hope. They offer something lasting, something that leads into the future. What is the value of any action or thought that is conceived without reference to the human being? Human beings and their deeds, human beings and their thoughts, belong together, and it is illogical to regard an evil deed, say an insult, as being expiated if the person who did this does not themselves redress it. The law of cause and effect tells us that human life is bound up with the human being who passes from incarnation to incarnation.

Lessing left us his book *The Education of the Human Race*[71] as summation of his whole life's work. The thought in which this book culminates is that we repeatedly return. Great minds, geniuses such as Lessing, thought nothing less than that the human soul develops onward from stage to stage, and that it continually re-experiences what it has caused. It will not be long before the teachings of reincarnation and karma are also acknowledged by outer science. And then humanity will receive something that materialistic science denied it: and that is hope.

Why do we understand the nature of past cultural epochs? Neither literature nor the history of art teach us the essence of what the Greeks left us: neither of them have much to say about it, and it's not even necessary to know these academic things. We possess the achievements of ancient Greek culture simply because we ourselves were alive then, because we experienced this epoch of culture; and we could not be what we are today if we had not lived through those times. Hebbel left behind notes[72] that he was no longer able to shape in dramatic form. He describes a teacher discussing Plato with his students. The reincarnated Plato is one of these students, and earns one bad mark after another from his teacher, is even punished because he—Plato—does not understand Plato! Here again the soul of a genius gives expression to the idea of reincarnation.

If the fruits of virtue did not depend on humankind, what would virtue be worth? How could evil be redressed if human beings themselves did not redress it? Lies would remain eternal if human beings themselves did not share in eternity, if their lies no longer concerned them. It is our continuing existence through many incarnations that constitutes hope, and only because of this can souls who are poor in hope, who cannot yet quench their thirst for hope, become sound again.

On Old Saturn the seed of the physical human being was laid down. How? It was implanted spiritually in what must live on, in hope. For this reason the physical body can rightly be called the hope body. The physical body's nature and property is its density. As the waves of soul life keep beating upon the shore of the human body, continually and increasingly penetrating it, it becomes permeated by hope, by the certainty that something will evolve from it that lasts eternally, that is imperishable. This longing for hope's satisfaction, for continuing existence, is a consequence of the soul's power of hope, and outward science deprives it of the nourishment it needs.

Anthroposophy, its ideas, thoughts and feelings, give it hope again, and that is the great mission of anthroposophy—to strengthen our faith, give us happiness in love and enduring existence in hope.

If we take the truths that anthroposophy conveys to us, and if we nourish the soul's power of faith with them, then manas will develop by itself: the transformation of the astral body into manas will occur by itself. If we take these truths and nourish love with them, buddhi will arise by itself. If we take these truths and nourish hope with them, spirit man, atman, will develop by itself.

This alone is why we work to cultivate anthroposophy, and not to satisfy theoretical curiosity. It is wrong to say there is no need to know all these things. That is a comfort-loving stance. Anthroposophic truths are drawn from the great universe, and they serve the human soul as living food, like bread, like the air we breathe. If we and humanity are not to suffocate, if humanity is to fulfil its mission, it needs this nourishment, now especially. It is urgently needed. That is the purpose of anthroposophic study, and not the quest for knowledge in itself, not curiosity, let alone other and perhaps worse impulses.

Lecture 14

SYMBOLISM AND IMAGINATION[73]
IN RELATION TO THE PLAY *THE SOUL'S PROBATION*

BERLIN, 19 DECEMBER 1911

Today I want to speak about the second of our Mystery Plays, *The Soul's Probation*.

As you will have seen, in all these plays, but especially *The Soul's Probation*, an attempt is made to bring dramatic portrayal to bear upon our spiritual-scientific worldview. Especially in this play, *The Soul's Probation*, an attempt has been made to fully embody the idea of reincarnation in its effect upon the reality of human soul life. I am sure I do not need to say that what happens in this play is not purely imaginary, but that it fully corresponds in a sense to esoteric observations. And the depiction is therefore in a sense fully realistic. This evening, I want to speak about the need that arose to create a kind of transition from Capesius's life so far to his immersion in and contemplation of a previous life, of a preceding incarnation.

Since *The Soul's Probation* was completed, I have often asked myself what can supply Capesius with a bridge leading him from life in a world in which he has—albeit in a keen and brilliant way—known only what outer sense perception of the world offers him, a form of perception bound up with the instrument of the brain; what can enable him to make the transition from this world into the world in which he then immerses himself, which is only available to occult sense organs? I have often asked myself why the fairy tale with the three figures necessarily creates this transition for Capesius. You see it is of course not a rational calculation or consideration that required the fairy tale to be introduced at this point in the play, but it arose imaginatively. Only after writing the play can one ask why such a fairy tale became necessary at this point. And in relation to this question concerning *The Soul's Probation*, perspectives arose for me that seemed illuminating for the poetry of fairy tales in general, and for poetry in connection especially with the anthroposophic worldview.

If people can come to the point of realizing in their lives, in practice, the categories of soul expressed in its division into sentient soul, mind soul and consciousness soul, then certain felt enigmas will arise for them in a purely primary, feeling way about their place in the world and their relationship to it. These enigmas cannot be expressed at all in our ordinary language and our ordinary conceptual forms, and this is simply because we live today in too intellectual an era to express in words, and in everything words facilitate, the subtle interplay that arises between these three aspects of the soul. We can do this instead by choosing a medium through which the soul's relationship to the world appears as a manifold and yet also very specific and manifest one. What runs throughout *The Soul's Probation* as a relationship of all the events it depicts to what is expressed in the three figures of Philia, Astrid and Luna, had to be conveyed not in sharp contours but in a way that nevertheless possesses, through certain soul energies, something that can render tangible and vivid our human relationship to the world. And the only way to do this was to show how, through the telling of this fairy tale, the three figures invoke in Capesius's soul a very particular urge, a very specific occurrence that makes him ready and mature enough to descend into the worlds that only now begin to become actual, real worlds for the human being.

I'd like first to recount this fairy tale and then to go on to link these reflections to it.

> Once there lived a boy, the only child
> of poor forest folk, growing up
> in lonely woodland. Besides his parents
> he knew few others.

His build was frail, his skin
almost transparent. Looking long
into his eyes, you'd glimpse
the deepest spirit wonders.
And though few encountered him,
he did not lack for friends:
when golden sunshine gleamed in nearby mountains,
the boy's pondering eyes would draw
the spirit gold into his soul;
and the nature of his heart
grew to be like the morning sun.
But when the rays of morning could not pierce
dark clouds and a mood of gloom had wrapped
the mountains in its shroud,
then his eye grew dim, his heart
grew full of melancholy.
Thus he was fully given up
to the spirit weaving of the world
that lay so close around him, which he felt
no stranger to him than his very being, than
his body's very limbs.
Friends he had also in the forest trees,
and in its flowers.
Spirit beings spoke to him from the swaying
tops and crowns of trees and from the chalices
of forest flowers.
He understood their murmurings.
The boy could eavesdrop on wondrous, secret worlds
whenever his soul communed
with what to others would be lifeless things.
Often in the evening, his anxious parents
found their much-loved son was missing—
close by he tarried where a spring
sprang forth from a rock, and spraying into mist
the water drops burst over stones.
When silver moonlight shone forth, magically
reflected in a sparkling play of colours
within the water spray, the boy for hours

could watch this wonder, seeing forms of spirit
that rose before his inner vision
within the water's pulse and in the flickering
moonlight shimmer. These formed themselves
to three female figures and spoke to him
of things for which his soul was thirsting.
Now on one mild summer night
when once again the boy sat at the spring,
one of these women clasped to herself a thousand
pearls of the waterdrops and gave them
to the second woman.
She formed from them a gleaming silver vessel
and passed it to the third of them, who filled it
with silver moonlight, whereupon she gave it
to the boy who watched this happening
in youthful seership. In the night
that followed this he had a dream in which
a wild dragon stole the cup from him.
Only thrice more after this night the boy
witnessed the wonder of the spring.
Then the ladies came no more
even though the boy still, musing, sat
beside the spring in moonlight's silver gleam.
Thrice three hundred and sixty weeks passed by:
the boy had long become a man, had left
his parents' house, the forest, and gone
to live in a far-off town. One evening tired
from hard work, he sat there musing
on what life might still hold in store for him; and then
he felt himself transported suddenly
back to the rock, the spring, and saw
the water ladies once again. But now
he heard them speak. The first said this to him:
'Think of me whenever you feel alone.
I draw the gaze of the human soul
into ether distances and starry breadths.
And give to any who with feeling seek me
the drink of hope in life from my wondrous cup.'

And then the second spoke:
'Do not forget me if at moments, courage
fails you, for I guide the human heart's
impulses into depths of soul and upward
to spirit's heights. To those who seek my powers
I forge the strength of faith in life
with my wondrous hammer.'
The third then spoke as follows: 'Raise
your eye of spirit to me if life's riddles
attack you from all sides, for I
spin the threads of thoughts
in labyrinths of life, in depths of soul.
And those who harbour trust in me,
for them I weave the rays of love for life
upon my wondrous loom.'
Each night that followed this, the man
dreamed that a wild dragon encircled him
in rings and yet could not approach him closer:
the beings he long ago beheld beside
the rocky spring protected him, for they
accompanied him from his home, had come to dwell
beside him in the far-off town.

It seems to me that the mood of fairy tale is altogether something that mediates between the outer world and everything that human beings once perceived in worlds of spirit in ancient, original clairvoyant vision, and which they can still perceive today if they raise themselves to these worlds of spirit, either through particular, abnormal capacities or through properly schooled clairvoyance. The world of the fairy tale is perhaps the most wholly justified intermediary between this latter world and the world of outer reality, and that of reason and the senses. It seems to me necessary to find a certain explanation for this whole place of the fairy tale and the mood of the fairy tale between these different worlds. Now it is extraordinarily difficult to build a bridge between these two realms. But then it occurred to me that this could be done in the form of a fairy tale itself. A very simple fairy tale[74] does indeed seem to me more apt here than all theoretical explanations. Such a fairy tale might run as follows:

> Once upon a time there was a poor lad who had a clever cat. And this clever cat helped the poor lad—who owned nothing apart from himself—to a great fortune. This is what she did: she persuaded the king that the poor lad owned a great, wondrous and remarkable estate, which the king himself would do well to see. And the clever cat succeeded in getting the king to set off on a journey to see it, and to travel through many, very remarkable regions. Wherever he went, the clever cat arranged for the king to be told that the great estate of this poor lad possessed great fields and meadows and all kinds of wonderful buildings. Finally the king arrived at a great and magical castle. But he arrived a little late, in the terms of a fairy tale, since it was already the time when the great giant or troll returned home from his travels through the universe and wished to enter his palace again. The king was inside the palace and wished to see all its magical wonders. The clever cat stretched out therefore in front of the gateway so that the king should not notice that all this actually belonged to the giant, the troll. When the giant returned home towards morning, the cat began to tell the giant a story, persuading him that he must listen to it. At great length she told him how the farmer ploughs his fields, how he manures it, how he must plough in the manure, how he fetches the seed that he wishes to sow, and then how he sows it. She told him such a long story that morning came and the sun rose. And then the clever cat told the giant, who had never seen this sight, to stay and look upon the golden virgin in the East, the sun. But there's a law to which giants are subject, and when he turned round to look at the sun, he burst asunder. And so, by delaying the giant in this way, the palace became the poor lad's property. He no longer had his estate by hearsay only, by the cat's machinations, but he now did truly own the giant's palace and everything that belonged to it.

This little, seemingly insignificant fairy tale is actually very central to what we can call the world history of the fairy-tale mood in our time. You see, if we consider human beings in their earthly evolution, most of them—as they have evolved on earth, passing through all incarnations, in all their current incarnations—are now comparable to the poor lad. Today, by comparison to other eras, we really are like the poor lad and possess nothing but a clever cat. But the clever cat is something we certainly possess, for this is our reason, our intellect. And what we possess through our senses today, what we have by virtue of our reason nowadays, which is bound up with the brain, is something very impoverished compared to the whole world of the cosmos, compared to everything we passed through in the conditions of Saturn, Sun and Moon. We are all, really, this poor lad, possessing only our power of reasoning which can set about ascribing to us an imaginary estate. In our present situation we are this poor lad. We are this in terms of our consciousness. But our I is rooted in hidden depths of soul life. These hidden depths of soul life are connected with countless worlds and countless cosmic occurrences, all of which play into human life. But the modern human being has become a poor lad and knows nothing of all this any more, can only at most, through the clever cat, through philosophy, explain all sorts of things about the meaning of what he sees with his eyes or perceives through his other senses. And when modern people wish after all to speak of something that surpasses the world of the senses, if they wish to acquire something that goes beyond the sense world, then they do so—and have been doing so for many centuries now—in art and poetry.

But our time especially—a remarkable time of transition in many respects—shows us very clearly that people do not get very far beyond this 'poor lad' sense of things even if they are able to integrate poetry and art into the world of senses as it currently surrounds us. In our era, you see, people have reached towards naturalism through a kind of lack of belief in higher art, higher poetry—a purely external reflection and representation of the outer world. It surely cannot be denied that our epoch has something of a mood of loss and regret, that, despite the inventiveness with which art and poetry represent reality, our age has an underlying sense that all this is illusory, and not truth. This mood does prevail in our time. The king within, who originates in the world of spirit, is in great need of persuasion by the clever cat, by the power of reason that we possess today, to accept that what imagination awakens in art, and endows it with, is indeed in some sense a true human possession. The human being, the king within, is persuaded initially. But this is not worth much, only convinces for a little while. Eventually—and we live at the beginning of such a time—people experience the need to gain access again to the higher, spiritual world, the actual world of spirit. People feel an urge—and this is becoming apparent everywhere today—to re-ascend into spheres of the world of spirit.

A certain transition has to arrive. And this transition can scarcely be better or more easily effected than by re-enlivening the mood of fairy tale. This atmosphere of fairy tales, to put this in purely outward terms, really has the capacity to prepare people's souls for experiencing occurrences that shine in upon us from higher, supersensible worlds. The very way in which a fairy tale presents itself to us without claiming in any way to represent outer reality, the way in which it simply and pluckily lifts itself beyond all laws of outer reality, enables the fairy tale to prepare our mood of soul to receive the higher world of spirit once again. The rough-and-ready faith achieved in olden times through primitive clairvoyance, has to burst asunder like the troll giant when faced by outward reality. He is subdued by the clever cat's questions, through the cat's narratives that are spun far and wide over outward reality. Certainly, we can spin such cat narratives for a long time, showing how reality now and then necessitates us taking refuge in spiritual explanations. We can expound in lengthy philosophical treatises how this or that question can be answered by referring to the world of spirit. In doing so we retain something like a reminiscence of olden times. We can hold the giant's attention for a while by relating things from the olden days. But faced by the clear language of reality, what has been salvaged in this way from olden times will not stand the test and will explode like the giant when he sees the sun rising. And this mood, the exploding giant, is something we need to know about. Here we touch on something that can in some degree illumine the psychology of the fairy tale. I cannot expound on these things theoretically—I can only discuss the psychology of the fairy tale in terms of inner observation, and I'd like to say the following about this.

Let us say that various aspects of the forms and configurations of the world of spirit—as we have described in brief in the lectures on pneumatosophy[75]—stand before someone in living imagination. Within anthroposophy, of course, we do relate many things concerning spiritual worlds. This must first stand in living fashion before a person's soul. But in terms of outer description or depiction not much would result if we were only to describe what unfolds there before a particular soul, even before the clairvoyant soul. A curious disharmony arises in the soul if we try to invest the grim web of modern thinking with truths, such as we expounded here in the last three sessions, about Saturn, Sun and Moon conditions.[76] We feel constricted everywhere in relation to the things that then stand before our soul. And the part of us that must capture mysteries of the higher worlds appears to us actually as very troll-like. We become clumping great troll-giants when we try to encompass the forms of the world of spirit. And of course in a sense we have to voluntarily let these forms of spirit explode in the sunlight of day to adapt them to the mood of the modern world; have to let their clairvoyance blow up when they encounter outer reality. And yet we can still retain something. We can retain what the poor lad retains. What we can come to possess in the immediacy of our modern souls is the transformation—but the sober and appropriate transformation—of the gigantic content of the imaginative world in the many layers of meaning of a fairy tale. Then such a human soul will indeed feel like a king who is led to what does not initially belong to this soul at all, what does not belong at all to the soul of the poor lad. The soul comes to possess this, when the gigantic troll bursts asunder, by relinquishing the imaginative world in the face of reality and introducing it into the palace that imagination can build. Whereas, in olden times, human imagination—the imagination of the poor lad—was nourished by the imaginative world, this is no longer possible for souls at our modern evolutionary stage. And yet, even if we first have to relinquish the whole imaginative world, and press it all into the multi-layered mood and meanings of fairy-tale, which does not adhere to external reality, then something that is a deep, deep truth can remain to us in the world of fairy-tale imagination. In other words, the poor lad, who has nothing really apart from the cat, the clever faculty of reason, can possess in the mood of fairy tale something he needs in modern life so that the soul can be educated to enter the worlds of spirit in a new fashion.

It therefore seems to me true to the psychology of Capesius—someone who has very much emerged from the contemporary world of thought—that, albeit from a more spiritualized view of the contemporary world, he enters the world of fairy tale, and that this discloses itself to him as something new, as a real relationship to the occult world. And therefore also something like a fairy tale has to be introduced at the place of Capesius's transition between outer reality and the world into which he is to descend to behold himself in a former incarnation.

What I say here as a purely personal perception, as the reason why it occurred to me to be necessary to place this fairy tale at this particular point in the play, accords with what we could call the development of fairy tale within the whole of humanity's evolution. Altogether, it accords extremely well with the way in which fairy tales arose within humanity. If we look back to past times of human evolution, we find a certain primitive clairvoyance everywhere in ancient peoples, a capacity to behold the world of spirit. In those times therefore we need to distinguish not only between alternating states of waking and sleeping, or, also at most a chaotic transitional state of dream, but we must also assume that ancient peoples possessed another transitional condition between sleep and waking life as well; and that this was not a dream state but a beholding of reality that enabled them to live in co-existence with the realm of spirit. Today people live in the world consciously during waking life, but only with a sensory consciousness and the power of reason. They have grown impoverished like the poor lad, who has nothing but his clever cat. But then they can also live in the world of spirit, during the night. And yet then they are asleep, they have no consciousness of spiritual worlds. Between these two conditions primordial people still had a third state, which conjured before their souls something like mighty pictures. They lived then in what the conscious clairvoyant, who has achieved the art of clairvoyant vision, also possesses—except that the latter is not in a dreamlike, chaotic state but can behold a world of reality. But in fact in ancient times people could also encompass their imaginations with clear consciousness. Primordial people lived in these three conditions. And when they felt their souls broadened into the spiritual cosmos, and connected everywhere with beings of spirit of various kinds, encountering the hierarchies, and beings of spirit living in the elements, in earth, water, air and fire, when they felt their being enlarged beyond the limits of their existence, then, in these intermediate states they experienced themselves as the giant who always bursts when the sun rises, whereupon they had to enter waking life.

These accounts, you see, are not so unrealistic. Nowadays, when people no longer feel the whole weight of words, they may assume that the word 'burst' is chosen at random, unthinkingly. But this bursting really does correspond to a kind of reality. People of ancient times felt their being growing out into a whole totality of worlds, and when the golden virgin of dawn came in the morning, and their eyes had to accustom themselves to outer reality again, the touch or blow of outer reality appeared to them like something that drove asunder what they had beheld before, that burst apart what they had been.

But the true king within human nature did not allow himself to be prevented from introducing into the world of ordinary reality something from the world in which the soul itself is rooted. And what was introduced from this world into ours is the projection, the shadow image of what is experienced there, the world of imagination, of true imagination, not fantasy which just ties life's rag-bag of odds and ends together, but real imagination whose seat is the inner soul, that is impelled from within outward in every aspect of creative endeavour. Naturalistic fantasy, on the other hand, pursues a path that is the very reverse of true imagination. Naturalistic fantasy seeks its motifs here and there in outer reality, and ties these rags together, combines them to produce combinatory images; and this sort of fantasy prevails only in times when art is in decline. In the shadow images cast by the light of imagination, on the other hand, something is at work that does not have this or that particular form, and does not initially know what outer forms it should create. From within outward, it seeks creative expression. Then, as if in a darkening of the light process, something emerges that bends toward true reality in surrender, creating, as it were, after-images of it. And this is precisely the opposite process from what we can so often observe today in modern art. From a centre everything is drawn toward this imagination which stands as spirit—initially of an imaginative reality—behind our sense reality. And what is here created is an imaginative reality that can legitimately grow into our reality out of spiritual worlds, can if you like become the legitimate possession of the poor lad—that is, of modern human beings who are confined to the poverty of the outer sense world. Of all forms of literature, fairy tales are least of all bound to outward reality. If we study sagas, myths and legends, we will always find that their traits, while hearkening to supersensible laws, are pervaded by the laws of external reality, that they trace a path from the world of spirit into the external world. And the sources of historical accounts, or those that are in some way connected with history, are of course connected with actual figures. Fairy tale alone does not allow itself to be configured in real or historical garb, but remains quite free in regard to them. It can draw as it likes on everything that exists in reality, and does so. Fairy tales are therefore the purest offspring of ancient primitive clairvoyance, are something like compensation for loss of ancient, primitive clairvoyance. Prosaic minds, pedants, who regard everything with a professorial eye, may not feel this. Nor do they need to, for the simple reason that they invariably want to establish the relation of any truth to outer reality.

A figure like Capesius seeks the truth above all else. He cannot be satisfied by asking how a truth relates to 'reality'. Is a truth confirmed, he asks himself, if we say it represents something that accords with the outer world? Things can be as true as you like, can be true and right and correct, yet may have as little connection with reality as the truth of that village lad who went to buy buns. His sums were correct but they bore no relation to reality: he worked out that, with his ten pennies, he should get five buns. This village lad behaved just like the philosophers who theorize about reality. But what he failed to consider was that in that particular village you got one free if you bought five. This was something that had no logic about it, and that no philosophy would have concluded. But nevertheless it was reality. So Capesius is not interested in how a particular idea, one or another concept, accords with 'reality'. Instead his first question was what the human soul experiences in relation to any concept it forms. In everything that can only be outer reality, the human soul experiences desiccation, aridity, the capacity for continual death in the soul; and so Capesius needs to be refreshed by Frau Felicia's fairy tale, needs something that need not be 'true' at all as far as external reality is concerned, a content that is real but that does not need to be true in the ordinary sense. And it is this content that helps prepare him to find his way into the occult world.

In the fairy tale we retain something like an offspring, an echo, of what people experienced in ancient clairvoyance. It is a form whose legitimacy is precisely due to the fact that no one who allows it to work upon them will assert that it bears a relationship to external reality. In the imaginative world of fairy tales, the poor lad who otherwise possesses nothing apart from his clever cat, takes ownership of a palace that protrudes into immediate reality. And so fairy tale can be a wonderful spiritual food for every age. When we tell children suitable fairy tales, we stir to life in the child's soul something that does not lead them only toward life in a way that requires every idea to accord with external reality—for such a relationship to reality desiccates and lays waste the soul. By contrast, the soul stays alive and fresh, so that it penetrates the whole human organization, if it feels a higher reality in the lawful forms and figures of fairy-tale images. These lift the soul entirely above the outer world. A person becomes more vigorous in life, can take hold of life with more vitality if fairy tales have acted upon their soul in childhood.

For Capesius, fairy tales kindle imaginative perception. It is not what they contain, not what they convey but the way they unfold, how one aspect links to the next, that works on in his soul. One feature allows soul forces to strive upward, another to strive downward, and in others, in turn, an interplay arises between ascending and descending powers. By these means his soul comes into movement, and there is drawn forth from it something that ultimately enables him to behold the world of spirit. For many, a fairy tale can be the most stirring, stimulating thing. And this is why we find in fairy tales that originated in earlier times something that shows how aspects of ancient clairvoyant consciousness played into them. Originally, fairy tales were not 'conceived' by someone, no one worked them out—unlike the theories of modern folktale scholars who 'explain' fairy tales. No, they were not authored in the way we conceive of this but are the last remnants of ancient clairvoyance, were experienced in dream states by those who still had such capacities. What was seen in dream was related, like the tale of Puss-in-Boots, which is simply another version of the fairy tale I told you today. All fairy tales first originated as the last vestiges of a primordial clairvoyance. And so a true fairy tale can only be created if—either consciously or unconsciously—the power of Imagination is present, projecting into the soul of the fairy tale creator. Otherwise a tale will not have that quality. A fairy tale simply worked out randomly can never be right. If someone nowadays chances to write a real fairy tale, this will only be because a longing awakens in them for the ancient times through which humanity once lived. This longing does exist, but sometimes it lurks very hidden in depths of the soul, and people misperceive how things that rise from these hidden depths play in to what they consciously create. They fail to see how much of this is also distorted by what they perform with their modern consciousness.

So here once again I want to emphasize that all poetry and literature can never draw on truth unless it can be traced back to a fulfilled longing for the ancient clairvoyant mode of engaging with the world, or unless it is connected with new and real clairvoyance. This need not come to full and apparent manifestation, but can still shine hidden in shadowy fashion within the depths of the soul. Nevertheless this connection is there. How many people today still feel the need for rhyme? How many people still feel that a rhyme has a necessity to it? In recitation nowadays, the deplorable custom has arisen to suppress the rhyme if possible, to skate over it and really only stress the meaning—that is, the aspect that corresponds to external reality. But this form of poetry, rhyme, is closely connected with a stage in language development that existed at the time when there were still echoes of the ancient clairvoyance.

End-rhyme is connected, you see, with the singular state of soul that expresses itself, after humankind entered its present stage of evolution, in the culture of the mind soul or rational soul. Basically the period when the rational soul or mind soul arose in us in the fourth post-Atlantean epoch, was also the time, in literature, when a memory dawned of the experiences of ancient times, of ancient capacities then to perceive imaginative worlds. This memory is given expression in end-rhyme, giving a regular shape and configuration to what shines out in the rational or mind soul. End-rhyme was cultivated chiefly as a prevalent aspect of everything that developed in the fourth post-Atlantean cultural epoch.

By contrast, everything that the culture of the fourth post-Atlantean epoch immersed itself in received a very decisive enlivening from Christianity and the influences of the Mystery of Golgotha. This poured itself into the European sentient soul. In Europe, the culture of the sentient soul remained at an earlier stage, awaiting a higher culture, a culture of the rational soul, that entered from central and southern Europe. This lasted beyond the fourth post-Atlantean cultural epoch so that what had developed in central and southern Europe, and in the Near East, could inform the old sentient-soul culture of central Europe, could be taken up into the strength of will and energy of will that primarily comes to expression in sentient-soul culture. And so we see, in all southern cultural influence, how regular end-rhyme informs poetry, while the will culture that takes up Christianity finds its fitting form in that other kind of rhyme, alliteration. In the alliteration of Norse lands and central Europe we can feel the unrolling will that pours itself into culture standing at the zenith of the fourth post-Atlantean cultural period, which is a culture of the mind soul.

It is curious to see how some poets, drawing on an original power of soul, seek to revive the original power of a particular region, trying to point back in a sometimes very unorganic fashion to what once existed. This happened with Wilhelm Jordan,[77] who sought to revive ancient alliteration in his *Nibelungen.* As a rhapsodist he travelled about and tried to revive alliterative verse. People couldn't work out what to make of this, since in our intellectual era people see language, speech, only as a vehicle for meaning, for content, and not what the sentient soul seeks to express with this alliteration, or what the rational soul seeks to express with end-rhyme.

The consciousness soul cannot really employ rhyme any more in the same way, and so people reach for other means. For this reason Miss von Sivers [Marie Steiner] will give you a sample now of alliterative verse to show how an artist like Wilhelm Jordan was trying to revive ancient conditions.

And the Norns now came near, whom no one beheld,
formed soundless rows, in silence surrounded
these two who had plighted their troth. These, drunk upon love,
thought it was wind that came murmuring in
to the hearth; but for other than earthly ears,
the Norn's song resounded, rang like the rush
of a tempest, descending to the night-world, the depths
of Nibelheim, and aloft to the clouds where Valhalla's
occupants lived:

> To you there belongs
> both salvation and downfall,
> your will and your wanting,
> your thinking and being.
> Now there comes chained
> in order eternal
> life-masks and illusory
> hosts of appearance;
> they draw the designs,
> they govern the goals,
> they stir up disgust,
> they waken your wishes;
> yet yours still the reflection
> but what you've become
> is the way you will turn,
> and we know the choice.
>
> From storehouse eternal
> our finger will form
> the fibre of your life,
> the thread of your in-
> escapable fate.

We spin and we spool,
we reel and unroll
the tapestry of deeds
on the loom of all life.
It was us long ago
who laid down the threads
of the weft, and yours only
the pattern to perfect!
But the lovelier you let
the mesh of the weave
form a picture, the greater
the power of envy.
Yes, the gods of the purer
light will not hold it
against you for slowly
enhancing the measure
of man, but the night world
is grim at all growth
of man, for it envies
his vaunt to Valhalla
and sheer depths have a share
in mortal material.
So it fuses forbidden
forms into the pattern,
and loyalty lapses,
oaths fail and a knot
knits up the fabric,
a nuisance that guilt's
scissors fast sunder.

The sun god, he sent
to the loveliest womb
the most luminous ray
for striving most pure.
But tempters, seducers
sent the desire
for gold, they dispatched
deceiving dreams—

> We knew the choice!
> For to you there belongs
> both salvation and downfall:
> destiny decides
> your heart and your hopes.
> Your star was ascending,
> but now, envied Siegfried,
> the song of the Norns
> is reversing it, turning it
> in a downward direction.
>
> And so to heaven and down to hell
> as if surf broke on rocks and raged,
> the storm of the song of the Three resounded.
> Unknowing that fate had chained them, still
> the hero and Krimhilde held each other
> lovingly, held each other fast:
> their souls shared in delirium, delighted
> in passion's heat and happiness,
> the glowing of their loving lips.

When Jordan himself declaimed these verses he emphasized the alliteration. That is something that a modern person no longer feels as quite appropriate. You see, to feel Wilhelm Jordan's intentions here, his programme,[78] one would have to experience the old era within the new in as imaginative way as happened in recent days in our assembly hall at the Architects' House, during the General Assembly,[79] when one could feel oneself enveloped in all the astral currents that express what was spoken there. And then one would have to feel how the various aspects of our impulse for knowledge that arose during those days would find figurative embodiment and realization in a Jordan phrase. Then we would properly experience what he recommended as a kind of programme, by means of which he sought to re-introduce a mood that unfolded in ancient Nordic times:

> …the spring of speech…
> needs only guidance to pour purer, to rush

>   in a speech-stream, a word-wave right to the rim
>   of the vessels of a former age, to fill them
>   a millennium later to make new again
>   the powerful, primordial wonder of the ancient
>   art of German poetry.

But something is needed for this—the kind of hearing that can feel the quality of speech sounds. And this in turn is intimately connected with the imaginations of the ancient era of clairvoyance, for that is where a feeling for speech sounds is rooted. But what is a speech sound? It is still an Imagination, an imaginative thought.

If you say 'light' and 'air', but mean nothing more by this than something bright or blowing, it is not yet Imagination. But words themselves are Imagination. And if we can still feel their imaginative content then, in the word 'Licht' [light], say, where the 'i' predominates, you can feel something radiant, bright and indeterminate, and in the 'u' of 'Luft' [air] you can sense something filled up and self-filling. And since the ray ['Strahl'] is something thinly filling, and air ['Luft'] gives rise to something wholly filling, therefore an alliteration has an inherent affinity with what fills and fulfils. It is not a matter of indifference if we place alliterating words such as 'Licht' and 'Luft' together, nor if we simply place the names of three brothers in random order, or instead in a way that gives a sense that the universal will united them—as Gunther, Gernot, Giselher. The sentient soul here felt the working of ancient Imagination in alliteration.

And in end-rhyme the mind soul would recognize itself in ancient Imagination. And for this reason too, if speech is given life, it can infuse certain imaginations into the soul, even infuse these into dreams, so that we can gain in dream-life some of what appears to clairvoyance as a true characterization, for instance of the elements. It is not always the case, but in the words 'Licht' and 'Luft' for instance, something arises that, if we feel it and it works on into dream-life, can in some circumstances allow to spring up in dream imagination itself a capacity to characterize these elements, those of light and air. People will only discern the diverse mysteries of language when it is led back to its origins, that is, particularly, to imaginative perception. You see, language originates from an era when we were not yet poor lads, and nor did we have the clever cat, but in a sense we still lived with the giant of Imagination; and through the limbs of the giant we experienced what had been implanted in speech sounds as audible Imagination. When Imagination encompasses the tone, and tone pours itself into it so as to fill it like a skin, then speech sound emerges, real speech sound.

I wanted to present these things to you today in an unexacting way, and without particular context. I wanted to show how, in a certain fashion, we need to re-enliven what we have lost, and what has been salvaged of it in our time; what must be regained, as Capesius does, so that human beings can grow on into the coming era, in which they can once again participate in higher worlds.

Lecture 15

CHRISTMAS—A FESTIVAL OF INSPIRATION

BERLIN, 21 DECEMBER 1911

In our work in the spiritual-scientific movement we look forward—forward into humanity's future; and we pervade our souls and hearts with something we believe we should incorporate into the currents of evolution and into the evolutionary forces of our human future. When we look upward to the great truths of existence, too, to the powers, potencies and beings who reveal themselves to us in the world of spirit as the causes and originators of what we encounter in the external sense world, there again we are inspired by the thought that the truths that we draw down from worlds of spirit are to gradually work their way into human hearts and souls in future.

Thus for the greater part of the year, our spiritual gaze is turned either toward the immediate present or toward the future. On days of celebration, therefore, at times of festival—which are like fixed memories of the thoughts and reflections of an earlier humanity, and stand there solidly for us still amidst the flux of time—we may feel ourselves all the more inclined to recall our connection with our precursors. We can immerse ourselves a little at such times in what led past human souls and hearts to establish these moments of celebration, these markers in the stream of time, which we know as the seasonal festivals.

While the festival of Easter, if we understand it, is one that awakens in us thoughts of human powers and of how higher forces can overcome lower ones, how the spirit overcomes all external physicality—a festival of resurrection, or awakening, one of hope and confidence in spiritual powers that can be awoken in the human soul—so by contrast the festival of Christmas is one that imbues us with a feeling of harmony with the whole cosmos, a festival of grace experienced, one that can repeatedly remind us of the following: Whatever happens around us, whatever doubts assail our faith, whatever disappointments sully our keenest hopes, however much the good things of life can prove unreliable, there is nevertheless something in our human nature and being—as the Christmas festival can teach us if we rightly understand it—that need only rise before the soul in living, spirit-filled form to show us continually that we originate from beneficent powers, from powers of rightness and truth. Accordingly, the Easter thought points us to powers in us that will be victorious in future, whereas the Christmas thought in a certain respect points us to our human origins in the most distant past.

Considering this we can see that our unconscious or subconscious human understanding and spirituality is a far, far loftier thing than we encompass with our conscious mind. We often have good reason to admire what human beings in past ages established out of hidden depths of soul as opposed to what they ordained through their rational thoughts, and all they could encompass conceptually. To us it seems infinitely wise to discover in the calendar that 'Adam and Eve' day is assigned to 24 December while 25 December celebrates the festival of the birth of Christ Jesus. During the Christmas period in medieval times, when Christmas plays were performed by people from one village or another, this was something, we can say, that the dim, subconscious creativity of those days revealed in vivid, spiritual ways. When the 'singers' as they were called, processed to perform their Christmas plays, the 'Tree of Paradise' was carried at the front of their procession. Just as 'Adam and Eve' day precedes the day of Christ's birth in the calendar, so these medieval Christmas plays paraded the Tree of Paradise in advance of the troupe of players who were going to perform. In other words, something in the hidden depths of people's souls once caused them to make a direct connection between our earthly human beginnings and the festival of Jesus' birth.

In the year 353, even in ecclesiastical Rome, 25 December was not yet celebrated as the day of Jesus' birth. Not until 354 was it celebrated on that day. Previously to this, people celebrated 6 January as a day of remembrance of the baptism by John at the Jordan. The sense they had of this was similar to the regard people later had for the festival of Jesus' birth. 6 January was celebrated as the day when Christ descended from spiritual heights and incarnated into the body of Jesus of Nazareth. Originally this was the birth of Christ within Jesus, a memory of the great, historical moment that is symbolically figured for us in the dove hovering over the head of Jesus of Nazareth. Thus 6 January was a day of remembrance of the birth of Christ within Jesus.

But in the fourth century, the encroaching materialistic worldview of the Western world meant that people no longer had any ability to understand the great thought of Christ's descent into and permeation of Jesus. This thought was present in the Gnostics, like a mighty though brief illumination. In a sense they had been contemporaries of the event of Golgotha, or came immediately after it, and they were still able to find this depth of wisdom about 'Christ within Jesus' in a way different from how modern clairvoyance must seek it again. Through the last flares of an ancient, original, human power of clairvoyance, the Gnostics were still able to discern, as if in the light of grace, much of what we must now rediscover about the great mysteries of Golgotha—thus in particular the secret of Christ's birth within Jesus at the Jordan baptism by John.

But like ancient clairvoyance in general, this remarkable flaring of the greatest clairvoyant powers, of the greatest Christmas light of humanity as the Gnostics possessed it, also faded. And by the fourth century, Western Christianity had long been unable to understand this great thought any more. At that time therefore, Western Christian culture no longer found any meaning in the festival of Christ's appearance within Jesus. People had forgotten the meaning of this festival of his appearance on 6 January. For a period, through into our modern era, any sense of the meaning of the figure of Christ for humanity's evolution was inevitably buried under the detritus of materialistic outlooks. But while people could no longer understand the sublime manifestation at the Jordan baptism, it did not run counter to materialistic consciousness to grasp that the bodily organization chosen to assimilate Christ was something very significant. And so the festival of the birth of the spirit, the manifestation at the Jordan baptism, was moved back to, and supplanted by, the festival of the birth of Jesus of Nazareth.

And yet, even though people scarcely ever gave this clear expression any more, significant feelings, sublime, lofty feelings still lived in humanity's sense of the Christmas festival. Whenever the Christmas festival approached, something important lit up in the human soul. And this was something we can express as follows: If we regard the world with the right outlook we can enliven our faith in humanity, can hold firm against all dangers and blows of destiny; we can enliven deep within us a feeling of love and peace that stands firm against all disharmony and conflict.

This is a light that continually dawns in relation to the Christmas festival. What was it, really, that people were recalling? Let us bring spiritual science to bear on this. We know what significant, great and mighty configurations were required in human evolution to enable the Mystery of Golgotha to dawn within it. Someone had to be born who was the reincarnated Zarathustra, one of the two Jesus boys. But one had to be born also whom the festival of Jesus' birth remembers: someone whose soul substance had remained behind in worlds of spirit. For the whole span of time during which humanity— all human souls except for this one—evolved up to the Mystery of Golgotha, passing through generational heredity, they had been absorbing destructive powers that infiltrated them right into their blood. Only a single soul-substance had remained throughout in worlds of spirit, guarded and protected by the purest mysteries and the purest centres of the rites. And this was then poured into humanity as the soul of the second Jesus boy, the one described in the Gospel of St Luke, to whose birth all accounts of the Christmas festival relate.

At Christmastide, people remembered their human origin, they intimated the human soul before it had descended into Adam's nature. It was as if they celebrated the birth in Bethlehem of the soul-substance that had not participated in humanity's decline and descent, but had remained behind and only entered a human body for the first time when it incarnated into the Luke Jesus child.

The human soul can feel its belief in humanity, its trust in humanity if it can direct its thoughts to this fact: Whatever conflict, lack of faith and disharmony have infiltrated human evolution—and they have indeed done so through everything that has poured into humanity from Adam's time through to the modern era—if we look back to the figure called 'Adam Kadmon' in ancient times, which then became the idea of Christ, trust can flame in the human soul for the right nature of human strength, trust in humanity's original loving, peaceful nature. And this was why the subconscious soul shifted the festival of Jesus' birth very close together with the day of Adam and Eve. In the Christ child who comes to birth, human beings see, really, their own nature, but they see it in its unspoiled innocence.

Why, for centuries, was the divine child placed before humanity as something that the human soul should so deeply revere? It was because, as we gaze upon the child—before the child has as yet reached the stage of saying 'I'—we can behold, we can know, that the child is still working upon the human body, upon the temple of the eternally divine; and because a child who does not yet say 'I' still clearly displays the signs of his origins in the world of spirit. By beholding our nature as children, we can learn to have complete trust in human nature. At a time when we can most easily engage in contemplation, when the sun shines least to warm the planet, when we are least occupied with outward daily concerns, when days are shortest and nights are longest, when, because of all these circumstances we can best gather our thoughts and go inward, where all outward delights, all outward beauties are removed for a while from our gaze, Western culture places the festival of the birth of the divine child—that is, of the human being who enters the world in unspoiled innocence, and by doing so can give us the very greatest trust in our divine origin at a time of deepest contemplation.

It is like an affirmation of the great truth that we can learn so much from children when we see that the festival of a child's birth is placed within the cycle of the year as a great, important festival of trust in human evolution. And so we can wonder at the subconscious, spiritual understanding of human beings of previous eras, who marked such a moment in the course of the seasons. Then we can feel how, in a sense, we can decipher remarkable hieroglyphs embodied in the script of time in the form of such a festival. We can feel united with these people of an older time. Whereas we otherwise turn our gaze futurewards, and are otherwise intent on placing our best powers at the service of the future, to affirm and strengthen our full faith in this future, on such festive days we try to live more in memories. These bring us, as if in embodied form, the insight, the teaching, that while in our own time we can only conceive in our particular way of the spirit underlying the external world, there was a time long ago when—in a different, but no less right, no less significant way—people thought and experienced sublime truth by feeling at one with humanity, with everything that would one day carry humanity into sublime heights. This is our spiritual-scientific ideal: to feel ourselves united with what human beings of olden times achieved, sometimes out of their most hidden depths of soul. And we are supported in this by festivals, especially the great festivals, as long as, through the truths of spiritual enquiry, we configure before our soul the meaning their hieroglyphs inscribe in the course of time, the cycle of the year.

Oh, it is a wonderful thought, that becomes wedded with a wonderful feeling in our soul, when we see how in the centuries that followed the fourth century—when the festival of Jesus' birth was changed to 25 December—a sense of the trust evoked by the nature of the child pours into the souls of people at that time. In painting, in the Christmas plays, everywhere we see how all earthly realms bow down before the divine child, before the divine origin of human beings. We meet the wonderful image of the crib, and see how beasts incline before this original human being. And then there are wonderful related tales such as this: that when Mary bore the Jesus child on the journey to Egypt, and had crossed into that land, a tree bowed down to her and the Jesus child, an ancient, primordial tree. And similarly, legends throughout Europe tell how trees bow before this great event in the Christmas night. In Alsace, in Bavaria, we meet legends everywhere that recount how certain trees bear fruit on Christmas night, how they bow down: all these wonderful symbols are to announce that the birth of the Jesus child is something that is connected with the whole life of the earth.

Let us recall what we have so often said, that primordial spiritual streams were given to humanity by the gods, and that people of ancient times possessed clairvoyant insights into the divine, spiritual world, that this clairvoyance gradually faded so that humankind could gain mastery of the I. And if we picture how in this process something occurs like a drying up and desiccation of the ancient powers of the gods, but how the Christ impulse, giving rise to the Mystery of Golgotha, pervades this aridity with a new water of life, then we have also a wonderful picture of this in Christmas legends that recount how the dried up and desiccated roses of Jericho sprang fresh and vigorous again during the Christmas night, unfolding in greeting when Mary passed as she bore the Jesus child on their journey to Egypt. It is a wonderful symbol for what happened with human-divine powers that even such dried-up, seemingly lifeless things as dead roses sprout and flower anew through the Christ impulse that intercedes in the course of evolution.

And in the festival of Jesus' birth we find an expression of what humankind was first endowed with in reality, of what it was accorded from the very beginning. Before Adam and Eve came into being, humanity—in the terms of the Christmas legend—was accorded the entirely unspoiled, divine nature of the child. But in truth, because of the influence of Lucifer, humanity could only acquire this after the whole course of evolution had unfolded from Adam and Eve to the Mystery of Golgotha.

Oh, it does indeed awaken a deep feeling in our soul when, as if compressed into a single night between 24 and 25 December, we can look back upon what occurred between Adam and Eve and the birth of Christ within Jesus, reflecting upon this and feeling what it means. If we can feel this, then we will feel the significance of this festival, and feel too what humanity has been shown through it.

Humankind, if it can really take the opportunity to meditate upon these markers within the year, can become aware of the purity of its origins in the cosmic powers of the universe. We can raise our gaze to the cosmic powers of the universe, and penetrate its secrets a little through Anthroposophia. And only then can we develop the maturity to understand that the festival of the birth of Christ, as once understood by the Gnostics, the festival that should by rights be celebrated on 6 January, is the festival of the birth of Jesus at a higher level: the festival of the birth of Christ in the body of Jesus of Nazareth. And to enable us to immerse ourselves in the twelve universal powers of the cosmos, we have the twelve holy nights between the Christmas festival and the festival that should be celebrated on 6 January, but which has now become the festival of the Three Kings.

Here, once again, without people knowing clearly why, these twelve holy nights stand there as if ordained by hidden depths of wisdom in the soul of humanity; as if they were telling us this: Feel the profundity of the Christmas festival, but then, during the twelve holy nights, immerse yourselves in the most sacred secrets of the cosmos, or in other words in the region of the universe from which Christ descended to earth. You see, only if humanity finds the will to be inspired by the thought of the human being's sacred, divine origin, by the wisdom that pervades the twelve powers, the twelve sacred powers of the universe, which are symbolically represented in the twelve signs of the zodiac, but which only spiritual wisdom can in fact reveal; only if humanity immerses itself in true spiritual wisdom and learns to perceive the course of temporal evolution within the great cosmos and within the individual human being, will it in future find the healing Inspiration, made fruitful by spiritual science, that can come from the festival of Jesus' birth, and enables us to move forward into the future with the greatest hope and confidence.

And so we may let the Christmas festival act upon our soul as a festival of Inspiration, as a festival that so wonderfully announces within us the thought of our human origin in the holy, divine child. The light that appears in the Holy Night, as a symbol of the light of humankind shining from our human origin itself, that light symbolized for us in modern times by the candles on the Christmas tree is, if rightly understood, the same light that can endow us with the best, the strongest powers for our soul as it strives for true, genuine, universal peace, for true, genuine, universal blessedness, for true, genuine, universal hope.

Such thoughts can bring home to us the wisdom of what was ordained and enacted in the past, can strengthen us for the impulses we invariably need for the future: Christmas thoughts, remembrances of humanity's origin, thoughts that are at the same time roots from which an authentic and most vigorous soul plant can spring for an authentic human future.

Lecture 16

THE BIRTH OF THE SUN SPIRIT AS EARTH SPIRIT

HANOVER, 26 DECEMBER 1911

WHEN we light the candles on the fir tree at this time of year, for the human soul it is as if a figure of something eternal arose before the eye of spirit, and as if this symbol could always have been the same since time immemorial. When outward nature gradually fades away in autumn, when outward sunlight's configurations, as it were, fall into slumber, and the human soul must turn its outward senses away from the world's sensory manifestations, then our soul has an opportunity—and not only the opportunity but it feels the necessity—of turning inward into its deepest being. It feels that the time has come, now outer sunlight shines least, warms us least, for the soul to withdraw in this outward darkness, and at the same time instead find paths toward its inner light of spirit. The candles on the Christmas fir tree appear to us as a figure of this inner light of spirit, kindled within the night of outward darkness. And because what we now feel as the shining of the soul's light of spirit into natural darkness appears to us something eternal, it may well seem as if the fir tree shining in the night of Christmas has done so in all ages that we might return through, journeying from incarnation to incarnation back to the primordial past.

The Christmas tree itself, however, is still relatively young—it has been the symbol of the Christmas thought and the feeling of Christmas for less than two hundred years. So it is a young symbol, but each year anew it announces a great, eternal truth to human beings, and for this reason it seems as if it must have existed back in the very ancient past. Each year anew the divine revelation of cosmic breadths and heavenly heights resounds again, as if from the Christmas tree itself. And we can feel this as our soul's most trustworthy powers of peace, springing forth from our good will. Such tones rang forth, according to the Christmas legend, also when the shepherds visited the place of birth of the child whose festival is celebrated on Christmas day. The visiting shepherds heard tones that revealed divine, primal powers from cosmic breadths and heavenly heights, entering human souls of good will as a deeply reassuring peace.

For many centuries the Christmas festival was not regarded as something that could ever have had a beginning. It was felt to be an eternal symbol. And this is why Christian worship clothed the eternal nature of what occurs on Christmas night in these words: Christ has arisen anew! Each year the soul was to feel anew something that could, however, only have happened once. The eternal nature of this symbol appears in its archetypal power before our soul if we feel it in the right way. And yet, back in 353 AD, the festival of Jesus' birth was not celebrated even in Rome itself. The Christmas festival as we celebrate it today was not inaugurated until 354. A festival of Jesus' birth was not previously celebrated on 24 or 25 December. Previously, those who knew something about the deep wisdom of the Mystery of Golgotha celebrated something very sublime on 6 January: the appearance of Christ. During the three first Christian centuries this was celebrated as a kind of festival of Christ's birth, to remind human souls of the descent of the spirit whom we know as the Christ spirit into the body of Jesus of Nazareth at the Jordan baptism enacted by John. People celebrated what they could understand of the Jordan baptism as a festival of the birth of Christ on 6 January, and did so until the year 353. In these early Christian centuries, the most difficult mystery to understand, that of the entry of Christ's being into the body of Jesus of Nazareth, still lived in people as, at least, a strong intimation.

What were the corresponding feelings of those who had a close relationship with the secrets of Christianity in these early Christian centuries? They were roughly as follows: The spirit of Christ pervades and infuses the world that is revealed to us through our senses and through our human spirit. In ancient times this Christ spirit revealed itself to Moses, resounding to him like the mystery of the human I, in the same way that this resounds for us from the Christmas tree in the symbolic sounds of IAO—alpha and omega, preceded by the I—when we allow this to resonate in the soul. This is how it resounded within Moses' soul when the Christ spirit appeared to him in the burning thorn bush.[80] And then the same spirit of Christ led Moses to where he was to perceive him in his truest being, expressed in the Old Testament in the words: 'Yahweh led Moses to the Mount of Nebo',[81] near Jericho, and showed him all that was to happen before this spirit could incarnate in a human body. And when this spirit stood face to face with Moses on Mount Nebo near Jericho, he said to him: 'But thou, to whom I have revealed myself beforetimes, with what thou bearest in thy soul thou mayest not enter the evolution of thy people that is to prepare what shall happen when the times are fulfilled.'

And after humanity had been prepared through its evolution, for century upon century, the same spirit that had held back Moses revealed himself. He revealed himself, becoming flesh, assuming a human body, in Jesus of Nazareth. Hereupon the whole of humanity was led upward from the stage of initiation that is indicated in the word 'Jericho', to that indicated in the passage through the Jordan. Those who understood the true meaning of Christianity in the early Christian centuries depicted Jesus of Nazareth being baptized in the Jordan, and the sun-earth spirit of Christ pouring itself into him. This was celebrated as a mystery, as the birth of Christ, in those early Christian centuries. And what we are nowadays readying ourselves for again through anthroposophy, what we are readying ourselves for through the wisdom of the fifth post-Atlantean epoch, shone forth for the Gnostics, perceived with the last inherited residues of ancient clairvoyance, at the time when the Mystery of Golgotha occurred. At the turning point of time, at the moment when the ancient era gave way to the new, the Gnostics, these singular theosophists, perceived the Christ Mystery in a different way from us, but nevertheless expressed the same content. What they said filtered through, and although what had actually occurred in the event that is symbolically depicted in the Jordan baptism was not generally understood, nevertheless people sensed and felt that the sun spirit had been born as earth spirit at that time, that a cosmic power had shone forth within an earthly human being. And so, in the early Christian centuries, 6 January was celebrated as the birth of Christ in the body of Jesus of Nazareth, as the appearance of Christ on earth.

But increasingly humanity lost sight, and even any intimation, of this profound mystery. A time arrived when people could no longer understand that what was called Christ dwelt for only three years in a physical human body. People will increasingly recognize that what occurred over three years in a physical human body had its incisive effect on the whole of earthly evolution, and that it is both one of the deepest wisdoms and one of the very hardest to understand. The human soul, as it prepared itself from the fourth century onward for the materialistic age that was to come, grew too weak to understand the great mystery that can only once again be increasingly understood from our own time onward. Thus as Christianity gained ever more outward power, it lost a deeper inner understanding of the Christ Mystery itself, and was no longer able to invest the festival of 6 January with any content. The birth of Christ was moved back thirteen days as if it was identical with the birth of Jesus of Nazareth. But in this very fact we encounter something that must fill us with deep satisfaction and awe. The 24 and 25 December are established as the day of Christ's birth due to the loss of a great truth, as we have just seen. And yet this very loss of wisdom had such wisdom in it that—although the people who ordained this knew nothing of it—we must feel astonished at the subconscious wisdom that held sway.

Divine wisdom also held sway in this. And just as we can read divine wisdom outside us in nature if we only know how to decipher everything revealed there, so we can discern divine wisdom active in the unconscious human soul if we consider one fact. Open the calendar and find 24 December, 'Adam and Eve' day there, followed by Christmas day. In other words, the loss of an old truth shifted Christ's birth for the earth backward by 13 days and instead identified it with the birth of Jesus of Nazareth; yet at the same time most wonderfully connected this birth with the thought of the human being's origins in earth evolution with Adam and Eve. And if we enquire into all the obscure feelings, all the wonderful intimations that prevail in the human soul in relation to this festival of the day of Jesus' birth without people being conscious of this, if we examine these feelings in the depths of the human soul, we find that they speak a wonderful language.

When it was no longer understood what actually flowed in toward humanity from cosmic breadths—since this should have been celebrated on 6 January—intuitively, as if through powers at work in hidden soul depths, people fell back upon a celebration of the nature of the human spirit-soul before it has passed fully through human physical corporeality, as it exists at the very outset of a human life as the human spirit-soul first takes possession of this human physical body. The child's soul at birth has not yet assimilated what is only invoked through immersion in physical corporeality. But more than this, the celebration recalls not only the child embarking on every human life but the child who existed before human beings arrived in earthly evolution at their very first physical incarnation; what the Cabbala calls 'Adam Kadmon': the human being who descended from divine, spiritual heights with everything he had acquired from the planetary stages of Saturn, Sun and Moon. A wonderful, divine wisdom was presented to humankind in the festival of Jesus' birth as the human being in spiritual form at the very outset of earthly evolution, now born through Jesus. When people could no longer understand what descended from cosmic breadths, from heavenly spheres to the earth, a memory of what the human being had been before the luciferic powers approached us in evolution, was lodged in human souls instead. And when people no longer understood the sublime event that occurred for humanity at the Jordan baptism by John—that a divine principle descends there from cosmic breadths and heavenly heights and penetrates the human soul, to bring the assurance of peace to those who are of good will—a different assurance was nevertheless given them. No longer understanding this celebratory moment and its symbols, they were instead shown that, before luciferic powers became active at the beginning of earthly evolution, human beings possessed a nature, an intrinsic essence, that is our sure foundation.

From previous accounts we know that the Jesus boy presented to us in the Gospel of Luke—and not the one in Matthew—is the child whom the shepherds worship; and that they hear within them the message of the divine revelation from cosmic breadths and heavenly heights, bringing peace to human souls who are of good will. And so, in those centuries when more sublime truths were no longer understood, a festival was initiated instead to remind us anew each year that, though we may not be able to gaze upon heavenly heights to discern there the great sun spirit, we bear within us in our child soul, before it immerses itself in outer physical embodiment, powers that can assure us that we can vanquish everything of our lower nature that adheres to us through Lucifer's temptation. And for this reason this festival of the birth of Jesus was moved, was immediately juxtaposed with a memory of Adam and Eve, showing us that, at a place the shepherds visit, a human soul is born who possesses the nature of the human soul before we had embarked upon our first earthly incarnation.

Instead of the God whose birth people no longer understood, the birth of the human being was celebrated. You see, there are two sources, really, of the peace, tranquillity and strength that can repeatedly reinvigorate us however much our powers threaten to wane, however much our pain and suffering seem to gain the upper hand. One of these sources can be discerned if we look out into cosmic breadths that are inwoven, illumined, pervaded and warmed through by what we can call the divine spirit. And if we can give ourselves up to the thought that, if we do not allow our strength to fade, we can imbue ourselves with the power of this divine spirit that pervades the weft of this world, if we can let this thought live in our hearts, then we grasp the thought of Easter through which, as it were, we draw cosmic assurance from the breadths of the universe. And the other source comes from the obscure intimation that before we succumbed to luciferic powers at the outset of earthly evolution, our soul-spiritual being was still a current in the stream of the same spirit which we now await from cosmic breadths and depths of space in the [Christmas*] thought. If we go to the source we can discern in the origin of our own being before the influence of luciferic powers took hold, we can say this: Whatever may come upon us, whatever may torment us and draw us down from the light-filled spheres of spirit, our own divine origin once existed, and must still reside within us, however deeply concealed within our depths of soul. If we can discern this inmost power of soul then we will find the assurance that we can and may once again ascend to those heights. And if we consider everything we can invoke in ourselves as childlike innocence that is as yet free of life's temptations, and remove from it everything to which human souls have succumbed through many incarnations since the beginning of earthly evolution, then we gain a picture too of that human soul who existed at the outset of evolution before our earthly incarnations began.

But only a single soul remained in this condition—the soul of whom the Luke Gospel speaks as the soul of one of the two Jesus boys. At the time when other human souls began to embark upon their incarnations in earthly evolution, this one soul was held back in the spiritual realm, preserved and protected within the most sacred mysteries through Atlantean times, post-Atlantean times, up to the time of the events in Palestine. And then it was conveyed into the body that was intended to receive it, that of one of the Jesus boys: the Jesus child whom the Luke Gospel describes.

Thus the festival of the birth of Christ became that of the birth of Jesus. If we rightly understand this festival then we must recognize that the symbolic birth we celebrate on Christmas night invokes the original nature of the human soul, the human being's childlike spirit as it existed at the outset of earthly evolution. If we regard this childlike nature as it was then, it will always teach us that it once descended as a revelation from heavenly heights. And if we feel it within our human breast, our soul will receive the feeling of the assurance of peace that can bear us to our lofty goals if we are of

---

* Translator's note: The word in brackets is 'Easter' in the German, but it seems to me that, since Steiner speaks here of 'two' sources, this must be a mistake, and Christmas fits the meaning better.

good will. Thus, if we can hear it, what speaks to us on Christmas night brings a powerful message.

And why exactly was the festival of the birth of Christ set back thirteen days and turned into the festival of Jesus' birth? If we want to understand this, we will need to penetrate deep mysteries of the human soul. We believe in outer nature because we see it with our own eyes; we observe in spring that the sun's rays entice life from the depths of the earth, then unfold this life through spring and summer in glorious beauty; we see how subsequently this life withdraws again into the earth's depths, at a time when the outward sun-sphere of the earth is darkest. We know that in these depths of the earth, in the seeds that lie there, is being prepared what will once again sprout the following year. Yes, believing in plant seeds, since we can see them, we acknowledge a seasonal cycle in which they must settle in depths of soil in order to reappear and unfold anew when the warmth and light of the sun awakens them in spring. But initially people do not know that the human soul itself can pass through such a cycle. They notice this only if they are initiated into the great mysteries of existence. Our own interiority of soul is connected, like the vigour of every plant seed connected with the physical powers of the earth, with spiritual earth powers. And just as the plant seed descends into depths of earth at the time we call Christmas, so the human soul descends into deep, deep regions of the spirit at this time, likewise drawing strength from these regions as the plant seed gathers strength to bloom again in spring. Ordinary human consciousness sees nothing of what happens to the soul in the earth's spirit depths. But for someone whose eyes of spirit have opened, this period of the thirteen days and thirteen nights is a profound period of spiritual experience.

Yes, parallel to our experience of the plant seed in the natural depths of the earth goes a spiritual experiencing within earth's spiritual depths. These two things run in parallel. And seers whose schooling enables them to do this, or who have naturally inherited powers of vision, can feel themselves descending into and penetrating such depths of spirit. During this period of thirteen days and thirteen nights, the seer can behold in the spirit what must come upon humankind because of our passage through these earthly incarnations—which have come to be as they are by the powers of Lucifer from the beginning of earthly evolution through to our own era. The kamaloka sufferings that have come upon us as human beings in the world of spirit as a result of Lucifer's influence since we first began to be incarnated on earth, can most clearly become apparent to our vision in the great and mighty imaginations that the soul can behold in the thirteen days and nights between the Christmas festival and the festival of 6 January, of Christ's appearance. If the plant seed spends its most important period in the depths of the earth at this period, so likewise the human soul has its profoundest experiences at this time. The human soul beholds everything that we must experience in worlds of spirit because we distanced ourselves under Lucifer's influence from the world's creative powers. The human soul beholds all this best during this period. And through this vision it is best prepared also for the Imagination which we can call the Christ Imagination, through which we perceive how Christ vanquishes Lucifer and in consequence becomes the judge of human deeds that arise from the incarnations subject to Lucifer's influence. And so the human soul, the seer's soul, lives from the festival of Jesus' birth to that of the appearance of Christ; and in doing so, the mystery of Christ dawns upon the soul. And thus during this period of the year we can most deeply discern what the Jordan baptism by John really means.

It is a singular fact that wherever the potential capacity for true spiritual vision arose in the Christian centuries, it also brought with it this remarkable connection with visions received by the seer's soul during the thirteen nights, the winter solstice period. Many seers, either schooled in the modern mysteries or possessing inherited powers of seership, have conveyed how, in the darkest time of winter, the soul can behold everything that we must endure through our removal from the spirit of Christ, and how we can also receive redress for this by virtue of the mystery of the Jordan baptism by John, followed by the Mystery of Golgotha. The visions of seers during these thirteen nights are crowned on 6 January by the Christ Imagination. It is right, therefore, to place the birth of Christ on 6 January, right to regard these thirteen nights as representative of human soul seership where we can perceive everything we must experience and endure because of our life in earthly incarnations from Adam and Eve onward to the Mystery of Golgotha.

I found it interesting to see this thought—reformulated here but similar to other lectures on the Christ Mystery—beautifully embodied in a legend and tale performed last year in Kristiania [Oslo]. This is the *Dream Song* as it is known, which has surfaced in the last ten or fifteen years in Norway and gained popularity there though it originates in olden times. This legend recounts in wonderful fashion how Olaf Åsteson is initiated as if by natural powers: falling asleep on Christmas Eve, he sleeps on through all the thirteen days until 6 January, witnessing all the horrors that we must endure as a result of our incarnations from the beginning of the earth through to the Mystery of Golgotha. As he approaches 6 January, Olaf Åsteson beholds how the Christ spirit, preceded by the spirit of Michael, intervenes in humanity. I hope that we will soon be able to perform this poem of Olaf Åsteson[82] so that you can see how awareness of such visionary powers during the thirteen days is still alive today, or rather is kindling to life again. I will read just the beginning verses to give you a sense of the poem:

> Listen all now to my song!
> I will sing to you
> Of a nimble, vigorous lad:
>
> I'll sing of Olaf Åsteson
> Who lay so long a-sleeping.
>
> He went to his rest on Christmas Eve,
> A sleep so deep encompassed him;
> And never did he awake again
> Until the thirteenth day when folk
> To church were all a-going.

This was Olaf Åsteson
Who lay so long a-sleeping.
Listen therefore to my song!

The tale continues as he is led in his dream during the thirteen nights through everything we must experience due to Lucifer's temptation. The song vividly conjures how Olaf Åsteson passes through all the regions we have described in accounts of kamaloka, into which streams the Christ spirit with Michael before him.

With Christ's advent in the spirit, as we may call it, human beings will increasingly receive the means really also to perceive how spiritual forces prevail, and pervade existence; how our festivals have not been arbitrarily established but originate through the cosmic wisdom holding sway throughout history in ways of which we are so often unconscious. This cosmic wisdom set the festival of Jesus' birth at the beginning of the thirteen days. Whereas the festival of Easter can always admonish us to find within ourselves, from our observations of the breadths of space, of the vast cosmos, powers to overcome everything of a lower nature, the Christmas thought teaches us that, if we understand our human origin, this origin of the divine human, we can recognize the meaning of the symbol we meet in the Jesus child on Christmas day. This human origin of ours continually urges us to find in ourselves the vigorous powers that endow us with what we can truly call peace of soul. You see, peace of mind, of soul, is only present when it is an assured peace—that is, when it enables us always to know that there lives in us something that can and must lead us upward to divine heights, to divine powers, if we only bring it to birth within us in the right way. The candles on this tree: they are symbols for us of the light so luminous within our own soul when we grasp what the symbol of the Jesus child, in all the innocence of his nature, announces to us on Christmas night: the inmost nature of the human soul itself, which is innocent, vigorous, peaceful upon its path toward the loftiest aims of earth existence. These candles can teach our soul that, if it ever grows weak, and believes it cannot find its way, or fulfil its aims, then it need only think of the human being's divine origins, perceive within the powers that are at the same time the powers of the highest love. Let us kindle all the strength we possess to perceive within us the powers that continually give us confidence and certainty in all our work, in all aspects of our lives, for all future times.

Appendix

THE THREEFOLD CALL FROM THE WORLD OF SPIRIT

NOTES FROM A LECTURE FOR THE INAUGURATION OF THE HEIDENHEIM BRANCH GROUP

HEIDENHEIM, 30 NOVEMBER 1911

We are here today to inaugurate the Heidenheim branch group. And we have been joined in this celebration by friends from various regions who have come to offer their support for this venture.

Over the years, a number of people have come together in this city, united in their inner desire for shared spiritual-scientific work.

Everything in life has its effect. If a person lies or falls into error, even if unaware of this in their conscious mind, nevertheless it resides in their subconscious, and is active there as a destructive energy not only for the individual themselves but for the whole of world evolution. In the same way, when someone connects with the powers of truth, this has a life-creating energy for the whole evolution of the world and humanity.

In our seven cultural epochs, there are three moments that are decisive for the further evolution of humanity. These are:

The first call to humanity, resounding in thunderous voice from Mount Sinai as the Commandments of Jehovah.

The second call in the desert, from John the Baptist, when he spoke to those who wished to hear, 'Change your ways, for the kingdom of heaven is at hand.'

And the third call, my dear friends, is the new revelation proclaimed from worlds of spirit through spiritual science or anthroposophy.

Conception, when the child's soul descends into this world from spiritual spheres, is a memory and a symbol of the first, thunderous call from Sinai in the Commandments.

And when the child begins to use speech in infancy, but as yet does so unthinkingly, learns to speak without employing slumbering capacities of thought, so this is a parallel within each person to the second call that resounded to humanity from John the Baptist, the voice crying out of loneliness.

And when, at a later stage in life, the child begins to understand speech by using and developing the powers of thinking, this is a reflection of the third call that resounds to humanity from spiritual science: the new revelation to comprehend what is enshrined in the Gospels concerning the Mystery of Golgotha.

Spiritual science brings us, as new revelation from worlds of spirit, a capacity to understand what was proclaimed in the second call by John, and was recorded in writing after the Mystery of Golgotha. Through spiritual science, the third call of our seven cultural epochs, we are given understanding of what Christ Jesus said: 'Behold, I am with you always, to the end of the earth's cycle'.[83]

In those days there were only a few who heard the second call, and similarly in our own era there will be only a small portion of humanity that hears the third call. But, my dear friends, if the call should pass by without being heard, humanity's evolution could not occur in the way intended by high spiritual beings.

In retrospect we may regard it as infinite grace that there were people back then who did hear the second call. We owe these souls our thanks that humanity's evolution could therefore continue. Those who understand how to read the signs of the times know what it means to hear the third call of the new, living revelation, or otherwise to let it pass unheard.

There was a time when it was said that there are only two paths for humankind: doing good would lead to eternal bliss after death while doing evil would cast us out into eternal damnation. But spiritual science offers a different teaching. My dear friends, we know that we are complex beings, that we possess a physical body, etheric body, astral body and I. If we now begin to believe in a world of spirit, to imbue ourselves with the powers of belief, this power of belief is a power of the astral body. Thus the astral body is the 'belief body'.

Through belief, and in the belief body, a person works their way upward to powers of love. These are the powers of the etheric or life body. Thus the etheric or life body is the 'love body'. If people were unable to work their way toward worlds of spirit through powers of belief, their capacities of thinking would become ever emptier, more ossified and arid. A person would be unable to raise themselves to the power of love. What would we be without love? We would inevitably become isolated, and gradually we would lose all connection with our fellow human beings and our fellow creatures in the natural world. We must be able to develop love. This alone gives us the true power of life, so that we renounce egoism and configure ourselves for true, unegoistic love in the love body or etheric body.

When we look out into nature, we learn to perceive the truth of the individual's soul's reincarnation. Behold the natural world. What kind of feeling would you have as the plant world dies in autumn if you were obliged to think that everything is dead, nothing sprouts or germinates any more, nothing blossoms. There is a proverb that says, 'No one knows what the morrow will bring'. But is this actually true? If we undertake our work today with enthusiasm and the most sacred sense of duty, do we really know nothing of what the morrow will bring? We know that the sun will rise and begin its journey across the skies, and set again in the evening. We know that the world order will continue. But how would it be for someone who never knew whether or not the sun would shine again in the morning, whether the powers of day and night, whether rain and sunshine, whether the regulated rhythms of the stars and planets would cease or change completely? We would embark on our tasks without courage or energy if we did not know that we can continue them the next day, and work further on what we have begun.

Just as truly as spring follows winter, and the slumbering seed, the inmost nature of a plant, is reawoken, so departing from the physical body the soul—the germ that remains—will be enlivened once again, and take up its life on the physical plane once more, further unfolding its own and humanity's evolution. Thus powers of hope grow forth from powers of love. The physical body is the 'hope body'. What would a person be without hope for the morrow, for completion of the work begun, without hope of being reunited with those they have loved in life? And thus the new revelation of the message of Christ, anthroposophy or spiritual science, can proclaim the teaching of reincarnation despite all the enlightened science and scholarship that holds sway in the external world and denies the existence of supersensible worlds. If people belittle or pity us for being so 'superstitious', we can look upon natural processes and find there proof of what the science of the spirit teaches.

If the third call were to pass unheeded, my dear friends, humanity's evolution could not continue; and those looking back from later times to the present age when we failed to heed it, would hold us responsible. But just as we look back in gratitude to the human souls who did heed the second call of John, so in later times human beings will look back in gratitude to those who now hear the present call, the third, and so enable humanity to continue to evolve.

In the Roman catacombs, the few early Christians gathered and held memorials together for their dead, while up above, in the arena, figures of power revelled in their power and dominion, casting these early Christians to wild animals or sacrificing them as burning torches. These figures of power were swept away, and today, similarly, we gather in premises that our friends provide us, rooms that might also be seen as spiritual catacombs. But the materialism that holds dominion in our time will be swept away too, and spiritual science will lead humanity further if the third call is heeded. Might it not be possible that one or other of you present here today heard and heeded the call of John? All of us, in one way or another, did hear that second call, and must hear the third so that humanity shall have the means to develop further.

To ensure that the teachings of the new revelation of Christ may be heard in this city, the spiritual powers have brought a number of human beings together here in the inner commitment of their hearts. Those high, spiritual individualities whose task is to convey this call to humanity, are humanity's guides and leaders.

Notes

Documents from which the text is drawn

No exact shorthand transcripts of the lectures exist, but only more or less detailed notes by participants. Only a few of the latter are known by name: Clara Michels, Alice Kinkel, Walter Vegelahn. The printed text is based on the most detailed transcript in each case, with any inaccuracies corrected by comparison with other transcripts. The text of the lecture of 28 March 1911 (Prague, 'Aphorisms on the Relationship between Spiritual Science and Philosophy'), which was first published in 1975, was largely replaced in 1989 with a different transcript. While the latter is somewhat shorter in places, it is substantially clearer and more comprehensible.

Readers should note that while the texts reproduce the content and structure of the lectures, they cannot always be regarded as Rudolf Steiner's actual original words. The quality of each transcript is of course determined to a great degree by the understanding and shorthand skills of the transcriber.

Lectures held at branch meetings of the Theosophical Society were not given titles in advance. The titles for each lecture in this volume are taken from their first publication in journals, and are largely attributable to Marie Steiner.

The German title of the volume itself was chosen by editors of the first, 1975, edition (taken from the lecture by Rudolf Steiner on 5 June 1911 that served as introduction to the cycle 'The Spiritual Guidance of the Human Being and Humanity').

(GA numbers refer to the original German edition.)

[1] Augustine, 354-430. Cf. the chapter 'Augustine and the Church' in *Christianity as Mystical Fact*, GA 8; and the lecture in Dornach on 22 May 1920, in GA 74.

[2] John Calvin, 1509-1564. Cf. the lecture in Dornach on 7 October 1917 in GA 177; and lectures in Dornach on 18 October and 2 November 1918 in GA 185.

[3] See GA 7.

4. See GA 7; in relation to Paracelsus and Boehme see also the lectures in Berlin on 26 April and 3 May 1906 in GA 54.
5. Kepler's laws: 1. All planets move about the sun in elliptical orbits, having the sun as one of the foci. 2. A radius vector (connecting line between the focal point of the sun and that of the planet) covers equal areas in equal lengths of time. 3. The squares of the sidereal periods of revolution of the planets are directly proportional to the cubes of their mean distances from the sun.
6. Isaac Newton, 1642-1727, *Observations upon the Prophecies of Daniel and the Apocalypse of St. John,* London 1733.
7. Cf. the lecture in Berlin on 3 July 1917 in GA 176; and lectures in Dornach on 22 May 1920 in GA 74.
8. In the Preface to the 2nd edition of the *Critique of Pure Reason*: 'I cannot even make the assumption—as the practical interests of morality require—of God, freedom, and immortality, if I do not deprive speculative reason of its pretensions to transcendent insight... I must, therefore, abolish knowledge, to make room for belief.'
9. See 'Anthroposophy and Antisophy', a lecture given in Berlin on 6 November 1913, GA 63.
10. Fichte's actual words were: 'That ideals cannot be embodied in the real world is something we others know perhaps as well as they, perhaps better. We assert only that reality must be judged according to them, and modified by those who feel they possess the strength to do so... While they may not be able to be convinced by them, they lose very little from their existence, and humanity loses nothing. But it becomes clear, merely, that no account of such non-idealists will be taken at the level of humanity's ennoblement. They will continue on their way. Let benevolent nature hold sway over them, and bring them rain and sunshine, good food and happy circulation of their fluids and—at the same time—keen thoughts!' Preface to *The Vocation of the Scholar,* 1794.
11. Cf. lectures in Bremen on 26 November 1910, and in Munich on 11 December 1910 in GA 125.
12. See Rudolf Steiner, *Autobiography,* GA 28, Chapter VI.
13. The poem by Goethe runs:
    Me an egoist! As if I knew no better!
    Envy is the greatest egoist;
    And whatever paths I may have taken
    By envy was I never shaken.

[14] Benvenuto Cellini, 1500-1571, goldsmith and sculptor. His autobiography appeared in Naples in 1758. Translation from Italian by Goethe published in Tübingen in 1803. There Cellini often stresses his love of truth, for example in Book III, Chapter 8 and in Book IV, Chapter 7, where he speaks of himself as a 'constant friend to truth and an enemy of lies'.

[15] Cf. the lecture in Breslau on 3 February 1912 in GA 143.

[16] See Plato, *Theaetetus*, p. 155 D; Aristotle, *Metaphysics* I, 2.

[17] Literally: 'A false doctrine cannot be refuted for it rests on the conviction that the false is true.' *Proverbs in Prose*.

[18] When this lecture was first published in the *Newsletter*, Marie Steiner prefaced it with the following introduction:

> Recalling memories that connect us with departed friends, we have chosen one of Rudolf Steiner's very important lectures from the year 1911, which has been preserved in the transcript by Clara Michels. Like various other lectures given in little-attended or newer branches of the Society, it gives a very lively, vivid and fundamental view of the manner in which the human bodies work together, before touching on particular problems current at that critical period. Because of the disconcerting and opaque occurrences transpiring in Adyar at that time, it had become necessary to awaken in listeners an understanding of how spirit beings or higher individualities intervene in an earthly soul. By this means, it was a matter, after all, of gradually cultivating understanding of the unique significance of the Mystery of Golgotha, and gaining insight into the confusions sown in Adyar to ensnare European seekers of Christ.
>
> Many of these lectures have survived only in note form, unfortunately. Other transcripts, such as those recorded by Agnes Friedländer, to whom we are very grateful for this, grew very abbreviated towards the end. Clara Michels knew how to do shorthand although she had little opportunity to improve these skills. Words by Rudolf Steiner referring to the nature of the Bodhisattvas can be found chiefly in the lectures of 1910, but also in those of 1911, as well as in the book *Buddha and Christ. The Sphere of the Bodhisattvas* [see GA 130] which was published at Whitsun. This Frankfurt lecture we are now publishing gives above all an insight into the way the hierarchies, and the retrograde spirits originating in their sphere, work upon the human soul.

[19] 8 January 1911, 'Goethe's Secret Revelation (exoteric)', 9 January 1911, 'Goethe's Secret Revelation (esoteric)'; no transcripts exist of either lecture. See lectures given on the same theme in Berlin on 22 and 24 October 1908, in GA 57.

[20] Galatians 2:20.

[21] Matthew 18:3.

[22] Eduard Suess, 1831-1914, geologist, palaeontologist, professor in Vienna, president of the Vienna Academy, from 1873 to 1896 a delegate in the Imperial Council. He designed the first mountain-springwater pipe system in Vienna.

[23] Leopold von Buch, 1774-1853, propounded the theory that mountains arose through sudden elevation of the ground following volcanic activity in the earth's interior (Plutonism). His Collected Works were published in 4 volumes in Berlin between 1867 and 1885.
Alexander von Humboldt, 1769-1859, met Buch during his studies at the mining college in Freiburg, in 1791. They remained friends, and Humboldt subscribed to Buch's views about the creation of the earth's surface. His Collected Works in 12 volumes were published in Stuttgart in 1889, and in 15 volumes between 1903 and 1920.

[24] In *Das Antlitz der Erde*, vol. I, section XII, 'Die Kontinente. Zusammenbruch der Lithosphäre', p. 778.

[25] Wilhelm Wundt, 1832-1920, philosopher and psychologist. See his *System der Philosophie*, section 4: 2. Idee der Einzelseele; 3. Idee der geistigen Gesamtheit. Leipzig 1889.

[26] Wilhelm Fliess, 1858-1928, a physician who became known for his theory of life's periodicity. His chief works are: *Vom Ablauf des Lebens*, Jena 1906; *Vom Leben und vom Tode*, Jena 1909; *Das Jahr im Lebendigen*, Jena 1918. See the lecture in Berlin on 9 November 1911 in GA 61.

[27] Galatians 2:20.

[28] Fichte: *The Vocation of the Scholar*, 1794, end of the third lecture.

[29] Zurich, 24 February 1911, 'Spiritual Science and the Future of Humanity', in GA 69.

[30] Heinrich Lhotzky, 1859-1930, priest in the German colonies in southern Russia; from 1901 he lived as a freelance writer at Ludwigshafen by Lake Constance. The book referred to, first edition 1904, sold 300,000 copies.

[31] Matthew 18:3.

[32] John 14:6.

[33] Matthew 28:20.

[34] John 16:12.

[35] Galatians 2:20.

[36] Mark 1:2; Mal. 3:1.

[37] Julius Duboc, 1829-1903, *Der Optimismus als Weltanschauung*, Bonn 1881; *Die Tragik vom Standpunkt des Optimismus*, Hamburg 1885.
Ralph Waldo Trine, 1866-1958, a pupil of Emerson whose teachings he popularized: *The Winning of the Best*, 1912; *My Philosophy and my Religion*, 1921.

[38] The best-known thyroid preparation is thyreodine, derived from the dried and pulverized thyroid of slaughtered animals. It is used primarily for growth disorders of the thyroid (myxoedema), falling sickness, goitre and cretinism.

[39] *Faust* I, Night, 784.

[40] Gerhart Hauptmann, 1862-1946. Hermann Sudermann, 1857-1928. Both writers were well-known representatives of naturalism. Cf. 'Prelude' and 'Interlude' in *The Portal of Initiation* by Rudolf Steiner.

[41] Galatians 2:20.

[42] See note 28.

[43] One of the biggest and most beautiful natural formations in Europe. The walls of the cave, extending for 113 metres, consist of series of hexagonal basalt pillars, 17 metres high crowned by a vault 70 metres long. According to Scottish and Hebridean legends, the cave was built by giants and served as the palace of the hero Fingal, whose deeds were celebrated in the Songs of Ossian.

[44] Ossian was a Celtic bard of the third century. According to the poems that bear his name, he was son of Fingal, the King of Alba, and went blind in old age. The oldest reference to the Songs of Ossian is found in the Book of Leinster, a manuscript from the twelfth century. It is assumed that the Songs of Ossian, in the form available to MacPherson (see the next note), originated in the eleventh century, but that their content is far older, and in fact can be traced back to very ancient battle songs and legends that were passed down through the generations in the bardic tradition. The customs, mores and laws described in Ossian's songs accord fully with the findings, not yet known in MacPherson's time, of modern research into the character and way of life of the ancient Gaels. There was only hunting and cattle-rearing but as yet no agriculture; the king held court in an open hall, and the daughters of chieftains lived in caves. No reference is made to the Viking/Norse conquests between 350 and 500, but there is mention of the invasion by the Viking/Norse King Suaron (see below) in the first half of the third century.

[45] James MacPherson, 1736-1796, a Scot and scholar. On his many travels through the Scottish highlands he collected ancient Celtic texts, publishing them under the titles *Fragments of ancient poetry collected in the Highlands*, *Fingal*, *Temora* and finally, in 1765, as collected works, *The Works of Ossian*. The songs and epics which MacPherson saved from oblivion at the last moment, were still alive then as oral tradition, and had been partially preserved in a few manuscripts. Soon after they were published, vitriolic doubt was cast on their authenticity. MacPherson handed the original documents he possessed to the Highland

Society in Edinburgh, which published them in two octavo volumes (*Dana Oisein mhic Finn*, London 1807).

46 Already in 1771, in Strasbourg, Goethe translated the *Songs of Selma* from the works of Ossian, and included some of it in his novel *The Sufferings of Young Werther* (first version 1774, second version 1782-86). Goethe's translation from *Temora* was published in the *Jahrbuch des Freien Deutschen Hochschulstift*, 1908 (facsimile and reprint of the German version). In *Poetry and Truth*, Part 3, Books 12 and 13, the poems of Ossian are mentioned three times in three different contexts.

Herder presents songs from *Temora*, rendered as 'Fillans Erscheinung und Fingals Schildklang' and 'Erinnerung des Gesanges der Vorzeit', in his *Stimmen der Völker in Liedern* at the beginning of the third volume of *Nordwestliche Lieder*. And also, in Goethe's translation, 'Darthulas Grabgesang'. In his treatise, Über Ossian und die Lieder alter Völker. Auszug aus einigen Briefen (in *Deutsche Art und Kunst, 1773*) and also in two reviews in Nicolai's *Allgemeiner Deutscher Bibliothek*, Herder takes a stand against the translation of Ossian's poems into hexameters, as undertaken by the Jesuit priest Denis (*Die Gedichte Ossians, eines alten celtischen Dichters, aus dem Englischen übersetzt von M. Denis*, Vienna 1768). Herder thought that translating the verses into a classical measure meant that their original bardic character was lost. Herder's essay 'Homer and Ossian' was published in 1795 in *Horen*. There he writes that Homer flourished amidst a young nation whereas Ossian was 'the last voice of a fast-dwindling heroic age'.

Napoleon ranked Ossian higher than Homer (see for instance Egon Friedell, *Kulturgeschichte der Neuzeit*, vol. II, Munich 1928, p. 332).

47 Finn Mac Cumaill or Fionn Mac Chumail, historical chieftain in Ireland, died 273 AD, and passed into legend in Celtic tradition in the same way as King Arthur. His son was Ossin (Ossian). The Irish immigration to Scotland brought these legends to the highlands of Scotland.

48 Ossian's *Fingal*, an epic poem in six songs, is given here in the words reproduced by MacPherson from Song 4. Selma is in Argyll and Bute. Suaron was the Viking/Norse king of west Gotland, who died in 240. Fillan was the son of Fingal and Clatho, and fell in battle against Cathmore. Ossian interred him in a cave above which his spirit was said to hover.

49 Proverb prefacing the *Preisschrift über die Grundlage der Moral, nicht gekrönt von der königlich dänischen Societät der Wissenschaften zu Kopenhagen, am 30. Januar 1840*.

50 Galatians 2:20.

51 GA 128.

[52] Lectures in Prague on 19 and 25 March 1911. Only inadequate notes of each lecture survive. See instead the two lectures in Berlin on 31 October and 7 November 1912 on the same theme, in GA 62.

[53] There is no transcript of the question and answer session.

[54] Otto Liebmann, 1840-1912, in his book *Zur Analysis der Wirklichkeit. Eine Erörterung der Grundprobleme der Philosophie*, 3rd edition, Strasbourg 1900, p. 28. The wording runs: 'Precisely because no thinking subject can in fact depart from the sphere of his subjective thinking, and precisely because such a subject can never establish what may or may not exist outside his subjectivity by overleaping his own consciousness, by emancipating himself from himself, it is useless to seek to assert that the object of his thinking does not exist outside of his subjective thought.'

[55] See GA 2 and GA 3.

[56] Eduard von Hartmann, 1842-1906. See Rudolf Steiner, *Autobiography*, GA 28, Chapter IX, and the essay 'Philosophy and Anthroposophy' in GA 35.

[57] There is a note in the transcript that states that Rudolf Steiner was here referring to the terms 'I' and 'Not-I' as Carl Unger uses them in his book *Das Ich und das Wesen des Menschen*, which had recently been published by the Philosophisch-Theosophischen Verlag. The essay is available today in Carl Unger, *Schriften*, Vol. 1.

[58] The planned lecture cycle had been postponed because Marie von Sivers was ill. See *Marie Steiner-von Sivers—Ein Leben für die Anthroposophie*, Dornach 1988, p. 183ff.

[59] Translator's note: In German, original sin is 'Erbsuende' or 'inherited sin'.

[60] Galatians 2:20.

[61] Matthew 28:20

[62] John 16:12.

[63] Following the General Assembly of the Scandinavian Theosophical Society, Rudolf Steiner prefaced the cycle 'The Spiritual Guidance of the Human Being and Humanity' with this lecture on 5 June. The three lectures of the cycle were reworked by him as a book publication (GA 15).

[64] Exodus 3.

[65] See GA 119.

[66] Socrates, 469-399 BC, was condemned to death due to supposed godlessness. His art of releasing concealed powers and insights in people through questions, was conveyed in Plato's dialogues. He himself left no written records.

[67] See Plato's dialogue *Menon, Laches and Protagoras*.

[68] Romans 8: 1-10 (Matthew 26:41 and Mark 14:38).

[69] In the version in which this lecture was published in the *Newsletter*, 1947, year 24, no. 37, a passage from *Anthroposophy* was included here. This quotation is not present in any of the transcripts, but it runs as follows: 'The I lives in the soul. While the highest expression of the "I" belongs to the consciousness soul, we must say nevertheless that this I, emanating from there, fills the whole soul, and exercises its effect upon the body through the soul. And in the I the spirit is living. The spirit shines into the I and lives within it as in its sheath, as the I lives in body and soul as its sheaths. The spirit forms the I from within outward, the mineral world from without inward. We will call the I-creating spirit, the spirit that lives as I, "spirit self", because it appears as the I or self of the human being... The spirit self is a revelation of the world of spirit within the I, in the same way that, from the other direction, sense experience is a revelation of the physical world within the I. In what is red, green, yellow, hard, soft, warm, cold, we discern the revelations of the corporeal world; in what is true and good, we discern the revelations of the world of spirit...'

[70] Paul, I Corinthians 13:13.

[71] *Die Erziehung des Menschengeschlechts*, Berlin 1780.

[72] 'After a migration of the soul it is possible that Plato might be punished at school for failing to understand Plato.' 'Neues Tagebuch no. 1336' in *Hebbels Werke*, edited by Th. Poppe, Deutsches Verlagshaus Bong & Co., Berlin/Leipzig/Vienna/Stuttgart, undated, Part 9: *Tagebücher I*, p. 202.

[73] The lecture began with the following words: 'This evening I will not continue the series of lectures that have been given in this branch as a kind of foundation for subsequent reflections on the Gospel of St Mark. To begin considering the Gospel of St Mark now would be to depart too radically from our reflections over recent evenings, and would be also an arduous undertaking. For this reason we will insert here some thoughts that have important relevance to what we have been considering in the last few days and also to our lectures in the autumn.' The lectures in question were the cycle published in GA 124.

[74] Rudolf Steiner broadly adheres in this tale to the version of the story of Puss-in-Boots which Ludwig Laistner gave in his book *Die Rätsel der Sphinx. Grundzüge einer Mythengeschichte*, Berlin 1889, vol. I, p. 26f.

[75] GA 115.

[76] See note 75 above.

[77] Wilhelm Jordan, 1819-1904, *Nibelungen*, 'Sigfridsage', Song 10.

[78] In the 1925 edition, we find the following footnote at this place: 'In the language of spiritual science we could say that Jordan had an instinctive desire to rekindle in the consciousness soul something that the sentient soul once developed as its natural form.'

[79] The General Assembly was on 10 December. Discussions took place on 12, 14 and 15 December.

[80] Exodus 3.

[81] Deuteronomy 32: 48-52.

[82] See the lecture 'The Dream Song of Olaf Åsteson', Hanover, 1 January 1921 in GA 158.

[83] Matthew 28: 20.

Rudolf Steiner's Collected Works

The German Edition of Rudolf Steiner's Collected Works (the *Gesamtausgabe* [GA] published by Rudolf Steiner Verlag, Dornach, Switzerland) presently runs to 354 titles, organized either by type of work (written or spoken), chronology, audience (public or other), or subject (education, art, etc.). For ease of comparison, the Collected Works in English [CW] follows the German organization exactly. A complete listing of the CWs follows with literal translations of the German titles. Other than in the case of the books published in his lifetime, titles were rarely given by Rudolf Steiner himself, and were often provided by the editors of the German editions. The titles in English are not necessarily the same as the German; and, indeed, over the past seventy-five years have frequently been different, with the same book sometimes appearing under different titles.

For ease of identification and to avoid confusion, we suggest that readers looking for a title should do so by CW number. Because the work of creating the Collected Works of Rudolf Steiner is an ongoing process, with new titles being published every year, we have not indicated in this listing which books are presently available. To find out what titles in the Collected Works are currently in print, please check our website at www.rudolfsteinerpress.com (or www.steinerbooks.org for US readers).

Written Work

CW 1 Goethe: Natural-Scientific Writings, Introduction, with Footnotes and Explanations in the text by Rudolf Steiner
CW 2 Outlines of an Epistemology of the Goethean World View, with Special Consideration of Schiller
CW 3 Truth and Science
CW 4 The Philosophy of Freedom
CW 4a Documents to 'The Philosophy of Freedom'
CW 5 Friedrich Nietzsche, A Fighter against His Time

CW 6	Goethe's Worldview
CW 6a	Now in CW 30
CW 7	Mysticism at the Dawn of Modern Spiritual Life and Its Relationship with Modern Worldviews
CW 8	Christianity as Mystical Fact and the Mysteries of Antiquity
CW 9	Theosophy: An Introduction into Supersensible World Knowledge and Human Purpose
CW 10	How Does One Attain Knowledge of Higher Worlds?
CW 11	From the Akasha-Chronicle
CW 12	Levels of Higher Knowledge
CW 13	Occult Science in Outline
CW 14	Four Mystery Dramas
CW 15	The Spiritual Guidance of the Individual and Humanity
CW 16	A Way to Human Self-Knowledge: Eight Meditations
CW 17	The Threshold of the Spiritual World. Aphoristic Comments
CW 18	The Riddles of Philosophy in Their History, Presented as an Outline
CW 19	Contained in CW 24
CW 20	The Riddles of the Human Being: Articulated and Unarticulated in the Thinking, Views and Opinions of a Series of German and Austrian Personalities
CW 21	The Riddles of the Soul
CW 22	Goethe's Spiritual Nature and its Revelation in 'Faust' and through the 'Fairy Tale of the Snake and the Lily'
CW 23	The Central Points of the Social Question in the Necessities of Life in the Present and the Future
CW 24	Essays Concerning the Threefold Division of the Social Organism and the Period 1915-1921
CW 25	Cosmology, Religion and Philosophy
CW 26	Anthroposophical Leading Thoughts
CW 27	Fundamentals for Expansion of the Art of Healing according to Spiritual-Scientific Insights
CW28	The Course of My Life
CW 29	Collected Essays on Dramaturgy, 1889-1900
CW 30	Methodical Foundations of Anthroposophy: Collected Essays on Philosophy, Natural Science, Aesthetics and Psychology, 1884-1901
CW 31	Collected Essays on Culture and Current Events, 1887-1901
CW 32	Collected Essays on Literature, 1884-1902
CW 33	Biographies and Biographical Sketches, 1894-1905
CW 34	Lucifer-Gnosis: Foundational Essays on Anthroposophy and Reports from the Periodicals 'Lucifer' and 'Lucifer-Gnosis,' 1903-1908
CW 35	Philosophy and Anthroposophy: Collected Essays, 1904-1923
CW 36	The Goetheanum-Idea in the Middle of the Cultural Crisis of the Present: Collected Essays from the Periodical 'Das Goetheanum,' 1921-1925

CW 37   Now in CWs 260a and 251
CW 38   Letters, Vol. 1: 1881-1890
CW 39   Letters, Vol. 2: 1890-1925
CW 40   Truth-Wrought Words
CW 40a   Sayings, Poems and Mantras; Supplementary Volume
CW 42   Now in CWs 264-266
CW 43   Stage Adaptations
CW 44   On the Four Mystery Dramas. Sketches, Fragments and Paralipomena on the Four Mystery Dramas
CW 45   Anthroposophy: A Fragment from the Year 1910

Public Lectures
CW 51   On Philosophy, History and Literature
CW 52   Spiritual Teachings Concerning the Soul and Observation of the World
CW 53   The Origin and Goal of the Human Being
CW 54   The Riddles of the World and Anthroposophy
CW 55   Knowledge of the Supersensible in Our Times and Its Meaning for Life Today
CW 56   Knowledge of the Soul and of the Spirit
CW 57   Where and How Does One Find the Spirit?
CW 58   The Metamorphoses of the Soul Life. Paths of Soul Experiences: Part One
CW 59   The Metamorphoses of the Soul Life. Paths of Soul Experiences: Part Two
CW 60   The Answers of Spiritual Science to the Biggest Questions of Existence
CW 61   Human History in the Light of Spiritual Research
CW 62   Results of Spiritual Research
CW 63   Spiritual Science as a Treasure for Life
CW 64   Out of Destiny-Burdened Times
CW 65   Out of Central European Spiritual Life
CW 66   Spirit and Matter, Life and Death
CW 67   The Eternal in the Human Soul. Immortality and Freedom
CW 68   Public lectures in various cities, 1906-1918
CW 69   Public lectures in various cities, 1906-1918
CW 70   Public lectures in various cities, 1906-1918
CW 71   Public lectures in various cities, 1906-1918
CW 72   Freedom—Immortality—Social Life
CW 73   The Supplementing of the Modern Sciences through Anthroposophy
CW 73a   Specialized Fields of Knowledge and Anthroposophy
CW 74   The Philosophy of Thomas Aquinas
CW 75   Public lectures in various cities, 1906-1918
CW 76   The Fructifying Effect of Anthroposophy on Specialized Fields
CW 77a   The Task of Anthroposophy in Relation to Science and Life: The Darmstadt College Course
CW 77b   Art and Anthroposophy. The Goetheanum-Impulse

CW 78   Anthroposophy, Its Roots of Knowledge and Fruits for Life
CW 79   The Reality of the Higher Worlds
CW 80   Public lectures in various cities, 1922
CW 81   Renewal-Impulses for Culture and Science—Berlin College Course
CW 82   So that the Human Being Can Become a Complete Human Being
CW 83   Western and Eastern World-Contrast. Paths to Understanding It through Anthroposophy
CW 84   What Did the Goetheanum Intend and What Should Anthroposophy Do?

Lectures to the Members of the Anthroposophical Society
CW 88   Concerning the Astral World and Devachan
CW 89   Consciousness—Life—Form. Fundamental Principles of a Spiritual-Scientific Cosmology
CW 90   Participant Notes from the Lectures during the Years 1903-1905
CW 91   Participant Notes from the Lectures during the Years 1903-1905
CW 92   The Occult Truths of Ancient Myths and Sagas
CW 93   The Temple Legend and the Golden Legend
CW 93a Fundamentals of Esotericism
CW 94   Cosmogony. Popular Occultism. The Gospel of John. The Theosophy in the Gospel of John
CW 95   At the Gates of Theosophy
CW 96   Origin-Impulses of Spiritual Science. Christian Esotericism in the Light of New Spirit-Knowledge
CW 97   The Christian Mystery
CW 98   Nature Beings and Spirit Beings—Their Effects in Our Visible World
CW 99   The Theosophy of the Rosicrucians
CW 100 Human Development and Christ-Knowledge
CW 101 Myths and Legends. Occult Signs and Symbols
CW 102 The Working into Human Beings by Spiritual Beings
CW 103 The Gospel of John
CW 104 The Apocalypse of John
CW 104a From the Picture-Script of the Apocalypse of John
CW 105 Universe, Earth, the Human Being: Their Being and Development, as well as Their Reflection in the Connection between Egyptian Mythology and Modern Culture
CW 106 Egyptian Myths and Mysteries in Relation to the Active Spiritual Forces of the Present
CW 107 Spiritual-Scientific Knowledge of the Human Being
CW 108 Answering the Questions of Life and the World through Anthroposophy
CW 109 The Principle of Spiritual Economy in Connection with the Question of Reincarnation. An Aspect of the Spiritual Guidance of Humanity
CW 110 The Spiritual Hierarchies and Their Reflection in the Physical World. Zodiac, Planets and Cosmos

Rudolf Steiner's Collected Works ∗ 217

CW 111	Contained in CW 109
CW 112	The Gospel of John in Relation to the Three Other Gospels, Especially the Gospel of Luke
CW 113	The Orient in the Light of the Occident. The Children of Lucifer and the Brothers of Christ
CW 114	The Gospel of Luke
CW 115	Anthroposophy—Psychosophy—Pneumatosophy
CW 116	The Christ-Impulse and the Development of I-Consciousness
CW 117	The Deeper Secrets of the Development of Humanity in Light of the Gospels
CW 118	The Event of the Christ-Appearance in the Etheric World
CW 119	Macrocosm and Microcosm. The Large World and the Small World. Soul-Questions, Life-Questions, Spirit-Questions
CW 120	The Revelation of Karma
CW 121	The Mission of Individual Folk-Souls in Connection with Germanic-Nordic Mythology
CW 122	The Secrets of the Biblical Creation-Story. The Six-Day Work in the First Book of Moses
CW 123	The Gospel of Matthew
CW 124	Excursus in the Area of the Gospel of Mark
CW 125	Paths and Goals of the Spiritual Human Being. Life Questions in the Light of Spiritual Science
CW 126	Occult History. Esoteric Observations of the Karmic Relationships of Personalities and Events of World History
CW 127	The Mission of the New Spiritual Revelation. The Christ-Event as the Middle-Point of Earth Evolution
CW 128	An Occult Physiology
CW 129	Wonders of the World, Trials of the Soul, and Revelations of the Spirit
CW 130	Esoteric Christianity and the Spiritual Guidance of Humanity
CW 131	From Jesus to Christ
CW 132	Evolution from the View Point of the Truth
CW 133	The Earthly and the Cosmic Human Being
CW 134	The World of the Senses and the World of the Spirit
CW 135	Reincarnation and Karma and their Meaning for the Culture of the Present
CW 136	The Spiritual Beings in Celestial Bodies and the Realms of Nature
CW 137	The Human Being in the Light of Occultism, Theosophy and Philosophy
CW 138	On Initiation. On Eternity and the Passing Moment. On the Light of the Spirit and the Darkness of Life
CW 139	The Gospel of Mark
CW 140	Occult Investigation into the Life between Death and New Birth. The Living Interaction between Life and Death
CW 141	Life between Death and New Birth in Relationship to Cosmic Facts

CW 142	The Bhagavad Gita and the Letters of Paul
CW 143	Experiences of the Supersensible. Three Paths of the Soul to Christ
CW 144	The Mysteries of the East and of Christianity
CW 145	What Significance Does Occult Development of the Human Being Have for the Sheaths—Physical Body, Etheric Body, Astral Body, and Self?
CW 146	The Occult Foundations of the Bhagavad Gita
CW 147	The Secrets of the Threshold
CW 148	Out of Research in the Akasha: The Fifth Gospel
CW 149	Christ and the Spiritual World. Concerning the Search for the Holy Grail
CW 150	The World of the Spirit and Its Extension into Physical Existence; The Influence of the Dead in the World of the Living
CW 151	Human Thought and Cosmic Thought
CW 152	Preliminary Stages to the Mystery of Golgotha
CW 153	The Inner Being of the Human Being and Life Between Death and New Birth
CW 154	How Does One Gain an Understanding of the Spiritual World? The Flowing in of Spiritual Impulses from out of the World of the Deceased
CW 155	Christ and the Human Soul. Concerning the Meaning of Life. Theosophical Morality. Anthroposophy and Christianity
CW 156	Occult Reading and Occult Hearing
CW 157	Human Destinies and the Destiny of Peoples
CW 157a	The Formation of Destiny and the Life after Death
CW 158	The Connection Between the Human Being and the Elemental World. Kalevala—Olaf Asteson—The Russian People—The World as the Result of the Influences of Equilibrium
CW 159	The Mystery of Death. The Nature and Significance of Middle Europe and the European Folk Spirits
CW 160	In CW 159
CW 161	Paths of Spiritual Knowledge and the Renewal of the Artistic Worldview
CW 162	Questions of Art and Life in Light of Spiritual Science
CW 163	Coincidence, Necessity and Providence. Imaginative Knowledge and the Processes after Death
CW 164	The Value of Thinking for a Knowledge That Satisfies the Human Being. The Relationship of Spiritual Science to Natural Science
CW 165	The Spiritual Unification of Humanity through the Christ-Impulse
CW 166	Necessity and Freedom in the Events of the World and in Human Action
CW 167	The Present and the Past in the Human Spirit
CW 168	The Connection between the Living and the Dead
CW 169	World-being and Selfhood
CW 170	The Riddle of the Human Being. The Spiritual Background of Human History. Cosmic and Human History, Vol. 1

Rudolf Steiner's Collected Works * 219

CW 171 Inner Development-Impulses of Humanity. Goethe and the Crisis of the 19th Century. Cosmic and Human History, Vol. 2
CW 172 The Karma of the Vocation of the Human Being in Connection with Goethe's Life. Cosmic and Human History, Vol. 3
CW 173 Contemporary-Historical Considerations: The Karma of Untruthfulness, Part One. Cosmic and Human History, Vol. 4
CW 174 Contemporary-Historical Considerations: The Karma of Untruthfulness, Part Two. Cosmic and Human History, Vol. 5
CW 174a Middle Europe between East and West. Cosmic and Human History, Vol. 6
CW 174b The Spiritual Background of the First World War. Cosmic and Human History, Vol. 7
CW 175 Building Stones for an Understanding of the Mystery of Golgotha. Cosmic and Human Metamorphoses
CW 176 Truths of Evolution of the Individual and Humanity. The Karma of Materialism
CW 177 The Spiritual Background of the Outer World. The Fall of the Spirits of Darkness. Spiritual Beings and Their Effects, Vol. 1
CW 178 Individual Spiritual Beings and their Influence in the Soul of the Human Being. Spiritual Beings and their Effects, Vol. 2
CW 179 Spiritual Beings and Their Effects. Historical Necessity and Freedom. The Influences on Destiny from out of the World of the Dead. Spiritual Beings and Their Effects, Vol. 3
CW 180 Mystery Truths and Christmas Impulses. Ancient Myths and their Meaning. Spiritual Beings and Their Effects, Vol. 4
CW 181 Earthly Death and Cosmic Life. Anthroposophical Gifts for Life. Necessities of Consciousness for the Present and the Future.
CW 182 Death as Transformation of Life
CW 183 The Science of the Development of the Human Being
CW 184 The Polarity of Duration and Development in Human Life. The Cosmic Pre-History of Humanity
CW 185 Historical Symptomology
CW 185a Historical-Developmental Foundations for Forming a Social Judgement
CW 186 The Fundamental Social Demands of Our Time—In Changed Situations
CW 187 How Can Humanity Find the Christ Again? The Threefold Shadow-Existence of our Time and the New Christ-Light
CW 188 Goetheanism, a Transformation-Impulse and Resurrection-Thought. Science of the Human Being and Science of Sociology
CW 189 The Social Question as a Question of Consciousness. The Spiritual Background of the Social Question, Vol. 1
CW 190 Impulses of the Past and the Future in Social Occurrences. The Spiritual Background of the Social Question, Vol. 2

CW 191	Social Understanding from Spiritual-Scientific Cognition. The Spiritual Background of the Social Question, Vol. 3
CW 192	Spiritual-Scientific Treatment of Social and Pedagogical Questions
CW 193	The Inner Aspect of the Social Riddle. Luciferic Past and Ahrimanic Future
CW 194	The Mission of Michael. The Revelation of the Actual Mysteries of the Human Being
CW 195	Cosmic New Year and the New Year Idea
CW 196	Spiritual and Social Transformations in the Development of Humanity
CW 197	Polarities in the Development of Humanity: West and East Materialism and Mysticism Knowledge and Belief
CW 198	Healing Factors for the Social Organism
CW 199	Spiritual Science as Knowledge of the Foundational Impulses of Social Formation
CW 200	The New Spirituality and the Christ-Experience of the 20th Century
CW 201	The Correspondences Between Microcosm and Macrocosm. The Human Being—A Hieroglyph of the Universe. The Human Being in Relationship with the Cosmos: 1
CW 202	The Bridge between the World-Spirituality and the Physical Aspect of the Human Being. The Search for the New Isis, the Divine Sophia. The Human Being in Relationship with the Cosmos: 2
CW 203	The Responsibility of Human Beings for the Development of the World through their Spiritual Connection with the Planet Earth and the World of the Stars. The Human Being in Relationship with the Cosmos: 3
CW 204	Perspectives of the Development of Humanity. The Materialistic Knowledge-Impulse and the Task of Anthroposophy. The Human Being in Relationship with the Cosmos: 4
CW 205	Human Development, World-Soul, and World-Spirit. Part One: The Human Being as a Being of Body and Soul in Relationship to the World. The Human Being in Relationship with the Cosmos: 5
CW 206	Human Development, World-Soul, and World-Spirit. Part Two: The Human Being as a Spiritual Being in the Process of Historical Development. The Human Being in Relationship with the Cosmos: 6
CW 207	Anthroposophy as Cosmosophy. Part One: Characteristic Features of the Human Being in the Earthly and the Cosmic Realms. The Human Being in Relationship with the Cosmos: 7
CW 208	Anthroposophy as Cosmosophy. Part Two: The Forming of the Human Being as the Result of Cosmic Influence. The Human Being in Relationship with the Cosmos: 8
CW 209	Nordic and Central European Spiritual Impulses. The Festival of the Appearance of Christ. The Human Being in Relationship with the Cosmos: 9

CW 210	Old and New Methods of Initiation. Drama and Poetry in the Change of Consciousness in the Modern Age
CW 211	The Sun Mystery and the Mystery of Death and Resurrection. Exoteric and Esoteric Christianity
CW 212	Human Soul Life and Spiritual Striving in Connection with World and Earth Development
CW 213	Human Questions and World Answers
CW 214	The Mystery of the Trinity: The Human Being in Relationship with the Spiritual World in the Course of Time
CW 215	Philosophy, Cosmology, and Religion in Anthroposophy
CW 216	The Fundamental Impulses of the World-Historical Development of Humanity
CW 217	Spiritually Active Forces in the Coexistence of the Older and Younger Generations. Pedagogical Course for Youth
CW 217a	Youth's Cognitive Task
CW 218	Spiritual Connections in the Forming of the Human Organism
CW 219	The Relationship of the World of the Stars to the Human Being, and of the Human Being to the World of the Stars. The Spiritual Communion of Humanity
CW 220	Living Knowledge of Nature. Intellectual Fall and Spiritual Redemption
CW 221	Earth-Knowing and Heaven-Insight
CW 222	The Imparting of Impulses to World-Historical Events through Spiritual Powers
CW 223	The Cycle of the Year as Breathing Process of the Earth and the Four Great Festival-Seasons. Anthroposophy and the Human Heart (Gemüt)
CW 224	The Human Soul and its Connection with Divine-Spiritual Individualities. The Internalization of the Festivals of the Year
CW 225	Three Perspectives of Anthroposophy. Cultural Phenomena observed from a Spiritual-Scientific Perspective
CW 226	Human Being, Human Destiny, and World Development
CW 227	Initiation-Knowledge
CW 228	Science of Initiation and Knowledge of the Stars. The Human Being in the Past, the Present, and the Future from the Viewpoint of the Development of Consciousness
CW 229	The Experiencing of the Course of the Year in Four Cosmic Imaginations
CW 230	The Human Being as Harmony of the Creative, Building, and Formative World-Word
CW 231	The Supersensible Human Being, Understood Anthroposophically
CW 232	The Forming of the Mysteries
CW 233	World History Illuminated by Anthroposophy and as the Foundation for Knowledge of the Human Spirit

CW 233a	Mystery Sites of the Middle Ages: Rosicrucianism and the Modern Initiation-Principle. The Festival of Easter as Part of the History of the Mysteries of Humanity
CW 234	Anthroposophy. A Summary after 21 Years
CW 235	Esoteric Observations of Karmic Relationships in 6 Volumes, Vol. 1
CW 236	Esoteric Observations of Karmic Relationships in 6 Volumes, Vol. 2
CW 237	Esoteric Observations of Karmic Relationships in 6 Volumes, Vol. 3: The Karmic Relationships of the Anthroposophical Movement
CW 238	Esoteric Observations of Karmic Relationships in 6 Volumes, Vol. 4: The Spiritual Life of the Present in Relationship to the Anthroposophical Movement
CW 239	Esoteric Observations of Karmic Relationships in 6 Volumes, Vol. 5
CW 240	Esoteric Observations of Karmic Relationships in 6 Volumes, Vol. 6
CW 243	The Consciousness of the Initiate
CW 245	Instructions for an Esoteric Schooling
CW 250	The Building-Up of the Anthroposophical Society. From the Beginning to the Outbreak of the First World War
CW 251	The History of the Goetheanum Building-Association
CW 252	Life in the Anthroposophical Society from the First World War to the Burning of the First Goetheanum
CW 253	The Problems of Living Together in the Anthroposophical Society. On the Dornach Crisis of 1915. With Highlights on Swedenborg's Clairvoyance, the Views of Freudian Psychoanalysts, and the Concept of Love in Relation to Mysticism
CW 254	The Occult Movement in the 19th Century and Its Relationship to World Culture. Significant Points from the Exoteric Cultural Life around the Middle of the 19th Century
CW 255	Rudolf Steiner during the First World War
CW 255a	Anthroposophy and the Reformation of Society. On the History of the Threefold Movement
CW 255b	Anthroposophy and Its Opponents, 1919–1921
CW 256	How Can the Anthroposophical Movement Be Financed?
CW 256a	Futurum, Inc. / International Laboratories, Inc.
CW 256b	The Coming Day, Inc.
CW 257	Anthroposophical Community-Building
CW 258	The History of and Conditions for the Anthroposophical Movement in Relationship to the Anthroposophical Society. A Stimulus to Self-Contemplation
CW 259	The Year of Destiny 1923 in the History of the Anthroposophical Society. From the Burning of the Goetheanum to the Christmas Conference
CW 260	The Christmas Conference for the Founding of the General Anthroposophical Society

CW 260a	The Constitution of the General Anthroposophical Society and the School for Spiritual Science. The Rebuilding of the Goetheanum
CW 261	Our Dead. Addresses, Words of Remembrance, and Meditative Verses, 1906-1924
CW 262	Rudolf Steiner and Marie Steiner-von Sivers: Correspondence and Documents, 1901-1925
CW 263/1	Rudolf Steiner and Edith Maryon: Correspondence: Letters, Verses, Sketches, 1912-1924
CW 264	On the History and the Contents of the First Section of the Esoteric School from 1904 to 1914. Letters, Newsletters, Documents, Lectures
CW 265	On the History and from the Contents of the Ritual-Knowledge Section of the Esoteric School from 1904 to 1914. Documents, and Lectures from the Years 1906 to 1914, as well as on New Approaches to Ritual-Knowledge Work in the Years 1921–1924
CW 266/1	From the Contents of the Esoteric Lessons. Volume 1: 1904–1909. Notes from Memory of Participants. Meditation texts from the notes of Rudolf Steiner
CW 266/2	From the Contents of the Esoteric Lessons. Volume 2: 1910–1912. Notes from Memory of Participants
CW 266/3	From the Contents of the Esoteric Lessons. Volume 3: 1913, 1914 and 1920–1923. Notes from Memory of Participants. Meditation texts from the notes of Rudolf Steiner
CW 267	Soul-Exercises: Vol. 1: Exercises with Word and Image Meditations for the Methodological Development of Higher Powers of Knowledge, 1904–1924
CW 268	Soul-Exercises: Vol. 2: Mantric Verses, 1903–1925
CW 269	Ritual Texts for the Celebration of the Free Christian Religious Instruction. The Collected Verses for Teachers and Students of the Waldorf School
CW 270	Esoteric Instructions for the First Class of the School for Spiritual Science at the Goetheanum 1924, 4 Volumes
CW 271	Art and Knowledge of Art. Foundations of a New Aesthetic
CW 272	Spiritual-Scientific Commentary on Goethe's 'Faust' in Two Volumes. Vol. 1: Faust, the Striving Human Being
CW 273	Spiritual-Scientific Commentary on Goethe's 'Faust' in Two Volumes. Vol. 2: The Faust-Problem
CW 274	Addresses for the Christmas Plays from the Old Folk Traditions
CW 275	Art in the Light of Mystery-Wisdom
CW 276	The Artistic in Its Mission in the World. The Genius of Language. The World of Self-Revealing Radiant Appearances—Anthroposophy and Art. Anthroposophy and Poetry
CW 277	Eurythmy. The Revelation of the Speaking Soul
CW 277a	The Origin and Development of Eurythmy

CW 278	Eurythmy as Visible Song
CW 279	Eurythmy as Visible Speech
CW 280	The Method and Nature of Speech Formation
CW 281	The Art of Recitation and Declamation
CW 282	Speech Formation and Dramatic Art
CW 283	The Nature of Things Musical and the Experience of Tone in the Human Being
CW 284/285	Images of Occult Seals and Pillars. The Munich Congress of Whitsun 1907 and Its Consequences
CW 286	Paths to a New Style of Architecture. 'And the Building Becomes Human'
CW 287	The Building at Dornach as a Symbol of Historical Becoming and an Artistic Transformation Impulse
CW 288	Style-Forms in the Living Organic
CW 289	The Building-Idea of the Goetheanum: Lectures with Slides from the Years 1920–1921
CW 290	The Building-Idea of the Goetheanum: Lectures with Slides from the Years 1920–1921
CW 291	The Nature of Colours
CW 291a	Knowledge of Colours. Supplementary Volume to 'The Nature of Colours'
CW 292	Art History as Image of Inner Spiritual Impulses
CW 293	General Knowledge of the Human Being as the Foundation of Pedagogy
CW 294	The Art of Education, Methodology and Didactics
CW 295	The Art of Education: Seminar Discussions and Lectures on Lesson Planning
CW 296	The Question of Education as a Social Question
CW 297	The Idea and Practice of the Waldorf School
CW 297a	Education for Life: Self-Education and the Practice of Pedagogy
CW 298	Rudolf Steiner in the Waldorf School
CW 299	Spiritual-Scientific Observations on Speech
CW 300a	Conferences with the Teachers of the Free Waldorf School in Stuttgart, 1919 to 1924, in 3 Volumes, Vol. 1
CW 300b	Conferences with the Teachers of the Free Waldorf School in Stuttgart, 1919 to 1924, in 3 Volumes, Vol. 2
CW 300c	Conferences with the Teachers of the Free Waldorf School in Stuttgart, 1919 to 1924, in 3 Volumes, Vol. 3
CW 301	The Renewal of Pedagogical-Didactical Art through Spiritual Science
CW 302	Knowledge of the Human Being and the Forming of Class Lessons
CW 302a	Education and Teaching from a Knowledge of the Human Being
CW 303	The Healthy Development of the Human Being
CW 304	Methods of Education and Teaching Based on Anthroposophy
CW 304a	Anthroposophical Knowledge of the Human Being and Pedagogy

CW 305	The Soul-Spiritual Foundational Forces of the Art of Education. Spiritual Values in Education and Social Life
CW 306	Pedagogical Praxis from the Viewpoint of a Spiritual-Scientific Knowledge of the Human Being. The Education of the Child and Young Human Beings
CW 307	The Spiritual Life of the Present and Education
CW 308	The Method of Teaching and the Life-Requirements for Teaching
CW 309	Anthroposophical Pedagogy and Its Prerequisites
CW 310	The Pedagogical Value of a Knowledge of the Human Being and the Cultural Value of Pedagogy
CW 311	The Art of Education from an Understanding of the Being of Humanity
CW 312	Spiritual Science and Medicine
CW 313	Spiritual-Scientific Viewpoints on Therapy
CW 314	Physiology and Therapy Based on Spiritual Science
CW 315	Curative Eurythmy
CW 316	Meditative Observations and Instructions for a Deepening of the Art of Healing
CW 317	The Curative Education Course
CW 318	The Working Together of Doctors and Pastors
CW 319	Anthroposophical Knowledge of the Human Being and Medicine
CW 320	Spiritual-Scientific Impulses for the Development of Physics 1: The First Natural-Scientific Course: Light, Colour, Tone, Mass, Electricity, Magnetism
CW 321	Spiritual-Scientific Impulses for the Development of Physics 2: The Second Natural-Scientific Course: Warmth at the Border of Positive and Negative Materiality
CW 322	The Borders of the Knowledge of Nature
CW 323	The Relationship of the various Natural-Scientific Fields to Astronomy
CW 324	Nature Observation, Mathematics, and Scientific Experimentation and Results from the Viewpoint of Anthroposophy
CW 324a	The Fourth Dimension in Mathematics and Reality
CW 325	Natural Science and the World-Historical Development of Humanity since Ancient Times
CW 326	The Moment of the Coming Into Being of Natural Science in World History and Its Development Since Then
CW 327	Spiritual-Scientific Foundations for Success in Farming. The Agricultural Course
CW 328	The Social Question
CW 329	The Liberation of the Human Being as the Foundation for a New Social Form
CW 330	The Renewal of the Social Organism
CW 331	Work-Council and Socialization
CW 332	The Alliance for Threefolding and the Total Reform of Society. The Council on Culture and the Liberation of the Spiritual Life

CW 332a   The Social Future
CW 333   Freedom of Thought and Social Forces
CW 334   From the Unified State to the Threefold Social Organism
CW 335   The Crisis of the Present and the Path to Healthy Thinking
CW 336   The Great Questions of the Times and Anthroposophical Spiritual Knowledge
CW 337a   Social Ideas, Social Reality, Social Practice, Vol. 1: Question-and-Answer Evenings and Study Evenings of the Alliance for the Threefold Social Organism in Stuttgart, 1919-1920
CW 337b   Social Ideas, Social Realities, Social Practice, Vol. 2: Discussion Evenings of the Swiss Alliance for the Threefold Social Organism
CW 338   How Does One Work on Behalf of the Impulse for the Threefold Social Organism?
CW 339   Anthroposophy, Threefold Social Organism, and the Art of Public Speaking
CW 340   The National-Economics Course. The Tasks of a New Science of Economics, Volume 1
CW 341   The National-Economics Seminar. The Tasks of a New Science of Economics, Volume 2
CW 342   Lectures and Courses on Christian Religious Work, Vol. 1: Anthroposophical Foundations for a Renewed Christian Religious Working
CW 343   Lectures and Courses on Christian Religious Work, Vol. 2: Spiritual Knowledge—Religious Feeling—Cultic Doing
CW 344   Lectures and Courses on Christian Religious Work, Vol. 3: Lectures at the Founding of the Christian Community
CW 345   Lectures and Courses on Christian Religious Work, Vol. 4: Concerning the Nature of the Working Word
CW 346   Lectures and Courses on Christian Religious Work, Vol. 5: The Apocalypse and the Work of the Priest
CW 347   The Knowledge of the Nature of the Human Being According to Body, Soul and Spirit. On Earlier Conditions of the Earth
CW 348   On Health and Illness. Foundations of a Spiritual-Scientific Doctrine of the Senses
CW 349   On the Life of the Human Being and of the Earth. On the Nature of Christianity
CW 350   Rhythms in the Cosmos and in the Human Being. How Does One Come To See the Spiritual World?
CW 351   The Human Being and the World. The Influence of the Spirit in Nature. On the Nature of Bees
CW 352   Nature and the Human Being Observed Spiritual-Scientifically
CW 353   The History of Humanity and the World-Views of the Folk Cultures
CW 354   The Creation of the World and the Human Being. Life on Earth and the Influence of the Stars

SIGNIFICANT EVENTS IN THE LIFE OF RUDOLF STEINER

1829: June 23: birth of Johann Steiner (1829–1910)—Rudolf Steiner's father—in Geras, Lower Austria.

1834: May 8: birth of Franciska Blie (1834–1918)—Rudolf Steiner's mother—in Horn, Lower Austria. 'My father and mother were both children of the glorious Lower Austrian forest district north of the Danube.'

1860: May 16: marriage of Johann Steiner and Franciska Blie.

1861: February 25: birth of *Rudolf Joseph Lorenz Steiner* in Kraljevec, Croatia, near the border with Hungary, where Johann Steiner works as a telegrapher for the South Austria Railroad. Rudolf Steiner is baptized two days later, February 27, the date usually given as his birthday.

1862: Summer: the family moves to Modling, Lower Austria.

1863: The family moves to Pottschach, Lower Austria, near the Styrian border, where Johann Steiner becomes station master. 'The view stretched to the mountains . . . majestic peaks in the distance and the sweet charm of nature in the immediate surroundings.'

1864: November 15: birth of Rudolf Steiner's sister, Leopoldine (d. November 1, 1927). She will become a seamstress and live with her parents for the rest of her life.

1866: July 28: birth of Rudolf Steiner's deaf-mute brother, Gustav (d. May 1, 1941).

1867: Rudolf Steiner enters the village school. Following a disagreement between his father and the schoolmaster, whose wife falsely accused the boy of causing a commotion, Rudolf Steiner is taken out of school and taught at home.

1868: A critical experience. Unknown to the family, an aunt dies in a distant town. Sitting in the station waiting room, Rudolf Steiner sees her 'form,' which speaks to him, asking for help. 'Beginning with this experience, a new soul life began in the boy, one in which not only the outer trees and mountains spoke to him, but also the worlds that lay behind them. From this moment on, the boy began to live with the spirits of nature...'

1869: The family moves to the peaceful, rural village of Neudörfl, near Wiener Neustadt in present-day Austria. Rudolf Steiner attends the village school. Because of the 'unorthodoxy' of his writing and spelling, he has to do 'extra lessons'.

1870: Through a book lent to him by his tutor, he discovers geometry: 'To grasp something purely in the spirit brought me inner happiness. I know that I first learned happiness through geometry.' The same tutor allows him to draw, while other students still struggle with their reading and writing. 'An artistic element' thus enters his education.

1871: Though his parents are not religious, Rudolf Steiner becomes a 'church child,' a favourite of the priest, who was 'an exceptional character.' 'Up to the age of ten or eleven, among those I came to know, he was far and away the most significant.' Among other things, he introduces Steiner to Copernican, heliocentric cosmology. As an altar boy, Rudolf Steiner serves at masses, funerals, and Corpus Christi processions. At year's end, after an incident in which he escapes a thrashing, his father forbids him to go to church.

1872: Rudolf Steiner transfers to grammar school in Wiener-Neustadt, a five-mile walk from home, which must be done in all weathers.

1873–75: Through his teachers and on his own, Rudolf Steiner has many wonderful experiences with science and mathematics. Outside school, he teaches himself analytic geometry, trigonometry, differential equations, and calculus.

1876: Rudolf Steiner begins tutoring other students. He learns bookbinding from his father. He also teaches himself stenography.

1877: Rudolf Steiner discovers Kant's *Critique of Pure Reason,* which he reads and rereads. He also discovers and reads von Rotteck's *World History.*

1878: He studies extensively in contemporary psychology and philosophy.

1879: Rudolf Steiner graduates from high school with honours. His father is transferred to Inzersdorf, near Vienna. He uses his first visit to Vienna 'to purchase a great number of philosophy books'—Kant, Fichte, Schelling, and Hegel, as well as numerous histories of philosophy. His aim: to find a path from the 'I' to nature.

October
1879–1883: Rudolf Steiner attends the Technical College in Vienna—to study mathematics, chemistry, physics, mineralogy, botany, zoology,

biology, geology, and mechanics—with a scholarship. He also attends lectures in history and literature, while avidly reading philosophy on his own. His two favourite professors are Karl Julius Schröer (German language and literature) and Edmund Reitlinger (physics). He also audits lectures by Robert Zimmermann on aesthetics and Franz Brentano on philosophy. During this year he begins his friendship with Moritz Zitter (1861–1921), who will help support him financially when he is in Berlin.

1880: Rudolf Steiner attends lectures on Schiller and Goethe by Karl Julius Schröer, who becomes his mentor. Also 'through a remarkable combination of circumstances,' he meets Felix Koguzki, a 'herb gatherer' and healer, who could 'see deeply into the secrets of nature'. Rudolf Steiner will meet and study with this 'emissary of the Master' throughout his time in Vienna.

1881: January: '... I didn't sleep a wink. I was busy with philosophical problems until about 12:30 a.m. Then, finally, I threw myself down on my couch. All my striving during the previous year had been to research whether the following statement by Schelling was true or not: *Within everyone dwells a secret, marvellous capacity to draw back from the stream of time—out of the self clothed in all that comes to us from outside—into our innermost being and there, in the immutable form of the Eternal, to look into ourselves.* I believe, and I am still quite certain of it, that I discovered this capacity in myself; I had long had an inkling of it. Now the whole of idealist philosophy stood before me in modified form. What's a sleepless night compared to that!'

Rudolf Steiner begins communicating with leading thinkers of the day, who send him books in return, which he reads eagerly.

July: 'I am not one of those who dives into the day like an animal in human form. I pursue a quite specific goal, an idealistic aim—knowledge of the truth! This cannot be done offhandedly. It requires the greatest striving in the world, free of all egotism, and equally of all resignation.'

August: Steiner puts down on paper for the first time thoughts for a 'Philosophy of Freedom.' 'The striving for the absolute: this human yearning is freedom.' He also seeks to outline a 'peasant philosophy,' describing what the worldview of a 'peasant'—one who lives close to the earth and the old ways—really is.

1881–1882: Felix Koguzki, the herb gatherer, reveals himself to be the envoy of another, higher initiatory personality, who instructs Rudolf Steiner to penetrate Fichte's philosophy and to master modern scientific thinking as a preparation for right entry into the spirit. This 'Master' also teaches him the double (evolutionary and involutionary) nature of time.

1882: Through the offices of Karl Julius Schröer, Rudolf Steiner is asked by Joseph Kürschner to edit Goethe's scientific works for the *Deutschen National-Literatur* edition. He writes 'A Possible Critique of Atomistic Concepts' and sends it to Friedrich Theodor Vischer.

1883: Rudolf Steiner completes his college studies and begins work on the Goethe project.

1884: First volume of Goethe's *Scientific Writings* (CW 1) appears (March). He lectures on Goethe and Lessing, and Goethe's approach to science. In July, he enters the household of Ladislaus and Pauline Specht as tutor to the four Specht boys. He will live there until 1890. At this time, he meets Josef Breuer (1842–1925), the co-author with Sigmund Freud of *Studies in Hysteria*, who is the Specht family doctor.

1885: While continuing to edit Goethe's writings, Rudolf Steiner reads deeply in contemporary philosophy (Eduard von Hartmann, Johannes Volkelt, and Richard Wahle, among others).

1886: May: Rudolf Steiner sends Kürschner the manuscript of *Outlines of Goethe's Theory of Knowledge* (CW 2), which appears in October, and which he sends out widely. He also meets the poet Marie Eugenie Delle Grazie and writes 'Nature and Our Ideals' for her. He attends her salon, where he meets many priests, theologians, and philosophers, who will become his friends. Meanwhile, the director of the Goethe Archive in Weimar requests his collaboration with the *Sophien* edition of Goethe's works, particularly the writings on colour.

1887: At the beginning of the year, Rudolf Steiner is very sick. As the year progresses and his health improves, he becomes increasingly 'a man of letters,' lecturing, writing essays, and taking part in Austrian cultural life. In August–September, the second volume of Goethe's *Scientific Writings* appears.

1888: January–July: Rudolf Steiner assumes editorship of the 'German Weekly' *(Deutsche Wochenschrift)*. He begins lecturing more intensively, giving, for example, a lecture titled 'Goethe as Father of a New Aesthetics.' He meets and becomes soul friends with Friedrich Eckstein (1861–1939), a vegetarian, philosopher of symbolism, alchemist, and musician, who will introduce him to various spiritual currents (including Theosophy) and with whom he will meditate and interpret esoteric and alchemical texts.

1889: Rudolf Steiner first reads Nietzsche *(Beyond Good and Evil)*. He encounters Theosophy again and learns of Madame Blavatsky in the theosophical circle around Marie Lang (1858–1934). Here he also meets well-known figures of Austrian life, as well as esoteric figures like the occultist Franz Hartmann and Karl Leinigen-Billigen (translator of C.G. Harrison's *The Transcendental Universe*). During this period, Steiner first reads A.P. Sinnett's *Esoteric Buddhism* and Mabel Collins's *Light on the Path*. He also begins travelling, visiting Budapest, Weimar, and Berlin (where he meets philosopher Eduard von Hartmann).

1890: Rudolf Steiner finishes Volume 3 of Goethe's scientific writings. He begins his doctoral dissertation, which will become *Truth and Science* (CW 3). He also meets the poet and feminist Rosa Mayreder (1858–1938), with whom he can exchange his most intimate thoughts. In September, Rudolf Steiner moves to Weimar to work in the Goethe-Schiller Archive.

1891: Volume 3 of the Kürschner edition of Goethe appears. Meanwhile, Rudolf Steiner edits Goethe's studies in mineralogy and scientific writings for the *Sophien* edition. He meets Ludwig Laistner of the Cotta Publishing Company, who asks for a book on the basic question of metaphysics. From this will result, ultimately, *The Philosophy of Freedom* (CW 4), which will be published not by Cotta but by Emil Felber. In October, Rudolf Steiner takes the oral exam for a doctorate in philosophy, mathematics, and mechanics at Rostock University, receiving his doctorate on the twenty-sixth. In November, he gives his first lecture on Goethe's 'Fairy Tale' in Vienna.

1892: Rudolf Steiner continues work at the Goethe-Schiller Archive and on his *Philosophy of Freedom*. *Truth and Science,* his doctoral dissertation, is published. Steiner undertakes to write Introductions to books on Schopenhauer and Jean Paul for Cotta. At year's end, he finds lodging with Anna Eunike, née Schulz (1853–1911), a widow with four daughters and a son. He also develops a friendship with Otto Erich Hartleben (1864–1905) with whom he shares literary interests.

1893: Rudolf Steiner begins his habit of producing many reviews and articles. In March, he gives a lecture titled 'Hypnotism, with Reference to Spiritism.' In September, volume 4 of the Kürschner edition is completed. In November, *The Philosophy of Freedom* appears. This year, too, he meets John Henry Mackay (1864–1933), the anarchist, and Max Stirner, a scholar and biographer.

1894: Rudolf Steiner meets Elisabeth Fürster Nietzsche, the philosopher's sister, and begins to read Nietzsche in earnest, beginning with the as yet unpublished *Antichrist*. He also meets Ernst Haeckel (1834–1919). In the fall, he begins to write *Nietzsche, A Fighter against His Time* (CW 5).

1895: May, *Nietzsche, A Fighter against His Time* appears.

1896: January 22: Rudolf Steiner sees Friedrich Nietzsche for the first and only time. Moves between the Nietzsche and the Goethe-Schiller

Archives, where he completes his work before year's end. He falls out with Elisabeth Förster Nietzsche, thus ending his association with the Nietzsche Archive.

1897: Rudolf Steiner finishes the manuscript of *Goethe's Worldview* (CW 6). He moves to Berlin with Anna Eunike and begins editorship of the *Magazin für Literatur*. From now on, Steiner will write countless reviews, literary and philosophical articles, and so on. He begins lecturing at the 'Free Literary Society.' In September, he attends the Zionist Congress in Basel. He sides with Dreyfus in the Dreyfus affair.

1898: Rudolf Steiner is very active as an editor in the political, artistic, and theatrical life of Berlin. He becomes friendly with John Henry Mackay and poet Ludwig Jacobowski (1868–1900). He joins Jacobowski's circle of writers, artists, and scientists—'The Coming Ones' (*Die Kommenden*)—and contributes lectures to the group until 1903. He also lectures at the 'League for College Pedagogy.' He writes an article for Goethe's sesquicentennial, 'Goethe's Secret Revelation,' on the 'Fairy Tale of the Green Snake and the Beautiful Lily.'

1898–99: 'This was a trying time for my soul as I looked at Christianity. . . . I was able to progress only by contemplating, by means of spiritual perception, the evolution of Christianity. . . . Conscious knowledge of real Christianity began to dawn in me around the turn of the century. This seed continued to develop. My soul trial occurred shortly before the beginning of the twentieth century. It was decisive for my soul's development that I stood spiritually before the Mystery of Golgotha in a deep and solemn celebration of knowledge.'

1899: Rudolf Steiner begins teaching and giving lectures and lecture cycles at the Workers' College, founded by Wilhelm Liebknecht (1826–1900). He will continue to do so until 1904. Writes: *Literature and Spiritual Life in the Nineteenth Century; Individualism in Philosophy; Haeckel and His Opponents; Poetry in the Present;* and begins what will become (fifteen years later) *The Riddles of Philosophy* (CW 18). He also meets many artists and writers, including Kothe Kollwitz, Stefan Zweig, and Rainer Maria Rilke. On October 31, he marries Anna Eunike.

1900: 'I thought that the turn of the century must bring humanity a new light. It seemed to me that the separation of human thinking and willing from the spirit had peaked. A turn or reversal of direction in human evolution seemed to me a necessity.' Rudolf Steiner finishes *World and Life Views in the Nineteenth Century* (the second part of what will become *The Riddles of Philosophy*) and dedicates it to

Ernst Haeckel. It is published in March. He continues lecturing at *Die Kommenden,* whose leadership he assumes after the death of Jacobowski. Also, he gives the Gutenberg Jubilee lecture before 7,000 typesetters and printers. In September, Rudolf Steiner is invited by Count and Countess Brockdorff to lecture in the Theosophical Library. His first lecture is on Nietzsche. His second lecture is titled 'Goethe's Secret Revelation.' October 6, he begins a lecture cycle on the mystics that will become *Mystics after Modernism* (CW 7). November–December: 'Marie von Sivers appears in the audience. . . .' Also in November, Steiner gives his first lecture at the Giordano Bruno Bund (where he will continue to lecture until May, 1905). He speaks on Bruno and modern Rome, focusing on the importance of the philosophy of Thomas Aquinas as monism.

1901: In continual financial straits, Rudolf Steiner's early friends Moritz Zitter and Rosa Mayreder help support him. In October, he begins the lecture cycle *Christianity as Mystical Fact* (CW 8) at the Theosophical Library. In November, he gives his first 'theosophical lecture' on Goethe's 'Fairy Tale' in Hamburg at the invitation of Wilhelm Hubbe-Schleiden. He also attends a gathering to celebrate the founding of the Theosophical Society at Count and Countess Brockdorff's. He gives a lecture cycle, 'From Buddha to Christ,' for the circle of the *Kommenden.* November 17, Marie von Sivers asks Rudolf Steiner if Theosophy needs a Western–Christian spiritual movement (to complement Theosophy's Eastern emphasis). 'The question was posed. Now, following spiritual laws, I could begin to give an answer. . . .' In December, Rudolf Steiner writes his first article for a theosophical publication. At year's end, the Brockdorffs and possibly Wilhelm Hubbe-Schleiden ask Rudolf Steiner to join the Theosophical Society and undertake the leadership of the German section. Rudolf Steiner agrees, on the condition that Marie von Sivers (then in Italy) work with him.

1902: Beginning in January, Rudolf Steiner attends the opening of the Workers' School in Spandau with Rosa Luxemberg (1870–1919). January 17, Rudolf Steiner joins the Theosophical Society. In April, he is asked to become general secretary of the German Section of the theosophical Society, and works on preparations for its founding. In July, he visits London for a theosophical congress. He meets Bertram Keightly, G.R.S. Mead, A.P. Sinnett, and Annie Besant, among others. In September, *Christianity as Mystical Fact* appears. In October, Rudolf Steiner gives his first public lecture on Theosophy ('Monism and Theosophy') to about three hundred people at the Giordano Bruno Bund. On October 19–21, the

German Section of the Theosophical Society has its first meeting; Rudolf Steiner is the general secretary, and Annie Besant attends. Steiner lectures on practical karma studies. On October 23, Annie Besant inducts Rudolf Steiner into the Esoteric School of the Theosophical Society. On October 25, Steiner begins a weekly series of lectures: 'The Field of Theosophy.' During this year, Rudolf Steiner also first meets Ita Wegman (1876–1943), who will become his close collaborator in his final years.

1903: Rudolf Steiner holds about 300 lectures and seminars. In May, the first issue of the periodical *Luzifer* appears. In June, Rudolf Steiner visits London for the first meeting of the Federation of the European Sections of the Theosophical Society, where he meets Colonel Olcott. He begins to write *Theosophy* (CW 9).

1904: Rudolf Steiner continues lecturing at the Workers' College and elsewhere (about 90 lectures), while lecturing intensively all over Germany among theosophists (about 140 lectures). In February, he meets Carl Unger (1878–1929), who will become a member of the board of the Anthroposophical Society (1913). In March, he meets Michael Bauer (1871–1929), a Christian mystic, who will also be on the board. In May, *Theosophy* appears, with the dedication: 'To the spirit of Giordano Bruno.' Rudolf Steiner and Marie von Sivers visit London for meetings with Annie Besant. June: Rudolf Steiner and Marie von Sivers attend the meeting of the Federation of European Sections of the Theosophical Society in Amsterdam. In July, Steiner begins the articles in *Luzifer-Gnosis* that will become *How to Know Higher Worlds* (CW 10) and *Cosmic Memory* (CW 11). In September, Annie Besant visits Germany. In December, Steiner lectures on Freemasonry. He mentions the High Grade Masonry derived from John Yarker and represented by Theodore Reuss and Karl Kellner as a blank slate 'into which a good image could be placed'.

1905: This year, Steiner ends his non-theosophical lecturing activity. Supported by Marie von Sivers, his theosophical lecturing—both in public and in the Theosophical Society—increases significantly: 'The German Theosophical Movement is of exceptional importance.' Steiner recommends reading, among others, Fichte, Jacob Boehme, and Angelus Silesius. He begins to introduce Christian themes into Theosophy. He also begins to work with doctors (Felix Peipers and Ludwig Noll). In July, he is in London for the Federation of European Sections, where he attends a lecture by Annie Besant: 'I have seldom seen Mrs. Besant speak in so inward and heartfelt a manner... Through Mrs. Besant I have found the way to H.P. Blavatsky.' September to October, he gives a course of 31 lectures for a small group of esoteric students. In October, the annual meeting of the German Section of the Theosophical Society, which still remains very small, takes place. Rudolf Steiner reports membership has risen from 121 to 377 members. In November, seeking to establish esoteric 'continuity,' Rudolf Steiner and Marie von Sivers participate in a 'Memphis-Misraim' Masonic ceremony. They pay 45 marks for membership. 'Yesterday, you saw how little remains of former esoteric institutions.' 'We are dealing only with a "framework" . . . for the present, nothing lies behind it. The occult powers have completely withdrawn.'

1906: Expansion of theosophical work. Rudolf Steiner gives about 245 lectures, only 44 of which take place in Berlin. Cycles are given in Paris, Leipzig, Stuttgart, and Munich. Esoteric work also intensifies. Rudolf Steiner begins writing *An Outline of Esoteric Science* (CW 13). In January, Rudolf Steiner receives permission (a patent) from the Great Orient of the Scottish A & A Thirty-Three Degree Rite of the Order of the Ancient Freemasons of the Memphis-Misraim Rite to direct a chapter under the name 'Mystica Aeterna.' This will become the 'Cognitive-Ritual Section' (also called 'Misraim Service') of the Esoteric School. (See: *Freemasonry and Ritual Work: The Misraim Service,* CW 265.) During this time, Steiner also meets Albert Schweitzer. In May, he is in Paris, where he visits Édouard Schuré. Many Russians attend his lectures (including Konstantin Balmont, Dimitri Mereszkovski, Zinaida Hippius, and Maximilian Woloshin). He attends the General Meeting of the European Federation of the Theosophical Society, at which Col. Olcott is present for the last time. He spends the year's end in Venice and Rome, where he writes and works on his translation of H.P. Blavatsky's *Key to Theosophy.*

1907: Further expansion of the German Theosophical Movement according to the Rosicrucian directive to 'introduce spirit into the world'—in education, in social questions, in art, and in science. In February, Col. Olcott dies in Adyar. Before he dies, Olcott indicates that 'the Masters' wish Annie Besant to succeed him: much politicking ensues. Rudolf Steiner supports Besant's candidacy. April–May: preparations for the Congress of the Federation of European Sections of the Theosophical Society—the great, watershed Whitsun 'Munich Congress,' attended by Annie Besant and others. Steiner decides to separate Eastern and Western (Christian–Rosicrucian) esoteric schools. He takes his esoteric school out of the Theosophical Society (Besant and Rudolf Steiner are 'in harmony' on this). Steiner makes his first lecture tours to Austria and Hungary. That summer, he is in Italy. In September, he visits Édouard Schuré, who will write the Introduction to the French edition of *Christianity as Mystical Fact* in Barr, Alsace. Rudolf Steiner writes the autobiographical statement known as the 'Barr Document.' In *Luzifer-Gnosis*, 'The Education of the Child' appears.

1908: The movement grows (membership: 1,150). Lecturing expands. Steiner makes his first extended lecture tour to Holland and Scandinavia, as well as visits to Naples and Sicily. Themes: St. John's Gospel, the Apocalypse, Egypt, science, philosophy, and logic. *Luzifer-Gnosis* ceases publication. In Berlin, Marie von Sivers (with Johanna Mücke (1864–1949) forms the *Philosophisch-Theosophisch* (after 1915 *Philosophisch-Anthroposophisch*) *Verlag* to publish Steiner's work. Steiner gives lecture cycles titled *The Gospel of St. John* (CW 103) and *The Apocalypse* (104).

1909: *An Outline of Esoteric Science* appears. Lecturing and travel continues. Rudolf Steiner's spiritual research expands to include the polarity of Lucifer and Ahriman; the work of great individualities in history; the Maitreya Buddha and the Bodhisattvas; spiritual economy (CW 109); the work of the spiritual hierarchies in heaven and on earth (CW 110). He also deepens and intensifies his research into the Gospels, giving lectures on the Gospel of St. Luke (CW 114) with the first mention of two Jesus children. Meets and becomes friends with Christian Morgenstern (1871–1914). In April, he lays the foundation stone for the Malsch model—the building that will lead to the first Goetheanum. In May, the International Congress of the Federation of European Sections of the Theosophical Society takes place in Budapest. Rudolf Steiner receives the Subba Row medal for *How to Know Higher Worlds*. During this time, Charles W. Leadbeater discovers Jiddu Krishnamurti (1895–1986) and proclaims him the future 'world teacher,' the bearer of the Maitreya Buddha and the 'reappearing Christ.' In October, Steiner delivers seminal lectures on 'anthroposophy,' which he will try, unsuccessfully, to rework over the next years into the unfinished work, *Anthroposophy (A Fragment)* (CW 45).

1910: New themes: *The Reappearance of Christ in the Etheric* (CW 118); *The Fifth Gospel; The Mission of Folk Souls* (CW 121); *Occult History* (CW 126); the evolving development of etheric cognitive capacities. Rudolf Steiner continues his Gospel research with *The Gospel of St. Matthew* (CW 123). In January, his father dies. In April, he takes a month-long trip to Italy, including Rome, Monte Cassino, and Sicily. He also visits Scandinavia again. July–August, he writes the first mystery drama, *The Portal of Initiation* (CW 14). In November, he gives 'psychosophy' lectures. In December, he submits 'On the

1911:
Psychological Foundations and Epistemological Framework of Theosophy' to the International Philosophical Congress in Bologna. The crisis in the Theosophical Society deepens. In January, 'The Order of the Rising Sun,' which will soon become 'The Order of the Star in the East,' is founded for the coming world teacher, Krishnamurti. At the same time, Marie von Sivers, Rudolf Steiner's co-worker, falls ill. Fewer lectures are given, but important new ground is broken. In Prague, in March, Steiner meets Franz Kafka (1883–1924) and Hugo Bergmann (1883–1975). In April, he delivers his paper to the Philosophical Congress. He writes the second mystery drama, *The Soul's Probation* (CW 14). Also, while Marie von Sivers is convalescing, Rudolf Steiner begins work on *Calendar 1912/1913*, which will contain the 'Calendar of the Soul' meditations. On March 19, Anna (Eunike) Steiner dies. In September, Rudolf Steiner visits Einsiedeln, birthplace of Paracelsus. In December, Friedrich Rittelmeyer, future founder of the Christian Community, meets Rudolf Steiner. The *Johannes-Bauverein,* the 'building committee,' which would lead to the first Goetheanum (first planned for Munich), is also founded, and a preliminary committee for the founding of an independent association is created that, in the following year, will become the Anthroposophical Society. Important lecture cycles include *Occult Physiology* (CW 128); *Wonders of the World* (CW 129); *From Jesus to Christ* (CW 131). Other themes: esoteric Christianity; Christian Rosenkreutz; the spiritual guidance of humanity; the sense world and the world of the spirit.

1912:
Despite the ongoing, now increasing crisis in the Theosophical Society, much is accomplished: *Calendar 1912/1913* is published; eurythmy is created; both the third mystery drama, *The Guardian of the Threshold* (CW 14) and *A Way of Self-Knowledge* (CW 16) are written. New (or renewed) themes included life between death and rebirth and karma and reincarnation. Other lecture cycles: *Spiritual Beings in the Heavenly Bodies and in the Kingdoms of Nature* (CW 136); *The Human Being in the Light of Occultism, Theosophy, and Philosophy* (CW 137); *The Gospel of St. Mark* (CW 139); and *The Bhagavad Gita and the Epistles of Paul* (CW 142). On May 8, Rudolf Steiner celebrates White Lotus Day, H.P. Blavatsky's death day, which he had faithfully observed for the past decade, for the last time. In August, Rudolf Steiner suggests the 'independent association' be called the 'Anthroposophical Society.' In September, the first eurythmy course takes place. In October, Rudolf Steiner declines recognition of a Theosophical Society lodge dedicated to the Star of the East and decides to expel all Theosophical Society members belonging to the order.

Also, with Marie von Sivers, he first visits Dornach, near Basel, Switzerland, and they stand on the hill where the Goetheanum will be built. In November, a Theosophical Society lodge is opened by direct mandate from Adyar (Annie Besant). In December, a meeting of the German section occurs at which it is decided that belonging to the Order of the Star of the East is incompatible with membership in the Theosophical Society. December 28: informal founding of the Anthroposophical Society in Berlin.

1913: Expulsion of the German section from the Theosophical Society. February 2–3: Foundation meeting of the Anthroposophical Society. Board members include: Marie von Sivers, Michael Bauer, and Carl Unger. September 20: Laying of the foundation stone for the *Johannes Bau* (Goetheanum) in Dornach. Building begins immediately. The third mystery drama, *The Soul's Awakening* (CW 14), is completed. Also: *The Threshold of the Spiritual World* (CW 147). Lecture cycles include: *The Bhagavad Gita and the Epistles of Paul* and *The Esoteric Meaning of the Bhagavad Gita* (CW 146), which the Russian philosopher Nikolai Berdyaev attends; *The Mysteries of the East and of Christianity* (CW 144); *The Effects of Esoteric Development* (CW 145); and *The Fifth Gospel* (CW 148). In May, Rudolf Steiner is in London and Paris, where anthroposophical work continues.

1914: Building continues on the *Johannes Bau* (Goetheanum) in Dornach, with artists and co-workers from seventeen nations. The general assembly of the Anthroposophical Society takes place. In May, Rudolf Steiner visits Paris, as well as Chartres Cathedral. June 28: assassination in Sarajevo ('Now the catastrophe has happened!'). August 1: War is declared. Rudolf Steiner returns to Germany from Dornach—he will travel back and forth. He writes the last chapter of *The Riddles of Philosophy*. Lecture cycles include: *Human and Cosmic Thought* (CW 151); *Inner Being of Humanity between Death and a New Birth* (CW 153); *Occult Reading and Occult Hearing* (CW 156). December 24: marriage of Rudolf Steiner and Marie von Sivers.

1915: Building continues. Life after death becomes a major theme, also art. Writes: *Thoughts during a Time of War* (CW 24). Lectures include: *The Secret of Death* (CW 159); *The Uniting of Humanity through the Christ Impulse* (CW 165).

1916: Rudolf Steiner begins work with Edith Maryon (1872–1924) on the sculpture 'The Representative of Humanity' ('The Group'—Christ, Lucifer, and Ahriman). He also works with the alchemist Alexander von Bernus on the quarterly *Das Reich*. He writes *The Riddle of Humanity* (CW 20). Lectures include: *Necessity and Freedom in World History and Human Action* (CW 166); *Past and Present in the*

Human Spirit (CW 167); *The Karma of Vocation* (CW 172); *The Karma of Untruthfulness* (CW 173).

1917: Russian Revolution. The U.S. enters the war. Building continues. Rudolf Steiner delineates the idea of the 'threefold nature of the human being' (in a public lecture March 15) and the 'threefold nature of the social organism' (hammered out in May–June with the help of Otto von Lerchenfeld and Ludwig Polzer-Hoditz in the form of two documents titled *Memoranda*, which were distributed in high places). August–September: Rudolf Steiner writes *The Riddles of the Soul* (CW 20). Also: commentary on 'The Chymical Wedding of Christian Rosenkreutz' for Alexander Bernus (Das Reich). Lectures include: *The Karma of Materialism* (CW 176); *The Spiritual Background of the Outer World: The Fall of the Spirits of Darkness* (CW 177).

1918: March 18: peace treaty of Brest-Litovsk—'Now everything will truly enter chaos! What is needed is cultural renewal.' June: Rudolf Steiner visits Karlstein (Grail) Castle outside Prague. Lecture cycle: *From Symptom to Reality in Modern History* (CW 185). In mid-November, Emil Molt, of the Waldorf-Astoria Cigarette Company, has the idea of founding a school for his workers' children.

1919: Focus on the threefold social organism: tireless travel, countless lectures, meetings, and publications. At the same time, a new public stage of Anthroposophy emerges as cultural renewal begins. The coming years will see initiatives in pedagogy, medicine, pharmacology, and agriculture. January 27: threefold meeting: 'We must first of all, with the money we have, found free schools that can bring people what they need.' February: first public eurythmy performance in Zurich. Also: 'Appeal to the German People' (CW 24), circulated March 6 as a newspaper insert. In April, *Towards Social Renewal* (CW 23) appears—'perhaps the most widely read of all books on politics appearing since the war'. Rudolf Steiner is asked to undertake the 'direction and leadership' of the school founded by the Waldorf-Astoria Company. Rudolf Steiner begins to talk about the 'renewal' of education. May 30: a building is selected and purchased for the future Waldorf School. August–September, Rudolf Steiner gives a lecture course for Waldorf teachers, *The Foundations of Human Experience (Study of Man)* (CW 293). September 7: Opening of the first Waldorf School. December (into January): first science course, the *Light Course* (CW 320).

1920: The Waldorf School flourishes. New threefold initiatives. Founding of limited companies *Der Kommende Tag* and *Futurum A.G.* to infuse spiritual values into the economic realm. Rudolf Steiner also focuses on the sciences. Lectures: *Introducing Anthroposophical*

Medicine (CW 312); *The Warmth Course* (CW 321); *The Boundaries of Natural Science* (CW 322); *The Redemption of Thinking* (CW 74). February: Johannes Werner Klein—later a co-founder of the Christian Community—asks Rudolf Steiner about the possibility of a 'religious renewal,' a 'Johannine church.' In March, Rudolf Steiner gives the first course for doctors and medical students. In April, a divinity student asks Rudolf Steiner a second time about the possibility of religious renewal. September 27–October 16: anthroposophical 'university course.' December: lectures titled *The Search for the New Isis* (CW 202).

1921: Rudolf Steiner continues his intensive work on cultural renewal, including the uphill battle for the threefold social order. 'University' arts, scientific, theological, and medical courses include: *The Astronomy Course* (CW 323); *Observation, Mathematics, and Scientific Experiment* (CW 324); the *Second Medical Course* (CW 313); *Colour*. In June and September–October, Rudolf Steiner also gives the first two 'priests' courses' (CW 342 and 343). The 'youth movement' gains momentum. Magazines are founded: *Die Drei* (January), and—under the editorship of Albert Steffen (1884–1963)—the weekly, *Das Goetheanum* (August). In February–March, Rudolf Steiner takes his first trip outside Germany since the war (Holland). On April 7, Steiner receives a letter regarding 'religious renewal,' and May 22–23, he agrees to address the question in a practical way. In June, the Klinical-Therapeutic Institute opens in Arlesheim under the direction of Dr. Ita Wegman. In August, the Chemical-Pharmaceutical Laboratory opens in Arlesheim (Oskar Schmiedel and Ita Wegman are directors). The Clinical Therapeutic Institute is inaugurated in Stuttgart (Dr. Ludwig Noll is director); also the Research Laboratory in Dornach (Ehrenfried Pfeiffer and Gunther Wachsmuth are directors). In November–December, Rudolf Steiner visits Norway.

1922: The first half of the year involves very active public lecturing (thousands attend); in the second half, Rudolf Steiner begins to withdraw and turn toward the Society—'The Society is asleep.' It is 'too weak' to do what is asked of it. The businesses—*Der Kommende Tag* and *Futurum A.G.*—fail. In January, with the help of an agent, Steiner undertakes a twelve-city German lecture tour, accompanied by eurythmy performances. In two weeks he speaks to more than 2,000 people. In April, he gives a 'university course' in The Hague. He also visits England. In June, he is in Vienna for the East–West Congress. In August–September, he is back in England for the Oxford Conference on Education. Returning to Dornach, he gives the lectures *Philosophy, Cosmology, and Religion*

(CW 215), and gives the third priests' course (CW 344). On September 16, The Christian Community is founded. In October–November, Steiner is in Holland and England. He also speaks to the youth: *The Youth Course* (CW 217). In December, Steiner gives lectures titled *The Origins of Natural Science* (CW 326), and *Humanity and the World of Stars: The Spiritual Communion of Humanity* (CW 219). December 31: Fire at the Goetheanum, which is destroyed.

1923: Despite the fire, Rudolf Steiner continues his work unabated. A very hard year. Internal dispersion, dissension, and apathy abound. There is conflict—between old and new visions—within the Society. A wake-up call is needed, and Rudolf Steiner responds with renewed lecturing vitality. His focus: the spiritual context of human life; initiation science; the course of the year; and community building. As a foundation for an artistic school, he creates a series of pastel sketches. Lecture cycles: *The Anthroposophical Movement; Initiation Science* (CW 227) (in Wales at the Penmaenmawr Summer School); *The Four Seasons and the Archangels* (CW 229); *Harmony of the Creative Word* (CW 230); *The Supersensible Human* (CW 231), given in Holland for the founding of the Dutch society. On November 10, in response to the failed Hitler-Ludendorff putsch in Munich, Steiner closes his Berlin residence and moves the *Philosophisch-Anthroposophisch Verlag* (Press) to Dornach. On December 9, Steiner begins the serialization of his *Autobiography: The Course of My Life* (CW 28) in *Das Goetheanum*. It will continue to appear weekly, without a break, until his death. Late December–early January: Rudolf Steiner re-founds the Anthroposophical Society (about 12,000 members internationally) and takes over its leadership. The new board members are: Marie Steiner, Ita Wegman, Albert Steffen, Elisabeth Vreede, and Gunther Wachsmuth. (See *The Christmas Meeting for the Founding of the General Anthroposophical Society,* CW 260.) Accompanying lectures: *Mystery Knowledge and Mystery Centres* (CW 232); *World History in the Light of Anthroposophy* (CW 233). December 25: the Foundation Stone is laid (in the hearts of members) in the form of the 'Foundation Stone Meditation.'

1924: January 1: having founded the Anthroposophical Society and taken over its leadership, Rudolf Steiner has the task of 'reforming' it. The process begins with a weekly newssheet ('What's Happening in the Anthroposophical Society') in which Rudolf Steiner's 'Letters to Members' and 'Anthroposophical Leading Thoughts' appear (CW 26). The next step is the creation of a new esoteric class, the 'first class' of the 'University of Spiritual Science' (which was to have been followed, had Rudolf Steiner lived longer, by two more advanced classes). Then comes a new language for

Anthroposophy—practical, phenomenological, and direct; and Rudolf Steiner creates the model for the second Goetheanum. He begins the series of extensive 'karma' lectures (CW 235–40); and finally, responding to needs, he creates two new initiatives: biodynamic agriculture and curative education. After the middle of the year, rumours begin to circulate regarding Steiner's health. Lectures: January–February, *Anthroposophy* (CW 234); February: *Tone Eurythmy* (CW 278); June: *The Agriculture Course* (CW 327); June–July: *Speech Eurythmy* (CW 279); *Curative Education* (CW 317); August: (England, 'Second International Summer School'), *Initiation Consciousness: True and False Paths in Spiritual Investigation* (CW 243); September: *Pastoral Medicine* (CW 318). On September 26, for the first time, Rudolf Steiner cancels a lecture. On September 28, he gives his last lecture. On September 29, he withdraws to his studio in the carpenter's shop; now he is definitively ill. Cared for by Ita Wegman, he continues working, however, and writing the weekly installments of his *Autobiography* and *Letters to the Members/ Leading Thoughts* (CW 26).

1925: Rudolf Steiner, while continuing to work, continues to weaken. He finishes *Extending Practical Medicine* (CW 27) with Ita Wegman. On March 30, around ten in the morning, Rudolf Steiner dies.

Index

A
acquisition, of language, 71
'Adam and Eve' day, 178, 181, 183, 189, 195
'Adam Kadmon', 181, 190
aggregation, 8
Agrippa of Nettesheim, 5
Ahriman, 19, 20, 31
    temptation of, 35
ahrimanic powers, 31
    in etheric body, 19
America statistics, 9
ancient Atlantean clairvoyance, 94
ancient Celts, 98
ancient clairvoyance, 38, 170, 179
    consciousness, 169
ancient Egypt, 39, 132
    in Egyptian culture, 53
    of fifth or fourth millennium, 40
ancient Greeks. *See* Greeks
ancient Nordic times, 174
ancient pre-Christian times, human beings, 40
ancient times
    'natural Inspiration and Imagination', 38
    physical body in, 38
animals, 127
anthroposophic movement, 122, 138, 139, 143, 146

anthroposophy, 4, 12, 15, 59, 60, 78
    academic curiosity, 153
    awareness, 16
    cultivate, 156
    endeavours, 113
    Fichte, Johann Gottlieb, 16, 92
    great mission of, 156
    human civilization, 101
    human morality, 109
    life and enquiry, 148
    moral consciousness, 103
    in nature, 18
    'Occult Physiology', 110, 112, 113
    opponents of, 111
    out of curiosity, 152
    outward processes, 113
    qualities of, 121
    realities, 112, 113
    Rosicrucian, 144
    teaches, 100
    teachings with Christ, 91
    thoughts and feelings, 152
    threshold of, 62
    treasures of, 83
    truths, 156
    whole earth organism, 104
    wisdom, 81
antisophy, 14
Apocalypse, 5
archangels/archangeloi, 30, 31

archetypal prefiguring, 69
Aristotle, 11
    doctrines of, 11
    nerves issue, 11
    spiritual science as promulgated by, 12
    teaching, 12
    work, 11
art beauty, Greeks, 41
ascendant powers, 48
assurance in life, 63
astral body, 7, 22, 37, 43, 52, 79, 149
    of children, 25
    earth's evolution, 38
    and etheric body, 19, 38–39, 42–43, 53, 87, 127
    evolution of, 126
    human beings, 47, 78, 128
    influence, 88
    luciferic powers in, 19
    nature of, 152
    during Old Moon, 64
    in sense, 19
    transformation of, 156
    transforms, 62
Augustine to Calvin, 2, 4, 6
austerity/acerbity, 61

B

bacilli-ghosts, 9
'bad Christians', 144
balance and equanimity, 81
bardic tradition, 95
belief body. *See* astral body
Bible, 75, 136
Boehme, Jakob, 5
brain
    function, 88
    injury, 83
    physical sheath, 43
Bruno, Giordano, 10, 11, 142, 143

C

Capesius, Victor, 157, 158, 166, 168, 169
Cellini, Benvenuto, 18–19
Celtic peoples, 96
centralization, 8
Chaldeans, 53
charlatanism, 35
childhood, primary powers of, 72
children
    astral body of, 25
    into spiritual world, 45
    thinking, 44
Christian era, 61
Christianity/Christ
    in accord with spiritual science, 136
    affirmation, 106
    birth, 189, 192
    broad-hearted and open, 73
    divine-spiritual thoughts, 7
    early impulses of, 94
    during earth evolution, 107
    event, 70, 143
    Greco-Roman period, 7
    heart's blood of, 105
    for humanity's evolution, 179
    impulse, 133–134
    knowledge, 106
    laws of gravity, 5
    mission, 73–74
    Mystery of Golgotha, 144
    new revelation of, 202
    Pauline phrase, 133
    perceive and absorb, 106
    personality, 133
    precursor, 75
    profounder aspects of, 125
    rise of, 2
    secrets of, 187
Christ Imagination, 194, 195
Christ-imbued spirit knowledge, 61

Christ Jesus, 91, 142, 178
Christmas festival, 178, 180, 184, 187
Christ Mystery, 188, 189, 195
Christ-resistance, 107
clairvoyance, 34, 78, 128, 161
    ancient, 38, 170
    ancient era of, 175
    communications based on, 88
    consciousness, 65
    primitive, 164, 166, 168
    primordial, 170
'class morality', 103
common knowledge, 16
communications, 88
conceptual analysis, 27
conceptual field, 114
confused hypotheses, 50
conscious awareness, 66
conscious mind, 198
consciousness, 43, 46, 69, 83
    ancient clairvoyant, 169
    approaches, 116
    clairvoyance, 65
    dream, 104, 111
    dull, 101
    materialistic, 103
    modern, 108
    moral, 103
    philosophical rigour and, 122
    picture, 111
    scope of, 116
    sensory, 166
    of spiritual worlds, 166
consciousness soul, 7, 8, 13, 15, 26–29, 31, 35, 150, 157, 172
    freedom in, 32
continual process, of degeneration, 48
Copernicus, Nicolaus, 5, 10, 54, 142, 143
cosmic powers of universe, 184

cosmic tendency, 42
cosmic wisdom, 196
cosmos
    spiritual, 85
    structure of, 143
    wisdom of, 57
cultivate anthroposophy, 156
cultural epochs, 53, 155

D
'Dark Ages', 54
Darwin, Charles, 5
death
    on Golgotha, 91
    and rebirth, 58–59
    in Resurrection, 91
deceitfulness, 18–19
    effect of, 20
degeneration, continual process of, 48
dependency
    on 'energy and substance', 85
    on matter and energy, 85
    on physical conditions, 84
destructive forces, 49
devotion, 59
differential and integral calculations, 16
discrepancy, 29
disintegration process, 50
divine-spiritual thoughts, 125
divine wisdom, 189
dreaming consciousness, 104, 111
Dream Song, 195
Druid, 95
dull consciousness, 101

E
early Indian culture, 44
    people in, 44
earth, 102
    Christ's birth for, 189

evolution, 48, 50, 52, 105, 144
   future evolution, 105
   geological epic, 49
   goal of evolution, 69
   human being on, 14
   humanity's evolution, 53
   Moon condition, 152
   natural depths of, 193
   organism, 102, 103
   physical human life on, 47
   and soil, development of, 49
   solid foundation, 50
   spirit depths, 193
Easter festival, 177–178, 196
echoes
   of ancient clairvoyance, 170
   of Greek art beauty, 41
Eckhardt, Meister, 4
education
   and culture, 25
   pictorial quality cultivated in, 25
Education of the Human Race, The
   (Lessing), 155
egoism, 13, 89, 100, 153
egoistic motivations, 100
Egyptian culture, 38, 39, 53
elasticity, of etheric body, 41
Elijah, 75
'endlessness of spiritual
   evolution', 50
end-rhyme, 170, 171, 175
'energy and substance', 84
   dependency on, 85
ephemeral value, 3
epistemology, 117
   conferences on, 121
   philosophy and, 121
   problem of, 116
   subjective in, 119
   writings, 117

epoch
   culture, 53
   epoch to, 7, 10–11
   of evolution, 135
   of humanity, 1–2
era, 141, 145
   of ancient culture, 39
   Egyptian and Chaldean, 7
   Greco-Roman, 39
   human body in Greek, 39
   of humanity, 1–2
   mechanical law of gravity in, 5
   of natural science, 6
   transitional, 9
erosion processes, 48
error, 145, 146
esoteric enquiry, 36, 106, 107
esotericism, 12, 70, 145
   asserts, 102
esotericists, 61
esoteric science, 2
establishing morality, 108
etheric body, 11, 37, 43, 52, 83, 88, 128,
   149, 152, 153
   ahrimanic powers in, 19
   astral body and, 19, 38–39, 42, 43,
      53, 87, 127
   definite form, 42
   development of, 129
   earth's evolution, 38
   elasticity of, 41
   human beings, 47
   incarnations form and penetrate, 62
   living effect of, 88
   matrix of, 153
   mood affects, 84
   during Old Sun, 64
   physical body and, 40
   quality inhering in, 20
   science of, 12

Europe
    culture, powerful impression on, 96
    in eighteenth century, 94
evangelical faiths, 12
evidence, 70
external human form, 39
external reality, 165, 168, 169
external science, 53, 55

F
Face of the Earth, The (Suess), 49
fairy-tale, 168
    development of, 166
    imaginative world, 165, 169
    mood, 161, 162, 164, 165
    psychology of, 164
faith, 150, 151
    knowledge and, 151
    power of, 152
    rough-and-ready, 164
    soul's power of, 156
'faith body', 152
Faust (Goethe), 90
'feelings', expression, 30
feeling soul, 29
Felicia, Frau, 169
festival of inspiration
    'Adam and Eve' day, 178, 181
    celebration moments, 177
    child's birth, 181
    Christmas, 178, 180, 184
    Easter, 177, 178, 196
    Jesus' birth, 178–182, 184, 187, 190, 192, 193
    soul as, 184
    spiritual-scientific movement, 177
    'Tree of Paradise', 178
    world of spirit, 177
Fichte, Johann Gottlieb, 16, 92
financial speculation, 8

Fingal's Cave, 93, 96–97
    ancient institution, 94
    musical inwardness, 94
Fliess, Wilhelm, 54–56
fluid-physical nature, 107
fundamental power of soul, 150, 152, 154

G
Galileo Galilei, 5, 11, 12, 142, 143
Goethe, Johann Wolfgang von, 19, 23, 26
Goethe's *Faust*, 90
Gospel of Matthew, 144
Gospel of St Luke, 144, 180, 191, 192
Gospel of St Mark, 75
Gospels, 73
'grace', 134
    Christian worldview, 124
    sin and, 134
Greco-Roman era period, 7, 39
Greeks
    art beauty, 41
    beauty, ideal of, 41
    culture, 155
    human body in, 39
    philosophers, 21–22
    physical body of, 39
    sculptors, 41
    self-sustaining quality, 41

H
Hauptmann, Richard, 91
Hebbel, Christian Friedrich, 155
Helsingfors (Helsinki), 124
Herder, Johann Gottfried, 94
'hope body.' *See* physical body
human being, 1, 31, 74, 104
    ancient pre-Christian times, 40
    and animals, 127
    architectural form, 68

astral body, 39, 47, 78, 128
Christ lives in, 32
configuration, spiritual-scientific
  view of, 4
by contrast, 71
death and rebirth, 58–59
decision as, 15
development, 40
different bodies of, 41
different levels/aspects, 37, 38
early Indian culture, 44
on earth, 14
Egyptian culture, 39
esoteric life, 99
etheric body, 39, 47
European peoples, 41
evolutionary process, 126
external human form, 39
Greek sculptors, 41
and humanity, 138
and human nature, 15
interrelationship of bodies/aspects
  of, 42
intrinsic and essential knowledge, 37
intrinsic interiority, 39
material science, 151
mission as, 42
moral responsibility, 127
nature and composition, 13
nature of, 62
Old Saturn period, 64
outer body, sculpt and model, 45
outer world and, 161
outward form, 39, 40
personality, 132–133
physical, 155
physical body, 42, 47, 149
primary mission of, 74
reincarnations, 38
Saturn condition, 104

skeletal system for, 102
spirit of eternal spirit, 92
with spiritual power, 95
unconscious or subconscious, 178
unhealthy soul, 151
human body, 69–70
  in ancient Greeks, 39
  interrelationship of, 37
  physical, 189
human civilization, 101
human conscience, 103
human culture, 2, 6, 7, 13, 57
human dignity, 30
human individuation, 50
humanity's evolution/humanity, 32, 46
  Christ for, 179
  cultural life, 3
  diverse eras of, 51
  on earth, 53
  eras and epochs, 1–2
  fairy tales, 166
  in general, 24
  history, 1
  with human beings. *See* human
    beings
human spirit, 11
intellectual and spiritual impulses, 140
mechanical law of gravity, 5
medieval period, 11
mission for, 2
moral evolution, 104
outward features of, 41
physical sense world, 126
placed us, 15
process of, 39
real mission in, 123
religious sensibility of, 124
self-knowledge, 16
spiritual and cultural movement, 4
spiritual guidance of, 145

spiritual-scientific movement, 1
successive eras, 1
transitional condition, 166
transitional period, 2
vision in, 143
humankind, 32, 135, 183
conscious powers of childhood, 72
expression of Jesus' birth festival, 183
living Christ, 136
paths for, 199
transitional stage of evolution, 127
virtue, 155
humanly educative, 91
human morality, 109
human nature, 7, 149
human being and, 15
possesses, 11
type of, 8
human organism, 106
human physical degeneration, 130
human soul, 154, 189
aspect of, 26, 27
consciousness soul, 26–27
evolution of, 26
experiences, 169
inner aspects of, 26
inner nature of, 26
inwardness, 5
life, 26–27, 34
mind soul, 26–27
mood of, 10
people's opinions, 28
relationship with outer world, 26
sentient soul, 26–27
humility, 59

I
ignorance, 108
imaginative thought, 175
imaginative world, 165

immoral action, karma, 101
immorality, 107, 108
and ignorance, 108
incarnation, 38, 162
'increased cultivation', 14
India, people culture in, 44
individualism, in religion, 13
individuality, 150
inflammatory process, 102
'ingenious' inventions, 51
ingenuity, 14
intellectual knowledge, 108, 143
intelligence, 14
and ingenuity, 14
and 'intelligent culture', 14
spirituality and, 14
'intelligent culture', 14
intermediate realms, 30
intrinsic interiority, 39
inward expression, 98
Isle of Staffa, 93

J
jealousy, 18–20
child, 19
consequence of, 20
and metamorphosis, 20
Jesus' birth festival, 178–182, 184, 187, 190
Jesus, Christ, 91, 142, 199
Jesus of Nazareth, 70, 73, 74, 144, 145, 179, 180, 184, 187, 189
John the Baptist, 75, 198, 199
Jordan baptism, by John, 47, 70, 73, 179, 180, 187, 189, 190, 194
Jordan, Wilhelm, 171–172, 174
Jupiter
condition, 106, 108
elements, 107

K

Kant, Immanuel, 12
Kant-Laplace theory, 77
karma, moral qualities on
    birth and death, in single life, 18
    children, 18
    cosmos, wisdom of, 57
    course of, 31
    deceitfulness, 18–19
    of earth, 47
    esoteric studies, 31
    experiences and observations, 17
    good and bad qualities, 18
    human soul life, 34
    immoral action, 101
    inner laws of, 56
    jealousy, 18–20
    mind soul. *See* mind soul
    perspective of, 124
    preceding factors, 17
    rational mind, 23
    reincarnation and, 50, 100, 139, 140, 154
    as self-evident, 21
    sense of responsibility, 36
    sentient soul. *See* sentient soul
    spiritual science, 17, 21
    spiritual-scientific movement, 34
    supersensible and sensory reality, 35
    surface of, 135
    workings, 18
Kepler, Johannes, 5, 11, 142, 143
    thoughts, 5
    three laws, 5
knowledge
    Christ, 106
    in common, 16
    and faith, 151
    intellectual, 108, 143
    outward thinking and, 7
    and powers of enquiry, 6
    spiritual, 60
    spiritual possessions, 83
    theory of, 112, 113, 115, 116
'knowledge is power', 151

L

language
    acquisition of, 71
    of reality, 164
laws of gravity, 5
laws of probability, 55
Lessing, Gotthold Ephraim, 155
Lhotzky, Heinrich, 64
liar/thief, 101
'Licht', 175
life body, 7, 200
living Christ, 135
living wisdom, 96
logical opinion, 31
logical reasonings, 28
logical thinking, 28
love body. *See* etheric body; life body
Lucifer, 19, 31, 127, 128, 183
    astral body through, 130
    temptation, 128, 191, 196
luciferic powers, 19
    and ahrimanic beings, 31, 32
    in astral body, 19
    beings, 30
'Luft', 175
Luther, Martin, 12

M

Macpherson, James, 95
mainstream science, 53, 54
materialism
    effect of, 86
    teachings of, 84
materialistic age, 14, 91, 189

materialistic consciousness, 103
materialistic medicine, 9
materialistic research, 11
materialistic science, 12, 151, 155
material realm, 120
mathematical thinking, 27
maya, 103
mechanical law of gravity, 5
medieval times, Christmas period in, 11, 178
mental health, 81
metamorphosis, as criticism, 20
Meyer, Julius Robert, 5
mind soul, 7, 26, 27, 29, 150, 157, 170, 171, 175
    gain freedom in, 31
    powers of, 27
    sentient soul and, 29–30
    unfreedom of, 35
mineral realm, 48
mission, as human beings, 42
modern consciousness, 108
modern materialism, 136
modern philosophy, 114
modern science, 55
monetary transactions, 8
mood
    of fairy tale, 161–163
    of human soul, 10
    of loss and regret, 163
    multi-layered, 165
Moon condition, 152, 165
moral consciousness, 103
moral qualities on karma. *See* karma, moral qualities on
moral sermons, 103
morbid fantasy, 77
multi-layered mood, 165
mysterious destinies, 93

Mystery in Palestine, 5
Mystery of Golgotha, 51, 70, 73, 91, 133, 144, 171, 180, 183, 187, 194–195, 199
Mystery Plays, 157

N

Napoleon, 94
natural depths, of earth, 193
'natural Inspiration and Imagination', 38
naturalistic fantasy, 167
nebulous mysticism, 123
negative qualities, of karma, 18
nervousness, 151
nervous person, 152
neurasthenia, 84
Nibelungen, 171
numerical factors, 55

O

'objective', 119
'Occult Physiology', 110, 112, 113
Occult Science, An Outline, 61, 92
Olaf Åsteson, 195–196
Old Moon, 61, 74
    for astral body, 64
    condition, 105
    'humanity' stage on, 75
Old Saturn, 61, 64, 155
    for physical body, 64
Old Sun, 61
    for etheric body, 64
organism, 86, 87
original sin, 130, 134
Ossian, 96, 98
outward perception, 114
outward science, 4, 53

P
Paracelsus, 5, 6
Pauline Christianity, 143
perception process, 26
personality, 131
    Christianity, 133
    Jesus of Nazareth, 145
    primary elemental power, 132
philosophical theories, 50, 51
philosophy
    branches, 111
    enthusiasm for, 122
    and epistemology, 121
    field of, 112
    lecture cycle on, 110
    modern, 112, 114
    primary concepts in, 114
    theory of knowledge, 112
physical body, 7, 37, 38, 43, 45, 52, 83, 87, 107, 128, 149, 155, 201
    of ancient Greeks, 39
    in ancient times, 38
    cosmic tendency, 42
    decomposes, 63
    degenerating, 63
    desiccation and decline as, 49
    earth's evolution, 38
    eternal imbues, 63
    and etheric body, 40, 42
    forces of, 63
    human beings, 42, 47, 149
    of Jesus of Nazareth, 144
    nature and property, 156
    Old Saturn for, 64
    resistance of, 40
physical health, 81
    moral and, 81
physical human brain, 66
physical nerve cords, 11
physical plane, 95

physical sciences, 5
physical substances, 58
physical world, 35, 36
physiognomy, 39
picture consciousness, 111
pneumatology, 12
pneumatosophy, 164
post-Atlantean period
    cultural epoch, 171, 188
    era, 15
    person's life in, 44
power of Imagination, 170
prayerfulness, 63
primitive clairvoyance, 164, 166, 168
primordial clairvoyance, 170
primordial people, 166
progressive spiritual movements, 33
prophetic stars, 9
psychology, of fairy tale, 164
public lectures, 110

R
rational mind, 23
rational soul, 27, 170–171
reality, 168
    external, 168, 169
    language of, 164
    religion in, 10
    reversal of, 91
    spiritual, 126
    of spiritual life, 12
realm
    intermediate, 30
    material, 120
    mineral, 48
    of spirit, 120, 166
    spiritual, 125
real science, 49
rebirth, death and, 58–59
red blood corpuscles, 102

reincarnated Plato, 155
reincarnation process, 24, 139
    and karma, 50, 100, 108, 139, 140, 154
religion, 7, 9
    individualism in, 13
    in reality, 10
    and science, 13
religious sensibility, of humanity, 124
reminiscence, 164
Renaissance of southern Europe, 41
renunciation, 145
resistance, of physical body, 40
Resurrection, 91
rhetorical glossing, 111
rhyme, 170
right conduct, 33
rise of Christianity, 2
Rishis, 44
Roman catacombs, 201
Roman culture, 2
Rose Cross movement, 138, 139
Rosicrucian anthroposophy, 144
rough-and-ready faith, 164

S

Saturn condition, 104, 149, 165
Schopenhauer, Arthur, 103, 116, 120
science, 7, 54
    of astronomy, 5
    in countless popular media, 49
    of etheric body, 12
    external, 53, 55
    in last century, 12
    mainstream, 54
    material, 12
    modern, 55
    outward, 53
    religion and, 13
    sort of, 102
    of spirit, 52

scientific theories, 4
self-assertion, 103
self-criticism, 34
self-development, 81
self-education, 122
self-evident, 36
self-knowledge, 16, 138
sense of responsibility, 36
sense-perceptible world, 114
sensory consciousness, 166
sensory world, 82
sentient soul, 26, 27, 150, 157, 171, 175
    gain freedom in, 31
    and mind soul, 29–30
    powers of, 27
seriousness, sense of, 3
shyness, 21
'sin'
    Christian worldview, 124
    etheric body, 129
    spiritual quality, 130
    temptation of Lucifer, 129
skeletal system, for human being, 102
social community, 7
social practice, 15
social relations, 23
Socrates, 148–149
Son of God, 46, 48, 67, 70, 76
Son of Man, 46–48, 67, 76
Soul of the Child, The (Lhotzky), 65
Soul's Probation, The, 157, 158
    fairy tale, 161–162
    Mystery Plays, 157
    perspectives, 158
    theoretical explanations, 162
speech sound, 175–176
spinal cord, 11
Spirits of Personality, 30
spiritual enquiry, for moral action
    egoistic motivations, 100

immoral actions, 101
  liar/thief, 101
  teachings and powers, 100
spiritual insights, into life
  anthroposophy, 78
  clairvoyance, 78
  harmful effect, 80
  least painful incident, 82
  Macpherson, James, 95
  magical connection with things, 89
  possession, 82
spirituality
  anthroposophic movement, 146
  concepts and ideas, 42
  and cultural movement, 4
  reality, 126
  realm, 125
  science teaches, 48
spiritualization process, 48
spiritual knowledge, 1, 52, 60
spiritual laws, 54
spiritual life
  reality of, 12
  stream of, 44
spiritual movement, 32–33, 40, 42, 124, 138, 139
  progresses, 36
  through revelations, 141
spiritual science, 7, 16, 20, 21, 59, 77, 105, 106, 199
  application, 17
  ascertains, 49
  certainty and strength, 52
  Christianity in accord with, 136
  consciously or unconsciously, 115
  deeper quality of, 64
  education and culture, 25
  employed in, 115
  light of, 21
  offers us thoughts, 81
  people's reaction to, 23
  and philosophy. *See* philosophy
  as promulgated by Aristotle, 12
  pupil of, 26
  and real science, 49
  role of, 14
  teachings of, 9, 60
  tenets of, 50
  truths of, 110
  world of spirit through, 199
'Spiritual Science and Our Human Future', 64
spiritual-scientific knowledge, 61, 65
spiritual-scientific movement, 34, 177
spiritual-scientific worldview, 1, 4, 6, 157
spiritual wisdom, 184
spiritual world, 40, 126
  children into, 45
  conscious assimilation of, 46
  consciousness of, 166
  'phone connection' to, 66
  powers of, 60
  reality out of, 168
  world of spirit, 164
statistics, 54
subjective sphere, 119
subjectivity, sphere of, 118–119
Sudermann, Hermann, 91
Suess, Eduard, 49, 50
Sun condition, 165
supersensible perception, 114
  and sensory reality, 35
sympathetic/unsympathetic qualities, 35

T

tangible reality, 41
Tauler, Johannes, 4
'telephone connection' to spiritual world, 66, 68

theory of knowledge, 112, 113, 115, 116
Theosophical Society, 132
Theosophy, 150
three laws of Kepler, 5
tormented soul, 150
transcendent reality, 116
'transitional eras', 2
trans-subjective reality, 116, 117
trans-subjectivity, 119
Tree of Knowledge, 151
'Tree of Paradise', 178
Trine, Ralph Waldo, 81, 85
true Christians, 137, 145
true religious feeling, 10

U
universal human beauty, 41
universal human quality, 39
unsympathetic qualities, 35

V
von Sivers, Marie, 172

W
Western Christian culture, 179
white blood corpuscles, 102

whole earth organism, 102–105
wisdom, 63, 108
    spiritual, 184
wondrous cathedral, 93
word-padding, 111
world of spirit, 30, 36, 38–40, 45, 47, 76, 94, 163
    ancient power of vision, 95
    childhood, primary powers of, 72
    forms and configurations of, 164
    forms of, 165
    human evolution, 142
    humility and devotion to, 59
    impulses working out, 95
    with philosophical concepts, 115
    physical world, 122
    powers of, 39
    resound in, 95
    teachings and powers, 100
    through spiritual science, 199

Z
Zarathustra, 34, 70

A NOTE FROM RUDOLF STEINER PRESS

We are an independent publisher and registered charity (non-profit organisation) dedicated to making available the work of Rudolf Steiner in English translation. We care a great deal about the content of our books and have hundreds of titles available – as printed books, ebooks and in audio formats.

As a publisher devoted to anthroposophy...

- We continually commission translations of previously unpublished works by Rudolf Steiner and invest in re-translating, editing and improving our editions.

- We are committed to making anthroposophy available to all by publishing introductory books as well as contemporary research.

- Our new print editions and ebooks are carefully checked and proofread for accuracy, and converted into all formats for all platforms.

- Our translations are officially authorised by Rudolf Steiner's estate in Dornach, Switzerland, to whom we pay royalties on sales, thus assisting their critical work.

So, look out for Rudolf Steiner Press as a mark of quality and support us today by buying our books, or contact us should you wish to sponsor specific titles or to support the charity with a gift or legacy.

office@rudolfsteinerpress.com
Join our e-mailing list at www.rudolfsteinerpress.com

RUDOLF STEINER PRESS